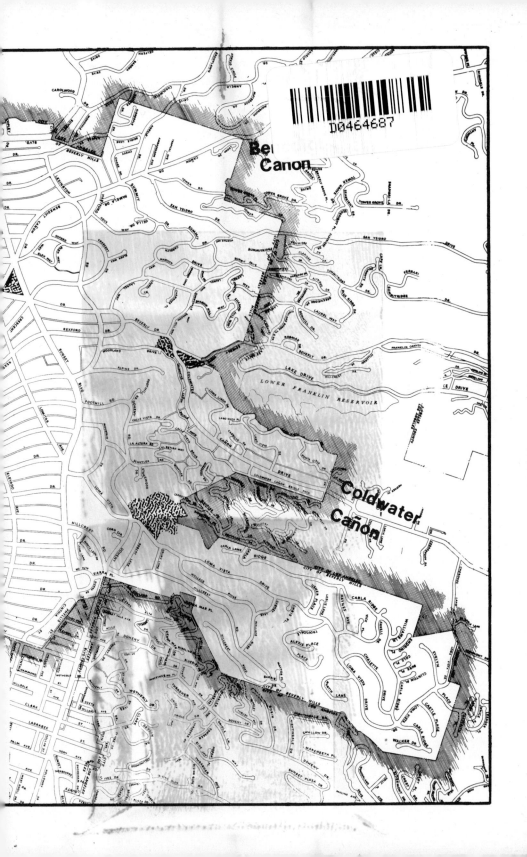

Beverly Hills

Inside the Golden Ghetto

Beverly Hills

Inside the Golden Ghetto

by Walter Wagner

Publishers · GROSSET & DUNLAP · New York
A FILMWAYS COMPANY

Endpaper map of Beverly Hills, courtesy of the City of Beverly Hills
Planning Department.

Library of Congress Catalogue Card number: 72-90861
ISBN 0-448-02163-3
First printing
Printed in the United States of America

For those who helped, especially:
Loriene Chase
Richard Laughran
Art Linkletter
Tony Mercatante
Ken Murray
. . . and my wife, Maxine

Contents

Photographic sections appear opposite pages 64 and 144.

Beverly Hills

Inside the
Golden
Ghetto

1.
Snow White's Boudoir

ONE HOT JULY morning, Douglas Fairbanks, Sr., tramped over his property on the highest point in Beverly Hills, rifle in hand, stealthily searching the wooded areas and underbrush. In April of 1919, he had purchased eleven acres, along with an abandoned, ugly two-story shooting lodge in the undeveloped township near Los Angeles. It had cost him $35,000—and a few sleepless nights from a coyote that prowled his acreage.

The screen hero fired a single shot and felled the offender, then walked back to his lodge, dressed, and slipped behind the wheel of his glass-enclosed, two-seater Rolls-Royce to keep a date with Mary Pickford. Fairbanks and Pickford were engaged to be married, and they were the King and Queen of Hollywood. After their marriage, they would live happily ever after here at the crest of Beverly Hills.

The modern myth of "The Beautiful, Wonderful World of Beverly Hills" had begun.

But Beverly Hills came to eminence thanks to some of the least admirable qualities of human nature. Greed, sex-laden scandals, and murder catapulted the town into the world-famous mecca for movie stars.

The original occupants of the area were a tribe of Indians named the Gabrielinos by the Spaniards, who first encountered them two

11

hundred years ago. The Gabrielinos were a civilized tribe by present Beverly Hills standards. They worshipped one God, Quaoar, and their tale of Creation was strikingly similar to Genesis. They had their own Adam and Eve, named Tobohas and Pobavit, and they believed in the immortality of the soul.

The Gabrielinos tossed big funerals, but rites for the departed were not as well-attended as weddings. They were also compulsive gamblers: many male Gabrielinos bet and lost turtle shells, livestock, and sometimes their wives in a game of guessing which hand held a small stick. Their favorite number was "4." For believers in numerology, the number "4" designates a quarrelsome personality, a penchant for amassing secret enemies, and an interest in liberal social reforms.

The big annual celebration for the Gabrielinos was the Eagle Feast. Each year the tribe's royal bird was honored at a special ceremony, then slaughtered and tossed into a sacrificial fire, after which the celebrants feasted into the wee hours, forgetting about the eagle. The tribesmen revered their medicine men above their chiefs, since the medicine men encouraged the notion that they could hold one-to-one conversations with Quaoar and effect supernatural cures for physical as well as mental ailments.

Coffee-brown in complexion, the Gabrielinos numbered a mere 10,000. They lived hardscrabble lives as hunters and gatherers, had no skill as farmers, and their dialect was so unintelligible that they actually could not communicate with other tribes residing less than thirty miles away. Their bodies were stunted, their limbs poorly developed, and the tallest of them were five feet in height. Their only weapons were crude knives made from stones and primitive bows that could fling arrows no more than twenty yards.

The natives were extremely friendly when a Spanish expedition came upon them in the afternoon of August 1, 1769. The two leaders of the expedition were Father Junipero Serra, a lame Franciscan fanatic, and Captain Gaspar de Portola, a heavy-set, professional military man loathed by his subordinates. Also in the party were Father Juan Crespi, who kept a diary of the expedition; chief scout José Francisco Ortega, who had once been court-martialed for sleeping with an officer's wife; and Juan Batista Valdez, a guide who is remembered mainly because one of his descendants would later own Beverly Hills and would sell it to a pair of American buccaneers. Unremembered are the twenty others in the party, who were blacks, mulattoes, and Indians.

The Spaniards gave the Gabrielinos a handful of beads and tobacco to establish Spanish equity in the area. It was a much better bargain than Peter Minuit's purchase of Manhattan from the Algonquins for twenty-four dollars' worth of trinkets. Indeed, the Spaniards paid even less for the 11,450 square miles of Los Angeles and Beverly Hills.

Before leaving, the expedition claimed Beverly Hills for the King of Spain and the Catholic Church, naming the territory El Pueblo de Nuestra Señora la Reina de Los Angeles.When they returned in 1771, the Spaniards introduced the Gabrielinos to Christ, conversion, baptism, smallpox, syphilis, tuberculosis, alcohol, the dawn-to-sunset working day, and the handy art of killing themselves. Approximately one thousand Gabrielinos soon learned it was a mercy to die by their own hand. They slashed their throats and wrists as the only alternative to the bestiality of Father Serra. Three thousand more died of starvation and disease while living in the Franciscans' concentration camp and working to build their mission. And by 1784, there was no trace left of the tribe, except possibly a few female Gabrielinos who had married Spaniards.

The first home in Beverly Hills was built by Maria Rita Valdez, a granddaughter of the Juan Batista Valdez who had served as guide on Serra's expedition. She formally applied to the Mexican government in 1841 for an official grant to the land, and was given it. But her experience as owner of the territory was not to be a pleasant one.

When war broke out between Mexico and the United States in 1846, she and her family fled. The U.S. troops, under the command of Lieutenant John C. Fremont, took Los Angeles without a fight, and the soldiers looted Maria's house, taking the trunk that contained her land grant. California was ceded to the United States in 1848. After a Board of Land Commissioners was set up in 1851 to pass judgment on grants issued during the Spanish and Mexican regimes, Maria filed her application. It took her three years to prove her case.

But back in her adobe home, at the juncture of what would one day become Sunset Boulevard and Alpine Drive, her problems continued. Her horses were continually running off, her cattle died from a lack of grass and water, and the roof of her house was crushed by a lightning storm. The final frustration came when three stray Apaches attacked her home. While fire-tipped arrows bounced off the adobe, one of her sons managed to slip away unnoticed, returning with a dozen vigilantes, who captured and killed the small band of Indians.

Surprisingly, Maria's suspicions were not aroused when a pair of fast-talking ranchers appeared at her door a few days later, offering her

$500 in cash and $3,500 in notes for Beverly Hills. Despite the possibility—or even likelihood—that the two men, Benjamin Wilson and Henry Hancock, had paid the Apaches a couple of bottles of rotgut to get rid of her and her family, Maria sold willingly.

During the next half-century, ownership passed from one unsuccessful American buyer to another, until Burton Green, one of the directors of the Amalgamated Oil Company, which had twice failed to locate oil on the land, decided to subdivide and sell the property as homesites. It was Green who gave it the name Beverly Hills—for his hometown, Beverly Farm, Massachusetts. The new town was incorporated in 1914 with a population of 550.

It probably would have forever remained just what it was then—a sleepy little village of anonymous homes occupied by anonymous people—if it had not been for the motion-picture industry. It took three greedy, unscrupulous men to get the motion-picture industry to California, and it took a single hypocrite to get the industry's denizens to Beverly Hills.

Until 1912, film production had centered in the East, and it might still be there except for the grasping, fledgling moguls who were using Thomas Edison's motion-picture patents without paying him. The most conspicuous offenders were Sam Goldwyn, Cecil B. DeMille, and Jesse Lasky. When Edison threatened to sue their company, the trio headed West.

The first film hammered out in Hollywood was the 1913 Goldwyn–DeMille–Lasky Western, *The Squaw Man*. At the time *The Squaw Man* was made, Hollywood had a population of about 100,000; distant Beverly Hills, less than 500. Hollywood had been organized as an independent city in 1903, but seven years later lost its autonomy by voting to join metropolitan Los Angeles in order to tap into its water supply.

By 1918, Hollywood was the center of the film industry, and the most important female star in films was the former Gladys Mary Smith of Toronto—renamed Mary Pickford by Broadway's David Belasco.

With a constant eye for the main chance, Mary Pickford had moved on from her great success in Cinderella films at D. W. Griffith's Biograph Studios to Adolph Zukor's Famous Players, the forerunner of Paramount Studios, where she was making $10,000 a week until she left to form United Artists with Douglas Fairbanks, Charlie Chaplin, and D. W. Griffith.

Unhappy with her marriage to Owen Moore, who was known as the

Beau Brummell of Biograph, she sought solace in the arms of Douglas Fairbanks. When America's Sweetheart asked Moore for a divorce, he responded by buying a revolver and threatening to shoot Fairbanks, "that climbing monkey," as he called him. Fairbanks bought his own freedom from his wife for $500,000; and finally Moore accepted a small fortune to let Mary go without gunfire.

Mary also promised Moore to do the "decent thing," by waiting a full year before remarrying. However, the divorce was final on March 1, 1920, and she married Fairbanks on March 28. The wedding ceremony was held in secret in the home of a Los Angeles minister, and the bridal supper and honeymoon were enjoyed in the refurbished hunting lodge in Beverly Hills, where Fairbanks had been living alone for a year.

News of the wedding was released three days later, and the announcement that the King and Queen of Hollywood had been married created a stir in the press tantamount to the Second Coming. The legality of Miss Pickford's divorce was questioned, with some newspapers intimating that Fairbanks had bribed a judge; and a rumor was spread that the couple's first heir was already on its way. But the validity of the Nevada divorce was upheld, and time dispelled the gossip about the bride's premature pregnancy. Soon the press was reporting that Mr. and Mrs. Fairbanks were enjoying a fairy-tale marriage, and they would undoubtedly live happily ever after.

Their life, as reported by the press, was idyllic—ensconced behind locked gates and high walls, served by butlers and maids, they rode in custom-built automobiles, and occasionally swam in Beverly Hills' first swimming pool. One reporter dubbed the place Pickfair, and the name stuck. In the press, its guest list, parties, and prestige eclipsed every home in the country, except possibly the White House.

They were the only movie stars living in Beverly Hills at the time, so—to the public across the country—the little community meant Douglas Fairbanks and Mary Pickford. But that was soon to change.

Although scandal—in the form of payoffs, intimidation, threats, blackmail, and infidelity—had been constant in the romance of Fairbanks and Pickford, it was mild by Hollywood standards. A series of far more sensational scandals would soon drive other Hollywood names to the Pickfair neighborhood.

On Labor Day weekend, in September 1921, Roscoe "Fatty" Arbuckle checked into San Francisco's St. Francis Hotel with a retinue of Hollywood friends. Fatty Arbuckle was radiantly happy because he had just signed Hollywood's first million-dollar contract to continue doing his highly successful slapstick comedies at Keystone, in which a young man named Charlie Chaplin was playing second banana. The occasion called for a party, and it was going to be as big a bash as the top Hollywood comedian could throw.

And, by all reports, it was—until the festivities ended with a bit-part actress named Virginia Rappe found dead, a Coke bottle protruding obscenely from her vagina.

Fatty Arbuckle was indicated for first-degree murder. After much legal maneuvering, the charge was reduced to manslaughter. Three sensational trials were held. The first two ended in hung juries, and in the third, Arbuckle was found innocent.

At the height of the newspaper coverage of the case, the Hearst press was grinding out thirteen editions a day replete with sexual detail. Demanding Arbuckle's scalp, Hearstian journalism kindled the fury of the self-declared guardians of the nation's morals—the Legion of Decency, random do-gooders and reformers, and the usually moderate clergy, along with the fundamentalists who predicted that the Arbuckle incident presaged the end of the world.

Although Arbuckle had been found not guilty, his career was shattered, and he would never again be able to appear on the screen. His studio couldn't even give his unreleased films away.

The Arbuckle mess cost the motion-picture industry millions in cash. No one could count the price in good will. And future box-office receipts were uncertain. Indeed the reputation of Hollywood as an iniquitous den was so deep and bitter that Adolph Zukor, Sam Goldwyn, William Fox, Carl Laemmle, and other studio brass went looking for someone who could change their bad press. They found Will Hays, the Postmaster General of the United States, who was on record as a foursquare opponent of sin, and they offered him a salary of $100,000 a year.

Hays was a forty-three-year-old religious fundamentalist, a Gable-eared, slick-haired slicker from Sullivan, Indiana. As national chairman of the Republican party in 1920, he had helped win the Presidency for Warren Harding, with the financial aid of two oilmen, Harry Sinclair and Beverly Hills' E. L. Doheny, who jointly donated $260,000 to Hays—supposedly loans for the Harding campaign, although the money was never repaid. When Harding was elected, Sinclair and Doheny felt sure that his administration could be bought, and they proceeded to buy it. In 1922, they gave Interior Secretary Albert Fall and Secretary of the Navy Edwin Denby $400,000 to transfer, with Hays' knowledge and agreement, government oil reserves at Elk Hills, California, and Teapot Dome, Wyoming, without competitive bidding.

When news of the under-the-table deal reached disapproving ears, there were rumblings about a Senate investigation, and Hays knew it was a choice moment to leave the Harding cabinet. By the time Teapot Dome hit the front pages in 1923, Hays was safely ensconced in his job as moral guardian of the movies.

However, he'd barely assumed his new post when he was faced with some prime examples of the sort of bad press he was supposed to keep from happening. The first example involved Paramount's leading director, William Desmond Taylor, who was found shot to death in his apartment in the Westlake section of Los Angeles. Two beautiful, highly paid stars—Mabel Normand and Mary Miles Minter—had called on Taylor on the night he was killed. Police learned that the director had been having affairs with both actresses, as well as with Minter's mother. The press had a field day. This scandal is said to have sold more newspapers than any other scandal in history.

The publicity ruined the careers of the two actresses. Like Arbuckle, they were banished from films. Minter settled into anonymous retirement, and Mabel Normand eventually died a drug addict—at the height of her addiction spending $2,000 a month for cocaine.

The next shocker brought to public notice occurred in January 1923, when Wallace Reid, the thirty-three-year-old movie idol, died in a padded cell, a morphine addict. Reid, one of the stars of *The Birth of a Nation*, was a strapping six-foot-three charmer who specialized in playing all-American heroes. Paramount's top leading man, he had been worth $2,000,000 annually at the box office.

The Hays attempt to clean up the industry included ordering studio chieftains to insert morality clauses in the contracts of stars, and picking through every script considered and every foot of film made, worrying—as someone put it—"how much leg and tit could be shown in Iowa."

Hays also obtained the cooperation of the studios to launch a propaganda campaign to give Hollywood an image of holiness. The movie moguls announced films with a religious base, and they issued public statements to try to cover up the memory of Arbuckle, Taylor, Normand, Minter, and Reid.

Cecil B. DeMille announced that his next project would be *The Ten*

Commandments, while hiding the fact that he was violating the seventh commandment, living with his wife but sleeping with the first of three mistresses with whom he would have long relationships.

Jesse Lasky proclaimed, "The future of motion pictures is as secure as the Rock of Gibraltar. Pictures have done much good in stimulating world thought; in arousing interest in history, drama, art, and letters; in presenting social and economic problems in a clear and graphic manner."

Carl Laemmle, the former manager of a clothing store in Oshkosh, Wisconsin, declared optimistically, "The motion picture has attained its full maturity. The art is already advanced to a plane with the legitimate theater, painting, music, and literature."

And Hays himself piously stated, "The motion picture has done more than amuse. It has carried the silent call for virtue, honesty, ambition, patriotism, love of country and of home. It is as great an institution as the church."

Meanwhile, Hays decided the best thing to do to cover up the sins of the stars would be to get the sinners out of town. As a sanctuary away from the temptations of Hollywood and Los Angeles, he suggested that little community where Mary Pickford and Douglas Fairbanks were giving the industry an aura of respectability by entertaining crowned heads—Beverly Hills.

The first to take the heavy-handed hint was Charlie Chaplin, who bought the lot next to Pickfair on Summit Drive. Soon Gloria Swanson, Harold Lloyd, and Conrad Nagel followed. So did Carl Laemmle and director Fred Niblo.

In pointing his stern finger in the direction of Beverly Hills, Hays touched off a real-estate boom. "Lots are sold so quickly and often out here that they are put through escrow made out to the twelfth owner," Will Rogers wrote in his nationally syndicated newspaper column. "They couldn't possibly make a separate deed for each purchaser; besides, he wouldn't have time to read the deed in the ten-minute time he owned the lot.

"Your having no money doesn't worry the agents. If they can just get a couple of dollars down, or an old overcoat, or a shotgun, or anything to act as first payment. Secondhand Fords are considered A-1 collateral.

"It's the greatest game I ever saw; you can't lose. Everybody buys to sell and nobody buys to keep. What's worrying me is who is going to be the last owner. It's just like an auction. Nobody ever gets stuck but the last one."

Despite his comments, Will Rogers did not live in Beverly Hills. But a barrage of stars, tycoons, studio executives, producers, directors, and writers—among them Tom Mix, Rudolph Valentino, Corinne Griffith, and John Barrymore—bought land, built houses, and moved in to stay.

The movie contingent was soon running the town. The film-makers had only to nod and the City Council bowed to their wishes. The nodding was done particularly when it came to the question of keeping property taxes as invisible as possible. In addition, a zoning change, a sidewalk, a free paved road to a home, virtually anything the film residents wanted could be had with a phone call, an invitation to a party, or—in extreme cases—a bribe.

For protection, the film elite hired the best police force money could buy—in effect, a private militia that would leave them alone but protect them from "outsiders." The cops of Beverly Hills have, as a result, swept more dirt under the rug than perhaps any other police force in the nation.

But this happy arrangement was threatened in the spring of 1923, when a group of non-famous, non-millionaire, not-very-influential citizens began a campaign to annex Beverly Hills to Los Angeles. Led by local real-estate men, who were angling to peddle more lots, the battle hinged on the question of water. The brokers knew the town required a large reliable water supply, and Los Angeles had one while Beverly Hills did not.

"There's more water in the swimming pool at Pickfair than I have on two large tracts I can't sell," one broker charged.

The anti-annexation campaign was led by eight film celebrities —Douglas Fairbanks, Mary Pickford, Tom Mix, Rudolph Valentino, Harold Lloyd, Will Rogers, Conrad Nagel, and Fred Niblo—whose homes had more than sufficient water. In his dining room, Tom Mix had a fountain that spouted fresh, non-recycled water in every color of the rainbow.

The movie people didn't give a hoot about any liquid except the kind that flowed from their bootleggers' bottles. They formed a committee, gave speeches, rang doorbells, pounded sidewalks, and buttonholed passers-by.

Left unsaid were the real concerns they had. Annexation to Los Angeles would mean the end of low taxes and other favors bestowed by the City Council. Gone would be their private police force. Annexation would bury their privileged sanctuary, which they were beginning to enjoy. It was amusing to have a city as a hobby, being big fish in a small pond. They had no desire to become part of the million run-of-the-mill taxpayers in Los Angeles.

"This is the most serious crisis we've ever faced," opined Fairbanks, who shortly would face far more serious crises both in his professional and in his personal life.

Will Rogers' motto was "I never met a man I didn't like," but what Rogers really liked was what money could buy—polo ponies and large landholdings. He was anything but the poor, self-effacing country bumpkin he portrayed. Born into a wealthy Oklahoma family, Rogers was as adroit in his business dealings as he was at poking jabs at politicians in the 350 daily papers that carried his column. He demanded outlandish prices for his services, and also insisted that vaudeville-house owners pay him in cash *before* every performance; otherwise, tradition notwithstanding, the show wouldn't go on.

In private, he was a surly, short-tempered, egocentric, heavy-drinking man. The police of Beverly Hills were so intimidated by him that he was never arrested for his frequent drunken driving. And when one of his kin became involved in a morals offense with a thirteen-year-old girl, the case was hushed up.

Rogers wrote his column under a Beverly Hills dateline. But since he didn't live within the boundaries of the city, he had no business inserting himself into the annexation dispute. In the course of that dispute, Rogers met many a man he didn't like—just about anybody who so much as hinted they were pro-annexation.

Mudslinging tactics, charge and countercharge, continued down to voting day. The battle had overtones and undercurrents of class warfare—between the haves and the have-nots, between the crowned heads of Beverly Hills and their restive vassals—and it would smolder and resurface again and again.

On April 24, the day the destiny of Beverly Hills would be decided by ballot, citizens found two items on their front doorsteps. The first was a copy of the Beverly Hills *Script* (a now-defunct newspaper) with a banner headline that read: FUTURE OF THE CITY HANGS IN THE BALANCE. The newspaper ignored the more trivial events occurring in the world news, such as the 500,000 coal miners on strike in Appalachia protesting wage cuts.

The second item on the doorstep was a bottle of foul, sulfurous water, with a label that read: *"Warning!* Drink sparingly of this water as it has laxative qualities! This is the odious water you drink! This is a sample of the water which the trustees of Beverly Hills propose as a water supply for our city!" The water in the bottles had been scooped from a swamp by pro-annexationists.

Voter turnout was extremely heavy—844 ballots registered in a town that had 800 homes. The tally went against annexation, 507 to 337.

With the annexation hassle behind it, Beverly Hills still had a water problem, but the city solved it temporarily by approving a $400,000 bond issue to expand tap facilities. Later, as population grew, Beverly Hills purchased the water system of West Hollywood.

The eight movie hotshots who had preserved the sovereignty of Beverly Hills were honored with a marker that is still standing in a remote corner of town. The guiding spirit behind this tribute was Corinne Griffith, who—after sound scuttled her career—invested in Beverly Hills real estate and made a bundle.

The stars had preserved their sanctum sanctorum, and the tiny monolith of Beverly Hills would continue to cast its independent, leviathan shadow across the planet. The celebrated residents knew the world would rather read about Pickfair than the poverty of pick-and-shovel miners. Their folklore, which consisted of one scabrous scandal after another, was much more momentous than the struggles of ordinary humanity.

Though Will Hays had commanded the stars to go ye into the hills of Beverly and sin no more, the royalty of the movies obeyed only the first part of his ukase.

2.
What Wasn't on Sale at Homer's Drugstore

WILL HAYS' PECULIAR NOTION that geography by itself would somehow tamp the misadventures of world-renowned stars who had stumbled into an industry that overpaid them and a city that overindulged them simply failed to pan out. But it didn't matter so far as the box office was concerned. The moviegoing public had executed a sharp about-face, and the studios quickly learned that scandal now sold tickets. Never again would careers be ruined for off-screen misconduct.

The stellar colonization of Beverly Hills, begun by Fairbanks and Mary Pickford, had included certain lurid aspects. Even so, their star status had survived. Though linked to scandal, the popularity of other Beverly Hills stars—among them Charlie Chaplin, Rudolph Valentino, Clara Bow, and Gary Cooper—was sustained in the Twenties. In later years, scandal boomed rather than busted the careers of Errol Flynn, Ingrid Bergman, Robert Mitchum, Lana Turner, Elizabeth Taylor, and Richard Burton.

The worst-kept secret scandal of the era involved William Randolph Hearst and Marion Davies. It was also the most hypocritical. Hearst's cross-country chain of powerful, opinion-molding newspapers boosted circulation with ribald accounts of the transgressions of Beverly Hills stars who were his neighbors. At the same time, Hearst was estranged from his wife and engaging in an illicit relationship with Miss Davies.

"When people spring from poverty to affluence within a few weeks, their mental equipment is not always equal to the strain," said Hearst's New York *Journal*. "They have money, an unaccustomed toy, and they spend it in bizarre ways. Many of them spend all they make, indulging in wild parties or other sinful forms of relaxation and excitement."

The editorial was a fairly precise summation of Hearst himself, except that he was born the scion of the Anaconda and Comstock mining bonanzas. Hearst, too, spent money in bizarre fashion. He spent, in fact, more than he could afford. He tossed a king's ransom away—$50,000,000—on his San Simeon castle, which dominated a 123-acre site. Antiques and entire rooms were purchased at random for him in Europe, many of which were never even uncrated. The castle had no unifying idea, lacked taste, and had no architectual style —unless hodge-podge can be considered style.

He also lavished millions on Miss Davies in jewels, stocks, bonds, and property. In the heart of the Depression, Hearst's spending caught up with him. He had to borrow money from Miss Davies, who wrote him a check for $1,000,000. Hearst raised another $2,000,000—to cover overdue notes—from the Rockefellers, and he did not get on his financial feet again until the entire economy began booming with the outbreak of World War II.

Following his death, Hearst's heirs abandoned the white elephant of San Simeon to the state of California. Today it is a tourist attraction, billed as an "historical site."

To fill his endless parties in Beverly Hills and at San Simeon, Hearst shanghaied the royalty of the golden ghetto. Nostalgia has tinted these affairs as one burnished bash after another, with wit and anecdote glancing off each other like rapiers in a duel. Actually, they were pathetic gatherings, the gaiety forced, the gossip tepid, the conversation for the most part a gob of deferential compliments to Hearst and Miss Davies. Mary Astor remembers: "The parties in Beverly and at San Simeon were ostentatiously dull." The only relief from monotony were the sex *soirées* the moguls and stars enjoyed in the late evenings in Hearst's guest bedrooms. There was so much action in the corridors, Errol Flynn once said, that Hearst should have hired a traffic cop.

During his years in Beverly Hills, Charlie Chaplin found himself embroiled in one mess after another. Shortly after he moved to Beverly, Chaplin wed teen-aged Mildred Harris when she claimed she was pregnant. However, as with Mary Pickford, time proved the pregnancy report false.

Visiting his next-door neighbors one day for a cup of spiritual cheer, Chaplin was told by Douglas Fairbanks that Mildred was sleeping around. Although he was sleeping around too, Chaplin was shocked.

Chaplin, who claimed he could never reach Mildred's mind because it was filled with what he called "pink-ribboned foolishness," divorced her and soon became infatuated with sixteen-year-old Lita Grey. She was his second shotgun marriage, but this nymphet *was* pregnant. During their brief wedlock, she mothered two sons, Sydney and Charles, Jr.

When Lita Grey Chaplin's petition for divorce was made public, it proved to be a document and a half. She charged that she had been seduced by Chaplin, that he had asked her to submit to an abortion of their first child, that she married him solely because she was pregnant and with a "reservation of the intention of divorce," that she was the recipient of "cruel and inhuman treatment," and that Chaplin was guilty of "immorality."

Lita Grey Chaplin also averred: "Whereas, four months before the separation of the Plaintiff and the Respondent, the Respondent suggested that a young girl who had the reputation of performing acts of sexual perversity spend the evening at their home and the Respondent told the Plaintiff that they could have some fun together."

Chaplin gave her the divorce. The unpleasant marriage had lasted two years. Chaplin also gave Miss Grey a hefty cash settlement—$1,000,000—which he could well afford. He was already the world's richest actor, a feat he accomplished by maintaining ownership of all his films and by investing wisely and luckily. His fortune is presently estimated at $100,000,000.

Handsome eighteen-year-old Rodolfo Guglielmi, a high-school dropout in Venice, Italy, hit New York City in 1913 and spent five inauspicious years working as a gardener, waiter, and taxi-dancer. He was also a part-time gigolo who catered to rich, bored women. Spotted in a nightclub by producer Emmet Flynn, he was given a couple of scenes in a 1918 picture, *Alimony*. He caught on and, as the titanically popular Rudolph Valentino, won success in *The Four Horsemen of the Apocalypse*, *The Sheik*, and *Blood and Sand*.

He built a home called Falcon's Lair at the timberline of Beverly's Benedict Canyon and furnished it all in black. Even the walls were painted black, and sunlight was held at bay by black leather drapes.

Valentino was briefly arrested for bigamy when he exchanged wives too swiftly. His divorce not yet final from Jean Acker, an aspiring actress, he had rushed into marriage with a set designer turned spiritualist who called herself Natasha Rambova. Natasha had divined that her real name, Winifred Shaughnessey, was too pedestrian for an investigator of the occult.

No star had a more virile image than Valentino, his dark good looks winning him the affection of millions of women. But down at Homer's drugstore—Beverly Hills' most popular dispensary for prescriptions, notions, ice cream, and gossip—the talk was that both of Valentino's wives were lesbians and that his marriages were a cover-up for his homosexuality. However, actress Claire Windsor, who died in 1973, was one patron at Homer's who was a living testament to Valentino's masculinity. On her first and only date with him, she said, Valentino had attempted to rape her.

Valentino's assertedly complex sex life was a little difficult to follow. But from Homer's rumor mill, the tales spread to the hinterlands. One Chicago paper called Valentino "a pansy," a shocker at the time. Valentino denied it, branded the statement libelous, but did not press the issue in court. Indeed, the fact that he endorsed such items as slave bracelets, gloppy gold jewelry, face cream and hair pomade didn't help Valentino prove his machismo. Nearly as many homosexuals as women bought the products he recommended.

The career and life of the star who, one critic said, "fulfilled all the fantasies of the romantic Latin lover" would be pitifully short.

It girl Clara Bow was the embodiment of the 1920s flapper. She was to movies what Fitzgerald was to the novel, Jack Dempsey to boxing, and Aimee Semple MacPherson to hellfire and brimstone. Her wanton screen personality apparently was a slice of life, straight from her red boudoir in the Beverly Hills Mediterranean she occupied.

Clara's secretary, Daisy DeVoe, sold an account of her employer's sex exploits to a newspaper. Among Clara's lovers, said Miss DeVoe, were Gary Cooper, Bela Lugosi, Western star Rex Bell, and—in one virtuoso performance—the entire football team of the University of Southern California! When the story broke, Paramount quickly raised Clara's salary to $5,000 a week and hurled her into three quickie pictures, all of which were ardently patronized.

No one named in the flaming headlines engendered by the DeVoe revelations was hurt. Gary Cooper remained a star until the end of his life. Bela Lugosi earned a handsome living in Dracula and Frankenstein films; he worked consistently and made his last picture in 1956, the year he died. Rex Bell married Clara Bow and later became lieutenant governor of Nevada. The University of Southern California and its football team still flourish. As for Miss Bow, sound and a changing economic atmosphere scuttled her professionally. She wasn't effective in talkies and, with the onset of the Depression, the flapper type she personified became obsolete. She made two unsuccessful come-back attempts in the early Thirties, and died in 1965, her last years flecked with a series of nervous breakdowns.

In 1927, the Jolson film *The Jazz Singer* rescued the studio owned by the Warner brothers and kept it from reverting to what it had been originally, a pig farm. But the development of talkies also ended many careers among the film luminaries of Beverly Hills. Besides Clara Bow, such idols as Theda Bara, John Gilbert, Billie Dove, Colleen Moore, and Norma Talmadge—as well as King Fairbanks and Queen Pickford—never quite made the transition to sound. The best work of Charlie Chaplin, Buster Keaton, and Gloria Swanson (except for her stunning reappearance in 1950's *Sunset Boulevard*) was behind them.

Most Beverly stars laid low by sound pictures lived on in a kind of squalid splendor, drowning themselves in drink, drugs, promiscuity, and vanished glory.

The downfall of Buster Keaton, born to vaudevillian parents in a trunk in Piqua, Kansas, was the most poignant. He was an established star by 1917. His deadpan antics in a torrent of side-splitting films had made him a hugely successful and rich superstar. Many knowledgeable Hollywoodites claim he was a greater, more inventive, and more talented comedian than Chaplin, the finest and funniest the movie factories ever produced.

Keaton's X-shaped Beverly Hills mansion sat on seven acres and was adorned with a cultivated lawn more than four hundred feet in length. There was a swimming pool, a garden conservatory, a vast playroom, and a projection room. His bedroom suite had a canopied bed, an elaborately carved ceiling, and a hand-chiseled fireplace imported intact from Italy. His private bathroom was large enough to hold a steam closet, massage table, and exercise equipment. It was a miniature San Simeon, one of *the* showplaces in Beverly Hills.

But, when the guillotine of talkies descended in 1927, the house, the fortune, and life at the top went completely. He ended as a Hollywood charity case. Metro-Goldwyn-Mayer and occasionally some of the other studios hired him as a "comedy consultant"—actually a glorified office boy. He died in 1966, a near-penniless alcoholic.

Although it had been only a scant ten years since Will Hays ordained it as an Eden for movie idols, by 1929 Beverly Hills was already a battleground strewn with casualties. The 1920s were rushing toward a punishing climax, and the nation would soon see fifteen million people unemployed. But, in the last pre-Depression months in Beverly Hills, the surviving stars remained aloof from the troubles of the rest of the country. It was not the studied, casual aloofness of a sophisticated aristocracy, but sheer, uncaring ignorance and lack of concern for anything except the gossip at Homer's and what occurred at the studios.

The stars of Beverly, over breakfast in bed, scanned their newspapers for industry tidbits. They laughed when the first photographs of a funny-looking little guy named Adolph Hitler began cropping up on the front pages. He might make it, they chuckled, as Chaplin's stand-in. But they ignored the realism of comparison shopping. A generous loaf of bread cost ten cents in Beverly; in Germany, the price for three rolls was a wheelbarrow of incredibly inflated currency. The select of Beverly Hills felt they could afford to ignore the outside world. Audiences were still flocking to the theaters, and there was plenty of hometown action to keep them occupied.

Oilman E. L. Doheny had just built Greystone, his twenty-acre palatial bastion. Visitors were butlered from the porte cochère through grilled double doors, and guided down a black-and-white marble stairway into his eleven-million-dollar, forty-room mansion. The ladies' lounge and powder room were done in pink marble. The west-wing drawing room had pegged oak floors covered by hand-woven Persian rugs. In the gentlemen's smoking room, the walls were wainscoted in light-brown marble, the moldings were gold-plated. The card room housed a cherub spouting water. In comparison, Pickfair was a slum.

The finishing touches had barely been put to Greystone when, on a Saturday night in 1929, gunfire bellowed from inside the mansion. Hugh Plunkett, the private secretary of E. L. Doheny, Jr., shot and killed his employer, then turned the pistol on himself. Plunkett's murderous rage had exploded when the junior Doheny refused his request for a raise in salary. Beverly Hills Police Chief Charles Blair investigated and concluded that Plunkett "undoubtedly had become suddenly insane."

The younger Doheny's sole claim to fame was that he had been the bagman for his father in the 1922 Teapot Dome scandal, delivering $100,000 in cash, in a black satchel, to Interior Secretary Albert Fall. Fall had been convicted of accepting a bribe and sentenced to one year in prison. Another participant, Navy Secretary Edwin Denby, had resigned in disgrace; co-conspirator Harry Sinclair, though found innocent of fraud, had served a brief jail-term for contempt of Congress; and the shock of Teapot Dome, said President Harding's intimates, had hastened his demise. But like ex-Postmaster General Will Hays, both Dohenys—Jr. and Sr.—had gotten off scot-free.

Doheny, Sr., lived lavishly in Greystone until his death in 1935 at the age of seventy-five. His direct legacy to his heirs was $100,000,000; his oblique legacy to America was Will Hays, who bowdlerized the movie industry but did nothing to enforce the morality clauses written into the contracts of Beverly Hills' pre-eminent players.

The Doheny murder and Plunkett's suicide, bereft of colorful sin, had a short run as a topic of conversation in Beverly. It had been merely a shoddy instance of a tightwad multimillionaire exploiting one of the hired help. Not much time was wasted discussing it at Homer's drugstore, where a cute couple at a rear table was spotted one afternoon tasting each other's ice-cream sodas.

Young Douglas Fairbanks, Jr., and Joan Crawford were exchanging soulful looks and giggling. Soon they would be wed, ostensibly another happily ever-after, fairy-tale marriage. But Mary Pickford and Douglas Fairbanks, Sr., who weren't up to the prospect of becoming Sweetheart grandparents, privately and violently opposed it. They needn't have worried; the childless marriage was to last only four years.

By the late 1920s, the practice of not permitting free citizens to walk freely on the streets of Beverly Hills was already in force. The police department, zealously overprotective of its wealthy constituents, was suspicious of pedestrians. Shanks'-mare sightseeing or exercise was pushily discouraged, especially in residential areas and especially with strangers. An Englishwoman staying at the Beverly Hills Hotel started out on foot one morning to explore Benedict Canyon. She passed the homes of Tom Mix, Corinne Griffith, and Harold Lloyd. Suddenly a prowl car whipped up and an officer asked disdainfully, "Lady, are you somebody's cook?"

Unaware of the unwritten statute against walking, the startled woman replied, "No, but I can toast crumpets." She was escorted back to the hotel, and her embarrassment became a joke at the station house.

By now Beverly's yearning for exclusivity had reached the point where the City Council passed an ordinance outlawing cemeteries in the golden ghetto. Celebrating the legislation, director Fred Niblo told a Chamber of Commerce luncheon meeting, "We are now the only city in the country without a cemetery. We live in Beverly Hills, but we're buried in Los Angeles." His audience gave Niblo a lusty round of applause. For some reason, Beverly Hills still glories in the fact that it doesn't have the decency to bury its own dead.

To carry the exclusivity even further, Douglas Fairbanks, Sr., proposed that a wall be built around the city to make it Fortress Beverly Hills. The Council seriously considered the idea for several months in 1929, dismissing it only when the merchants and the company running the tourist buses through town objected on grounds that too much privacy would keep cash customers away.

Another nettlesome problem existed for the wealthy stars of Beverly. It was publicly exposed when an unsigned letter appeared in the *Script* from a self-styled "prominent actor," charging that "all the servants in our fair city are swindlers. I know one famous star whose butler systematically knocked down a fortune over a period of six years and another whose chauffeur bought and paid for a business out of two years of graft."

"Of course there's graft," a letter of rebuttal said the next week. "Most of the people we work for are bums and we have to teach them etiquette. They even ask us to word invitations. All that is worth extra, but we don't get it. So we take it out by stealing a little. Most of them throw their money away anyhow, so why shouldn't we get a slice?"

It wasn't the first or last time that grievances between the rich and poor, the powerful and the powerless, would surface in Beverly Hills. Indeed, in the star versus servant battle, it was difficult to find sympathy for the movie lords, since one of America's least-known, least-examined economic miracles was occurring in Beverly Hills. As the rest of the nation was sinking into poverty, Beverly and its Hollywood suzerainty were enjoying unprecedented prosperity.

The public, as the dreadful decade of the Thirties shuffled in, was patronizing the theaters in numbers that would never be surpassed. Ninety million people a week sought escape in the dark sanctuary of the movie houses. For the nation, the joy ride of the Twenties was over; for Beverly Hills, the joy ride continued.

"Beverly Hills was settled by a group of wealthy people who wished to withdraw from the tumult of American life," the *Script* wrote nonchalantly as the nation struggled with financial disaster. "There is so much gaiety in Beverly Hills that the community suggests nothing so much as Queen Victoria turned Follies girl, wearing a blonde wig and doing a toe-dance in pink tights."

Beverly Hills could well afford to thumb its nose at hard times. In the midst of bust, its population had soared to 22,000, and it was the fastest-growing city in the nation. There were no bread lines, soup kitchens, or apple sellers in Shangri-La because 90,000,000 troubled people were keeping it lavishly afloat—and because the Beverly Hills police force barred the hungry and jobless from entering.

Everything in Beverly Hills was in mint condition—except the psyches of its more prominent citizens, who had discovered that no matter how much they were willing to spend, happiness, serenity, contentment, and peace of mind weren't on sale at Homer's drugstore.

3.
Such as It Was, the Dream Dies

BY THE 1930s, mergers and buy-outs had pole-vaulted five studios to the top of the Hollywood heap—Metro-Goldwyn-Mayer, Paramount, Warner Brothers, Twentieth Century-Fox, and RKO. The Beverly Hills titans who ran them had the best contacts with the banks to finance their films, owned the contracts of the most important stars, owned the majority of the nation's 16,000 theaters, and had a virtual monopoly on distribution.

Universal, Goldwyn, Columbia, Disney, Republic, and Monogram had to depend on the giants for scheduling their own releases in the important theaters in the big cities. Indeed the lesser studios relied totally on the majors. It is doubtful, for example, whether Columbia would have survived had not Louis B. Mayer decided to "punish" Clark Gable by lending him to Harry Cohn for *It Happened One Night*. The picture won Oscars for Gable, co-star Claudette Colbert, director Frank Capra, and writer Robert Riskin. It also allowed Harry Cohn to buy a mansion in Beverly Hills.

Grinding out 750 pictures a year, the film business was enjoying a higher rate of employment than any other industry in the nation. Hollywood prosperity meant prosperity for a fortunate few in Beverly Hills. And the economic contrast between the majority of Americans and the small movie minority in Beverly Hills could not have been more stark and striking; their wolfhounds and poodles were eating better than the average American.

Novelist Upton Sinclair gave a speech to the film elite at the Beverly Hills Hotel in October 1932, reminding them that the country wasn't a paradise from sea to shining sea. "Natural resources belong to all the people and should not be controlled by private interests," Sinclair said. "The present Depression will end only when the American people work out a new economic system."

The lip-service movie liberals listened to Sinclair's socialist ideas politely and applauded him warmly. But the last thing they wanted was a new economic system. They saw nothing wrong with the have/have-not status quo. Their reasoning was selfishly simple: so long as the rest of the country remained poor, Beverly would continue to enjoy riches.

During the Depression, a surprisingly large number of new, almost unbelievably opulent mansions were rising in Beverly Hills, conspicuous consumption amid conspicuous poverty. The services of those who occupied them came high; the services of those who built them and the materials they used came dirt-cheap.

Starting as a $3-a-day extra at Universal, Harold Lloyd had worked a pair of horn-rimmed glasses, a straw hat, death-defying acrobatics and pure love for pure heroines into a $25,000-a-week salary. But the shrewd lad from Burchard, Nebraska decided he didn't need the salary. He formed a company that produced and owned his films, a move that led to his amassing a $65,000,000 fortune. He named his sixteen-acre, two-million-dollar Italian Renaissance home Green Acres. Among its amenities: forty-four rooms in the main house, twenty-six bathrooms, kennel facilities for seventy-seven dogs, quarters for thirty-three servants, Olympic swimming pool, game pavilion, lighted tennis court, canoe lake, indoor handball court, and a theater organ in the living room.

A kid from Pittsburgh named William Powell didn't do badly either. He got a late start, not reaching Hollywood until he was twenty-eight, and his first roles were as the bad guy in the black hat, in sagebrush shoot-'em-ups. Powell hit the jackpot in six Thin Man pictures, playing the urbane Nick Charles. His mansion had a whitewashed brick exterior, a vestibule paneled with primavera wood imported from Guatemala, parquet floors, and a gallery connecting the front and rear wings of the house. A private master suite occupied the entire second floor. There was a thirty-foot solarium and twin tennis courts with a gallery for spectators.

The Powell place, however, was dwarfed by the Colonial erected next door on ten acres by Eric Lobban Cord, one of a small number of wealthy businessmen and socialites who'd found Beverly Hills preferable to such bastions of the rich as Newport or the lakeshore area outside Chicago. "To the American man in the street," said *Time* magazine in 1937, "the name Cord means a low-slung automobile, rare and swank, which is entirely too expensive for him to own. To that class that can afford the car, the name means a profane, bespectacled young capitalist whose life has been a garage mechanic's dream."

Cord was on the board of directors of a dozen companies. He controlled the firm that produced the Duesenberg, said by car buffs to be the most illustrious automobile ever manufactured. House buffs called his Beverly Hills place the most illustrious ever erected in Beverly Hills.

More than a million bricks were used to construct the two-story, five-pillared, 87-room main house, which had 36,000 square feet of walking area. The furniture was Chippendale, the walls mahogany, the drapes blue satin, and the floors white marble. There was an immense formal ballroom, crystal chandeliers, and a cocktail loggia reached by way of a curving marble staircase. The upper story had a billiard room, a shooting gallery, a taproom, and an organ chamber. Mrs. Cord's bathroom had 14-karat gold fixtures. There was an eighteen-car garage, and over it five apartments for chauffeurs and other servants. The play area on the park-like grounds was five hundred feet from the house. It consisted of a 100-foot swimming pool, a 50-foot playroom, a dining room, a kitchen, a projection room, and mahogany-paneled dressing rooms.

In the midst of such splendor, the eccentric Cord added a bucolic touch; he built what was undoubtedly the ritziest chicken coop of all time. For Cord's roosters and hens, it was chicken heaven. No expense was spared, the coop having mahogany walls, red-brick flooring, satin drapes, and gold vessels from which the chickens ate and drank. Chicken-raising was a Cord hobby, and many an American would unhesitatingly have changed places with the magnate's high-living fowl.

When moguls Mayer, Goldwyn, Selznick, and Cohn saw the Cord palace—all had been entertained there—they went home to their own modest million-dollar mansions wondering how they had failed.

Harry Cohn, as usual, was the bluntest commentator. "Those fucking chickens are better off than I am. All they do is eat and screw like goddamn kings. *They* don't have to worry about working their asses off running a goddamn studio."

As if coddled chickens weren't enough, more bad taste took place in Beverly Hills when "Depression parties" became a vogue. Socialite Clara Bell Walsh tossed one that had Bea Lillie, Grace Moore, Gracie Allen, and Fanny Brice in attendance. The girls cavorted in calico instead of finery—a grotesque gesture of "roughing it" like their fellow Americans. The spoiled and pampered stars chatted gaily and danced into the night. They ate from heaping French Regency tables piled high with delicacies. The press was invited to the calico gala; pictures were snapped and widely published. "It was a fun party," Gracie Allen said.

Such splashy displays of fiddle-playing while Rome burned stirred so many vituperative letters to the studios that Joan Crawford stepped forth as spokeswoman for the industry. In a remarkable *Photoplay* magazine interview, Miss Crawford, who'd made it to Beverly Hills via a Broadway chorus line, declared that it was her duty to enjoy her high living standard. Her public demanded that she reside in Beverly Hills, have diamonds, furs, and a limousine. Her public insisted that she continue to thrive in such fashion as an inspiration to them. She saw nothing wrong with her fans participating in her good fortune vicariously. Miss Crawford also had a solution to the Depression—believe in the dollar and revive the economy by spending. "I believe in the dollar," she said. "Everything I have, I spend." Miss Crawford, however, failed to explain how those who had nothing to spend could follow her selfless example to revive the economy.

The Sunset Strip nightclubs began to flower in this era. The Trocadero, Mocambo, Ciro's and a gambling den called the Clover Club were five minutes away from Beverly Hills, and they were crowded every night. Certainly Beverly Hills wasn't aware that the Roaring Twenties were supposedly over. Drunken producers tipped headwaiters $100 and tore the dresses from starlets. At one of the clubs one evening, a ranking female star publicly committed fellatio on a director. Down the street Robert Benchley, Charlie Butterworth, and Dorothy Parker (earning $5,000 a week as a scenarist) led a group who were making the Garden of Allah a spurious legend. At the bungalow-hotel they brawled and cursed, fornicated and drank, and pitied themselves for "selling out" to Hollywood. To pacify their collective consciences,

Dorothy Parker attempted with notable non-success to create a Beverly Hills branch of New York's Algonquin Roundtable in her home. Without George S. Kaufman, Alexander Woollcott, Heywood Broun, and Franklin P. Adams (all confirmed New Yorkers), the salon's repartee fell flat. Meantime up and down the Sunset Strip, men wearing sandwich boards advertised themselves as available for work. *I'm Hungry. I'll Do Any Honest Labor. I'm Not Proud,* said one.

The moguls of Beverly weren't proud either. They were doing business any way they could, and with anyone they could, to squeeze every dime they could from the nation's tattered jeans. In New York, they filed a successful legal action that wiped away the Sunday ban against moviegoing. In California, Louis B. Mayer threatened to move the film industry out of the state when legislators slapped a new inventory tax on the studios, and his pressure got the tax rescinded. In the worst of times, only the underworld was sharing the best of times with the residents of Beverly Hills. There was much similarity in their ethics.

Howard Hughes, for example, had lucked-in with his 1930 flying epic *Hell's Angels,* which made a star of blonde sexpot Jean Harlow. What he did for Harlow, he promised scores of girls, he could do for them. He was to use his star-maker leverage for fourteen years, making more girls than stars.

Hughes lived in a $100-a-day Beverly Hills Hotel bungalow and, part-time or overnight, in half a dozen homes he owned or rented in Beverly Hills.

Not until 1944 did Hughes make another star, and that was a freak success. Non-actress Jane Russell zoomed to popularity in *The Outlaw* because of a ton of breast publicity and because, for a time, the censors would not permit the picture to be shown.

In what Beverly Hills insiders call "the son-of-a-bitch sweepstakes," Louis B. Mayer ran a photo-finish with Hughes. An armload of books and magazines and newspaper articles have been printed concerning the excesses and tyranny of the ex-junk dealer who ruled Hollywood's powerhouse studio. One heretofore unpublished story involves the late Johnny Mack Brown, who had helped earn millions for MGM, co-starring in pictures with Greta Garbo and Joan Crawford.

When Mayer returned to his office on November 28, 1933, from a studio party celebrating his twenty-sixth year in show business, Brown was waiting for him. Mayer spotted him, and his party mood vanished quickly.

"You were like my own son," he told the startled actor. "Why couldn't you trust me? Why did you send a lousy agent in here to negotiate for you when you know I've always treated you fairly? You're through. Get out!"

What had transpired was that Brown had hired an agent, who simply and reasonably asked Mayer to increase his client's salary from $750 to $1,250 a week. The agent had been a former assistant of Mayer's at MGM, and Mayer himself had urged him to go into the agency business.

But Mayer's ire ruined both men. Blacklisted by Mayer, the agent committed suicide. Brown's career was confined to low-budget Monogram and Republic Westerns. He ended as an alcoholic, and years before he died in the Motion Picture Country Home in 1974, he had lost his house in Beverly Hills.

Two of the nation's most discussed events in the 1930s involved a pair of Beverly Hills' leading ladies, the first of them being Mary Pickford. After a run of fifteen years, the Fairbanks-Pickford fairy tale was over.

Shortly before the news broke, Will Rogers cracked, "My most important duty as mayor of Beverly Hills is directing folks to the home of Mary Pickford and Doug Fairbanks."

Now Pickfair became the sole property of Mary Pickford. Fairbanks gave her the estate as part of the divorce settlement when he left her for Lady Sylvia Ashley, a former chorus girl who had married and divorced an English title. The happily-ever-after marriage, *the* fairy-tale romance in the perfect setting, had lasted a long time by Beverly Hills standards.

But there was another fairy-tale romance to take its place. "Everybody in Hollywood who was in Hollywood Sunday attended the wedding reception of Paul Bern and Jean Harlow," according to *The Hollywood Reporter* of July 5, 1932.

Three months later, Bern killed himself, leaving the Benedict Canyon house to his wife. A brief five years later, Harlow died, burned out at the age of twenty-six.

Another Beverly Hills fairy tale that suddenly appeared to be tottering was that the town was immune to the Depression. There was a flash of terror when news reached Beverly that hard times had finally caught up to the movie business. One-third of the nation's theaters had closed, grosses were down, and for the first time since its founding, MGM's profit statement showed a loss.

Beverly Hills and its Hollywood tributary were the last to feel the Depression, but they were also the first to recover. Few of the film princes and princesses were hit hard or hit long. Emphasis on better quality, big-budget pictures helped. So did bank night, bingo, free dishes, air-conditioning the theaters, and the introduction of the double feature. Soon moviegoers were waiting in line for an hour or more, even at the neighborhood Loew's or RKO outlet, to take advantage of the bonuses and the low admission prices.

Life reeled on in the golden ghetto with surface smoothness. Each month the city collected 314 tanks of garbage, liberally spiked with empty bottles of post-Prohibition booze and with the bodies of at least twenty-five dead animals—everything from cats and dogs to sea lions and donkeys. The bodies were sold as feed to hog farmers in Los Angeles.

The Beverly Hills Police Department, always alert as to how it might better protect the better people, began fingerprinting every salesman who wanted to enter its environs. Indeed, Beverly was the first city to put such a policy into effect, though its constitutionality was doubtful. The Beverly cops assumed, as they still do, that hometown folk were innocent until proven guilty, but that precisely the reverse was true for non-residents.

Ordinarily the highest level of efficiency for the men in blue of Beverly Hills was flagging down pedestrians, handing out parking tickets, and nabbing speeders—especially at the city's busiest intersection, Wilshire and La Cienega, where 40,000 vehicles passed through daily. In a rare example of effective police work, and with the help of a fortuitous telephone tip, they apprehended a four-man gang that planned to kidnap Mary Pickford. After that, a pack of watchdogs became a part of the atmosphere at Pickfair. Mary Pickford, no longer "America's Sweetheart," had to be content with her new sobriquet, the "First Lady of Beverly Hills," and with her new husband, Buddy Rogers, a smiling, unassuming, all but invisible man.

Prosperity, long lurking around the corner in America, finally made the turn when the Japanese attacked Pearl Harbor. And Beverly Hills graciously consented to join the nation in the hostilities, pledging itself to fight, after a fashion, down to the last millionaire.

When a rumor spread that the Japanese had landed at Santa Monica, calls flooded the Chamber of Commerce and the police department. One woman asked if the water was safe to drink—she'd heard it was poisoned. Several residents wondered if the roads were safe enough for them to evacuate to their homes in Palm Springs. A man on North Camden Drive said he wanted the Chamber of Commerce to arrange a charter plane so he, his family and a number of like-minded patriots could reach the sanctuary of Acapulco.

John Barrymore chose to remain staunchly on the home front. He phoned the police and offered his house, atop what he considered the strategic knoll of Tower Road, as an anti-aircraft gun emplacement. Barrymore suggested that his swimming pool be drained and used to store emergency rations.

In the first rush of war, only one local casualty was reported. On December 8, 1941, with a blackout already in force, a teen-ager collided with his basement door and gashed his head.

Beverly Hills police, a trim strike-force, met invasion with counter-invasion. They fearlessly attacked the mansions of Beverly and grabbed every Japanese gardener and house servant in sight. The Japanese of Beverly went to U.S. concentration camps just as the Gabrielinos of Beverly once had been confined by Father Serra. Many local Japanese died at the Manzanar camp on the high desert near Lone Pine, California, never understanding why they were imprisoned. All were loyal; most had never seen Japan.

Beverly Hills did what it could to win the war with a checkbook. In 1942, more than $100,000,000 in interest-bearing bonds were sold in Beverly, an average purchase of $3,333 for each of the 29,000 people who resided in the city. A 1943 money drive resulted in $1,750,000 for the financing of a Flying Fortress which was christened "The City of Beverly Hills."

Beverly High added three new war-oriented courses to its curriculum. The police announced a crackdown on violators of the dim-out law. A simulated air raid was staged, with several dozen "enemy" parachutists landing in town during the mock exercise. Some locals speculated that, had the Japanese chosen Beverly Hills instead of Pearl Harbor for the first surprise hit of the war, the rest of the country would have capitulated immediately. If America's Garden of Eden went, what would be left that was worth fighting for?

The war brought the Beverly Hills–Hollywood moviemakers a billion-dollar bonanza, new prosperity heaped on old prosperity. Just as they had needed escape from Depression poverty, Americans now craved diversion from the grim headlines of world conflagration. The major leading men—Clark Gable, Jimmy Stewart, Tyrone Power, and Robert Taylor—were in uniform, but they weren't sorely missed. The studios turned out more schlock than at any other time in their history and discovered to their delight that patrons would pay to see anyone in anything.

Bob Hope, a resident of Beverly Hills before he moved to the San Fernando Valley, began his thirty-year career of entertaining GI audiences, men who were so eager to be diverted from the horrors of war that they would have welcomed an accordion player in drag.

Clark Gable, whose career was never to reach its pre-war heights after his discharge, served bravely and with as little fanfare as possible in the Air Force. He was forty years old when the war began; Bob Hope was thirty-seven. Hope came out of the war a solidly established, flag-waving star, far richer than Gable, who had been the king of Hollywood.

The war proved to be the high-water mark for Beverly Hills. Afterward the supermansion, the superstudio, and the superstar—the three entities that gave the town what distinctiveness, prestige and glamour it had—were to vanish.

The dream that Beverly Hills represented, never much even at its apex, was dead. What followed was a city living on reflected glory, borrowing from its past in a vain attempt to shore up its future.

The decline began with the disappearance of the huge estate. Land, servants, construction labor, and materials were no longer cheap. No more could anyone afford to acquire vast acreage and build and maintain a supermansion. Aside from the money involved, huge homes were out of beat with changing tastes. New buyers, including multimillionaires, preferred smaller houses and modern design.

The Cord mansion and Charlie Chaplin's villa fell to the wrecker's ball, and the grounds were subdivided. Harold Lloyd's Green Acres became the property of a non-profit foundation, then was sold to a subdivider. Greystone is rented to the American Film Institute for one dollar a year. Pickfair, one of the few remaining privately occupied supermansions, is slated to be turned into a Jewish home for the aged. That's her way, Miss Pickford says, of showing her gratitude to the Jewish moguls who made her career possible.

The studios, too, are either gone or survive only as a pale shadow of themselves—their demise hastened by television, by changing public tastes, and by a Supreme Court ruling that compelled the film factories to divest themselves of their theater chains. Fewer than 5,000 movie theaters now dot the American landscape.

Harry Cohn's Columbia lot has been abandoned, the remnants of his empire combined with the remnants of the studio sold by Jack Warner. The surviving amalgamation is called The Burbank Studios, which is poorly run and ridden with debt. MGM, RKO, Republic and Monogram are no more. Paramount is for sale. The Goldwyn lot survived by renting space to television production companies. The bulk of Disney's income is now derived, not from films, but from television and from its amusement parks in California and Florida. Twentieth Century–Fox sold off its back lot to the Aluminum Company of America, which used the land to develop Century City, a high-rent office building and apartment house complex adjacent to Beverly Hills.

Less than one hundred films a year are produced now, and the industry has appealed to Washington for government aid, calling Hollywood a job-short disaster area. The unemployment rate in most craft guilds is 40 to 50 per cent. William Howard, president of the Hollywood Film Council, says joblessness among actors is 85 to 90 per cent.

As for the superstars, there's only one left whose name alone will draw profitable patronage. But John Wayne is sixty-eight years old, running to fat, drinking too much, and smoking again after licking cancer and temporarily giving up cigarettes.

Many of the once-great stars had tragic finales. Rudolph Valentino, when he died of peritonitis in 1926 in New York, was physically and emotionally burned-out and totally alone. More than 100,000 hysterical mourners passed his bier at a Manhattan funeral home. Several committed suicide. Benito Mussolini sent a wreath. The services held for the consummate Latin Lover at Good Shepherd Church in Beverly Hills were more orderly, but his burial in the Court of the Apostles of Hollywood Memorial Park was tastelessly marred by Rudy Vallee, who sang, "There's a New Star in Heaven Tonight—Rudy Valentino." A sprinkling of dogged fans still visit his grave. The stay of the falcon of Falcon's Lair had been sad and swift, eerie and unhappy. He had lived only thirty-one years.

Will Rogers and his pilot Wiley Post were killed in a 1935 plane crash near Point Barrow, Alaska, on a flight to the Orient. In Rogers' memory, time has stopped at his ranch: the living-room clock is frozen at 8:17, the moment the plane went down. The cowboy wit had died prematurely at age fifty-six. Warned of the dangers, Rogers had made the needless flight anyway—simply to ward off boredom.

Douglas Fairbanks also died at age fifty-six, exhausted, overweight, deluding himself that he was still youthful by avoiding mirrors. His death came in 1939. His last film had been made in 1934. Fairbanks "was forced to retire because his romantic, zestful image could not fight middle-age spread," says film historian Leslie Halliwell. Before he died, Fairbanks said he had experienced everything life had to offer. He was tired of life. "Death is the only challenge left."

Tom Mix, another giant whose popularity waned after the coming of sound, dissipated his fortune. In his last years, the Pennsylvania-born cowboy became a heavy drinker. He died in a 1940 automobile crash at age sixty, after not having made a picture in seven years.

And the man who had once found it a source of amusement that he couldn't be buried in Beverly Hills *was* buried there—in a professional sense. After talkies, Fred Niblo worked infrequently, and he never topped his *Ben Hur* triumph. His end was painful when he died in 1948 at age seventy-four. His last film, in 1941, was an unremembered dreg, *Three Sons O'Guns.*

Conrad Nagel starred on the stage and in films from *Midsummer Madness* in 1920 to *The Man Who Understood* in 1959. After that he played only minor character roles. The seventy-four-year-old Nagel, always a reliable Beverly Hills tub-thumper, was reduced to running a school for actors before he passed away in 1970.

Following an unsuccessful attempt to revive his career, Harold Lloyd spent the final decades of his life in frustration, engaging himself in the trifling civic affairs of Beverly Hills. In *Sunset Boulevard*, the character played by William Holden described Lloyd's Green Acres, where much of the film was shot, as "the kind of a place that crazy movie people built in the crazy Twenties." Lloyd in his last years did little entertaining and indulged himself in such offbeat, if not "crazy" pleasures, as letting his garish Christmas tree remain standing and lit the year round. Lloyd would call a few intimate friends and discuss his family. "They're lost, just lost, that's all I can say," was the way he summed up his wife and Harold Lloyd, Jr., both of whom preceded him in death.

The younger Lloyd, after an unsuccessful fling at show business, died owing money to all his professional contacts. "Go sue me," he told his press agent, while refusing to pay a $1,300 tab. Harold Lloyd did not go gently into that good night when he died in 1971 at the age of seventy-eight. The crosses he carried with him to the grave were his son's homosexuality and his wife's alcoholism.

Two other personalities who indirectly and directly had much to do with the creation of Beverly Hills as a homeland for the caudillos of celluloid are long departed. "Whatever happened to Fatty Arbuckle?" King Alphonso asked Douglas Fairbanks when the squire of Beverly Hills visited Spain. Arbuckle's sole contact with films after the San Francisco scandal was as the director of three shorts for Warner Brothers. He worked under the ironic pseudonym of Will B. Good. Forty-six years old, he died in 1933.

After reigning as movie czar from 1922 to 1945, Will Hays was replaced by public relations expert Eric Johnston as president of the Motion Picture Association of America. Living to a ripe seventy-five, Hays died in 1954, self-righteous to the end, certain that his reign over Hollywood and the role he had played had bought him his ticket to heaven.

Indeed, dead or inactive are all the moguls who helped build Beverly's reputation as Hollywood's bedroom. Laemmle, Mayer, De-Mille, Selznick, Cohn, Goldwyn, and three of the Warner brothers are gone. At age eighty-two, Jack Warner is ailing, suffering from a serious eye infection. Adolph Zukor, retired since 1965, is one hundred and three years old. Darryl Zanuck, since being deposed from his throne at Fox in 1971, has resided in sullen anonymity in New York. The former owner of RKO, Howard Hughes, makes headlines now only for his eccentricities.

Fresh postscripts to old legends enliven the Beverly Hills landscape from time to time, such as when Charlie Chaplin returned, in April 1972, to receive a special Academy Award. The Los Angeles *Herald-Examiner*, recalling an earlier romance, headlined: CHAPLIN BACK TO LITA GREY HOME IN THE WEST. So controversial was his reappearance that the Academy had to hire five round-the-clock bodyguards to protect him at his Beverly Hills Hotel bungalow.

It was his first visit to the golden ghetto since his departure twenty years earlier. He'd left after having been involved in still another scandal, a paternity suit filed by his freckle-faced girl friend, Joan Berry, who claimed that her infant was conceived at The Little Tramp's estate on Summit Drive. "I spent many evenings with Mr. Chaplin at his home," she testified. At the time of their romance, Chaplin was fifty-four, Miss Berry, twenty-three. Chaplin was ordered to pay child support.

Chaplin had also been caught up in a good deal of nasty wrangling with the government. The Justice Department had assailed him for "moral turpitude." Government agents had invaded his estate and questioned his servants about his private life. Conducting its own investigation, the House Committee on Un-American Activities had chastised him for not becoming a United States citizen and had charged that such films as *The Great Dictator, City Lights,* and *Modern Times* smacked of Red propaganda. In addition, Chaplin had a tax squabble with the Internal Revenue Service. Faced with all these problems, Chaplin had fled to Switzerland in 1952, to a 95-acre estate near Lake Geneva.

In the subsequent two decades, much had been forgiven and forgotten, but much was not. When Chaplin received his Academy Award for "the incalculable effect he has had in making motion pictures the art form of this century," most of Hollywood stood up and cheered. But the letters that poured into Chaplin's bungalow and to the Academy ran about two to one against him.

"A traitor to this country," read one that was typical.

"His political beliefs of whatever persuasion should not be allowed to obscure his comedic brilliance," said a typical supporter.

In the view of Ronald Reagan, then governor of California, there had been a "noble forgetfulness" of the eighty-three-year-old comedian's past troubles. Chaplin was a genius, said Reagan; however, the government officials who had drummed him out of the country should not feel guilty because "they were not wrong."

The Los Angeles *Times,* on the other hand, felt that Chaplin had been a victim of political persecution and that he should receive a formal apology from the government in addition to his Academy Award.

William C. Jordan, in charge of the detail guarding Chaplin at the hotel, revealed that the comedian "expected to be shot" during his visit. According to Jordan, Chaplin commented, "They killed Mr. Kennedy, didn't they?"

"I can't give the exact number of death threats," Jordan reported, "but there were at least a dozen. They were all anonymous and most of them came by telephone. But they said they were going to kill Chaplin.

"With anonymous phone callers there isn't much you can do, so we had to assume that someone would try. Sometimes they specified they were going to blow him up or shoot him. Sometimes they didn't specify how it would be done. Chaplin went away so fast, I think, because he was fearful."

The comedian's visit had lasted four days.

Mary Pickford was asked by an interviewer how she felt about the praise that had been heaped on Chaplin by the Academy and the press. The twice-divorced First Lady of Beverly Hills, married to her third husband, said of the twice-divorced Chaplin, married to his third wife, "I think they should ask some of his ex-wives what they think of him." She called Chaplin "a stinker," and said she disapproved of his leftist leanings. Regarding their one-time business association as partners in United Artists, Miss Pickford said, "As Sam Goldwyn would say, 'I can tell you in two words: Im-possible.' "

The former next-door neighbors didn't see each other during Chaplin's return. In fact, they had not seen each other since 1951.

Another figure from the past, an actress who had done her share in making Beverly Hills the home of the stars, resurfaced after Chaplin's visit; she appeared before Los Angeles Superior Court Judge Benjamin Landis on March 26, 1973. No one recognized her until she identified herself as Mary Miles Minter.

She was now a seventy-one-year-old, gray-haired, portly woman. It had been fifty-one years since she had been exiled from the film industry because of her involvement in the William Desmond Taylor murder case.

Miss Minter had filed a $350,000 suit against CBS, Rod Serling, and two sponsors—the Mentholatum Company and Van de Kamp's Bakeries. She charged that in two segments of *Rod Serling's Wonderful World of Crime*, televised on CBS, she had been "placed willfully in a context of murder . . . by relating her—after a philosophical homily upon crime—to the events preceding and surrounding the assassination of William Desmond Taylor." She claimed invasion of privacy.

Judge Landis called Miss Minter's action a "non-suit," and he refused to submit the case to a jury.

"It is clear from the evidence," the judge said, "that the scope of [Miss Minter's] privacy, at least with regard to the 1922 murder of William Desmond Taylor, is more limited than a normal individual's scope of privacy. . . . The evidence shows that the [murder] was and still is a historical event of continuing interest, particularly to this locale."

He added that it was clear the defendants had not intended any malice or recklessness in producing the programs, which were neither offensive nor objectionable.

Defeated and haggard, Mary Miles Minter lumbered heavily out of the courtroom.

Of the eight film luminaries who kept Beverly choked off from annexation to Los Angeles in 1923, only Mary Pickford survives—and she is confined to her Pickfair bedroom, an eighty-two-year-old recluse, plagued by ill health. Since 1972, she has attempted to spark interest among theater owners in reshowing some of her outmoded silents—*My Best Girl*, in which she co-starred with Buddy Rogers, *Little Lord Fauntleroy*, *Suds*, *Little Annie Rooney*, and *Rebecca of Sunnybrook Farm*—and a talkie, *Taming of the Shrew*, her only film with Douglas Fairbanks. Miss Pickford spent $250,000 on new prints of her old films and new musical scores. Failing to attract an audience, the venture proved a pathetic, expensive, empty valedictory.

Clearly, the changes wrought in the movie business have drastically altered the complexion, the beat, the atmosphere, and the personality of Beverly Hills. No longer the home of moguls and stars, it is instead a petulant little community struggling for survival. The blonde wig of "Queen Victoria turned Follies girl" is tattered and frayed.

4.
Behind the Palm-Tree Curtain

THE MYTH of Beverly Hills dies hard.

Despite its well-publicized movie-star tragedies, the image of Beverly Hills as the ultimate American Dream is alive and well—thanks to the media and to misrepresentation by the local Chamber of Commerce.

Virtually all Americans still think of the place as a town occupied solely by film celebrities and consider it the last frontier of elegance, style, charm, and wit.

In truth, the palm-tree façade hides a gross, neglected, decaying community that struggles unsuccessfully with many of the same problems afflicting other cities in the United States. Beverly also has problems that are unique unto itself, foremost among them being a highly mobile, younger generation that is just as miserable amid affluence as their predecessors were.

Since 1950, when the population was 29,032, there have been 4,384 "seekers of the dream" who have made it to Beverly Hills. The official head-count, according to the 1970 census, is 33,416.*

*A 1975 U.S. Census Bureau update revealed that Beverly's population curve was down by 702 people, despite the proliferation of multi-unit apartment buildings and condominium complexes.

Half the dream-chasers who move to Beverly do not stay for any length of time. Fifty per cent of the residents, says the Census Bureau, left between 1965 and 1970 and were replaced by newcomers. The heavy turnover, which continues to the present day, provides a perpetual windfall for the town's 341 real-estate brokers, who are unusually adept at selling the old, tattered dream to new believers. A city that overhauls its population so drastically and so swiftly cannot, by any stretch of the imagination, be designated an "ideal residential community," which is the way the Chamber describes it.

According to one long-time broker in Beverly: "There's hardly a house in the city that isn't for sale. Some people, including what's left of the old show-business crowd, hang on because they can't get the price they're asking. In general, there's very little loyalty to the city because so many come and go so rapidly. This isn't a town where people sink roots. It's more motel than city."

While driving a friend through Beverly in his Cadillac, Irwin Zucker, a book promoter and public-relations man who lives across the street from Doris Day, points out dozens of vacant homes. "There's one," he says, "that has a price tag of $350,000. It was owned by a family named Jones. They moved, I suppose, because they couldn't keep up with all the other Joneses."

The Joneses presumably left Beverly for the same reasons so many others leave—the overhead is too high, the quality of life is disappointing, the reputed quality of the police protection and of the school system is a mirage. Ex-Beverlyites discovered they were paying a premium for what they could get better and more cheaply elsewhere.

As cities go, Beverly Hills is unusually small in area, a mere 5.7 square miles. Instead of gold, its streets are paved with plebeian concrete, much of it broken, pocked, stained and strewn with garbage. It has 41 miles of alleys, which are slum-filthy, and 160 miles of sewers and storm drains badly in need of repair. It is beset by the slam-bang noise of low-flying airplanes, by screeching bumper-to-bumper automobile congestion, and by one of the heaviest concentrations of smog in Southern California. The thick gunk in the air is the reason why Frank Sinatra and thousands of others have either put their homes on the block or spent as little time as possible in the golden ghetto. Among those few who have the money and leisure for frequent travel or who have a second or third home away from Beverly, the local pad is used only when it is necessary to be in town on business. Sinatra spends forty weeks a year at his Palm Springs layout.

For necessity, luxury, or sin, Beverly Hills is among the world's most expensive cities in which to live and shop on a day-to-day basis. The moment anyone steps into Beverly, the cost of living, no matter what is being purchased, rises anywhere from 20 to 2,000 per cent. Even the outlay for a prostitute can run $300 a night. The same girl providing the same service to a patron outside Beverly Hills will charge as little as $25.

In emotional wear and tear, the city extracts a fearful penalty. The town leads the nation in the per capita number of residents who have been or are in therapy. Its suicide rate is twice the national average.

For its size and population, Beverly is also the most snobbish of cities, a charge denied by Bob Burns of the Chamber of Commerce. "I don't find snobbery among the people who live in Beverly Hills," he says. "If there is snob appeal concerning Beverly Hills it is from persons who don't live here but come to Beverly Hills, either to shop or to patronize an attorney, a doctor, a bank. I hear constantly from people, 'I've got to see my attorney in Beverly Hills.' Or, 'I went to my dentist yesterday in Beverly Hills.' To me this is the type of snob appeal we have."

The Chamber's own prose, however, belies that position. Trading handily on snob appeal, one of its brochures asserts ridiculously, "Never in the history of the world has such a small community attained so much influence on the entire international scenes of entertainment, fashion, sports, the amenities of everyday living. The city exerts profound world-wide influence. It is a wonderful place to live."

It requires little investigation to discredit such pap. But the Beverly Chamber must be heeded because, unlike most chambers of commerce in American cities, the Beverly propaganda outfit wields considerable influence. As spokesman, activist, under-the-table shaker and mover, and front for 1,700 businessmen, it is the town's most important power bloc, next to the City Council. The Chamber, acting as a lobby, often initiates legislation that the Council supinely approves.

In some respects, the Chamber is more important than the Council. It is Beverly's window to the world, projecting the town's supposedly rich, sophisticated image. From the Chamber's portals flow millions of pieces of misleading literature each year. Its hirelings write the specious ads that appear in magazines with high-income readership, such as *The New Yorker*, singing the praises of Beverly as a convention city and tourist attraction.

Actually, no convention of any size is held in Beverly. Its three major hotels, the Beverly Hills, the Beverly Wilshire, and the Beverly Hilton, are too small. Among many other well-attended affairs, the Academy Awards and the star-laden SHARE show, which raises about $250,000 a year for handicapped children, have transferred their annual gatherings to the copious Santa Monica Auditorium. There are *no* tourist attractions in Beverly Hills, unless visitors wish to contemplate the outside walls and foliage of movie-star homes which, with few exceptions, are no longer occupied by movie stars. A brief attempt to open Harold Lloyd's Green Acres estate to the public, on a paid-admission basis, failed when neighbors complained of noise, litter, and traffic.

The Chamber also selectively gathers statistics that give the world an impression of Beverly Hills the Bountiful and Beautiful. However, as with the sham brochures and ad copy, the surface statistics are not what they appear to be. The entire town has a net worth, the Chamber proclaims, of two billion dollars, and about three billion dollars repose in its twenty-six banks and ten savings and loan institutions. The five-billion-dollar total puts all the assets of Beverly well within the economic reach of such superbillionaires as Howard Hughes, computer king Ross Perot, Doris Duke, Barbara Hutton, Christina Onassis, J. Paul Getty, the Mellons of Pittsburgh, the heirs of the late H. L. Hunt, or the Rockefeller, Ford, and Kennedy clans. Any of them—all far richer than anyone in Beverly—could buy the city lock, stock, and problems.

Interestingly, none of the superbillionaires have found it necessary or desirable to spend their lives in Beverly. J. Paul Getty, returning from fifteen years of residence in England, announced he planned to live in Malibu, not Beverly Hills.

In its stream of paper drivel, the Chamber unfailingly refers to Beverly as "America's most affluent community," implying it is united, lacks poor people, is financially homogeneous—a whipped-cream heaven where everyone feasts daily on lobster and Dom Perignon. But as rich or richer than Beverly Hills are such well-off enclaves as Grosse Pointe, Michigan; Shaker Heights, Ohio; Lake Forest, Illinois; Palm Beach, Florida; Scarsdale, New York; Westport, Connecticut; and Belvedere, a suburb near San Francisco.

Nevertheless, the Beverly Chamber blithely claims that average income per household—$35,000—is the highest in the nation. Moreover, the Chamber adds, Beverly Hills is a "municipality where spendable income of its residents is at least four times as high as that of the average city in the United States—a per capita buying power of $30,000 per household."

It isn't made clear how a Beverly Hills family can have an income of $35,000 and $30,000 to spend. In the $35,000 income range, a family, before deductions, is subject to a 25 to 36 per cent Federal tax bite. There are also city, county, and state taxes. Too, the "typical" family in Beverly has unusually heavy fixed costs—high mortgage or rent payments, as well as exorbitant local prices for food, clothing, and utilities and ferocious bills for upkeep of the house beautiful. Rather than having an annual $30,000 to spend, a family in Beverly is fortunate, once overhead is subtracted, to break even at the end of the year. Most do not.

The far more objective figures of the Census Bureau show that, in four of Beverly's six census tracts, average household income is considerably less than $35,000 a year, and two-thirds of the population live in those four tracts.

The wealthiest neighborhoods in Beverly Hills are the two tracts in the northern section of the city. The Census Bureau divides these two into western and eastern. In the western tract, where some of the old mansions still exist, average family income is $50,000. In the eastern tract, which includes the overpriced and pedestrian Trousdale Estates, the norm is $48,370. However, in the four southern tracts of the city, annual income slides to $18,202; $17,258; $16,190; and $14,411. This is the 66 per cent of the city that obviously finds it impossible to spend the Chamber's $30,000 per family.

Beverly Hills isn't even the richest city in Los Angeles County. According to the Federal census arithmetic, Beverly Hills doesn't match the wealth of coastal Palos Verdes or San Marino, which abuts Pasadena and was the birthplace of General George Patton. Nor does Beverly measure up to those two in educational levels, the yardstick considered by many economists and social scientists to be a principal factor in determining income. A table of comparison, drawn from Census Bureau statistics follows.

Out of a total of 15,385 households in Beverly Hills, the census also discloses, only 3,678 families have incomes *above* $25,000. Of the 3,678, according to information from the IRS, less than one hundred families have a net worth of $1,000,000, and less than fifty are multimillionaires. There lies the joker in the Chamber's misleading claim. The income of

	Average Family Income	Per Cent of Families with Incomes Above $15,000	Median School Years Completed	Per Cent Who Completed 4 Years of High School or More
Beverly Hills	$20,434	62.2	13.0	79.4
Palos Verdes	$23,760	84.3	15.8	93.1
San Marino	$25,103	78.4	15.8	91.3

the rich and the super-rich are averaged into the earnings of the remainder of the city.

The true picture that emerges from the government's data is that Beverly Hills is a tight economic circle. Of the 10,131 people who live in the north, in private homes occupying well over half the city's land area, fewer than 1 per cent are measurably rich. These are the storybook people of storybook Beverly Hills. Among the anonymous 23,285 who reside in modest homes and apartments in the south, income is unspectacular. And for many, income is virtually non-existent, though the Chamber of Commerce declares, "The reputation for affluence within Beverly Hills is neither ephemeral nor illusory."

How ephemeral and illusory affluence is for almost 25 per cent of Beverly's citizens can be gauged by the number living in want. Amid the trappings of plenty, 4.5 per cent of the residents exist below poverty level, which the Department of Labor defines as a yearly maximum income of $2,100 for a single person and no more than $5,000 for a family of four. The census, additionally, uncovered another 19.4 per cent of the city's residents whose incomes ranged from $4,001 to a top of $7,000. The majority of the 23.9 per cent at the lowest rung of the economic ladder are senior citizens. The poor of Beverly Hills, who manage to survive by living two or three to an apartment and by eating cheap, starchy foods, are twice damned by the mystique of the town. They pay a bonus for a Beverly Hills address and at the same time are treated callously by the City Council and the northern nobility.

One of the most salient realities of Beverly is that it is *two* cities —economically, socially, and geographically—with no viable communication between north and south. The dividing line is Santa Monica Boulevard, along which run the Southern Pacific railroad tracks, still used late at night by the "Beverly Cannonball" (top speed: fifteen miles an hour) to haul freight into town. Everything above Santa Monica Boulevard is north, and north is definitely right, while south is definitely wrong.

One old-timer, wise in the ways of Beverly Hills, sums it up this way: "The closer you live to Olympic Boulevard [at the southern extremity of the city] the poorer you are. Each block north of Olympic means that you must have an income of at least $5,000 to $10,000 more a year. When you get north of Santa Monica, you really have to be in good financial shape and have a speaking acquaintance with the president of the bank, not just the local manager. In some of those places way north of Sunset Boulevard, you have to own the bank or have a speaking acquaintance with God Almighty."

Santa Monica Boulevard in effect is Douglas Fairbanks, Sr.'s cherished wall, separating and insulating the wealthy from the less wealthy and the have-nots.

A final statistic, repeated endlessly as an inducement for living in Beverly Hills, is its low property-tax rate. Of the seventy-seven incorporated cities in Los Angeles County, Beverly Hills does have the lowest rate, but it is not that low. Homeowners pay $9.66 per $100 of assessed valuation. (Assessed valuation is computed at the rate of one-fourth the market value of the home.) In Burbank, primarily a blue-collar town and the location of Lockheed, NBC, Disney Studios and Warner Brothers, the bill is $10.54, only $.88 higher. In Los Angeles city, which has the most punishing rate in the county, the bite is $12.87, which is $3.21 more than in Beverly Hills. But the Beverly Hills homeowner winds up paying a much greater amount because the high market value of his house breeds a higher assessed valuation.

Whatever minor tax advantage presently accrues to the Beverly Hills householder is canceled out, not only by the elevated cost of everything purchased locally, but by the horrendous price of maintenance. In a typical instance, the proprietor of a house on North Hillcrest Drive replaced his water pipes and much of his electrical wiring. The cost, even after he took the lowest of three bids, was $10,000. The same job almost any place else in the county would have been one-third to one-half that amount. Beverly Hills property owners are being taken. They know it, the skilled craftsmen who serve them know it, but the system persists.

Moreover, the days of Beverly as a tax paradise are numbered. Irwin Zucker attests his property taxes hurtled more than 150 per cent between 1966 and 1975. And he is not an exception.

"We're seeing a great deal of taxpayer resistance, which is relatively new in Beverly Hills," says one high-ranking municipal administrator. "Beverly Hills is running into more tax problems than heretofore."

Ignoring galloping inflation, which has raised the amount spent for all goods and services purchased by the city, and disregarding at least three million dollars' worth of bureaucratic fat in Beverly's budget, the administrator lays the blame for rising taxes solely and squarely on municipal workers, who merely want to keep pace with the rise in their cost of living and to gain wage parity with employees of adjoining communities.

The administrator adds: "The police and fire departments have militant employee representatives who make what seem like unreasonable demands, and this, in turn, sometimes makes the administration over-react with a very hard-nosed, adversary stand. Labor-management relations in Beverly Hills need to be overhauled and improved. Excessive demands from the unions, which is part and parcel of collective bargaining, may result in a reduction or lowering of public services if more money cannot readily be raised."

At its current tax level, the city amasses an annual revenue of $22,000,000 (excluding financing for schools), and that isn't enough to provide even essential services.

One example is protection against fire, which is a shockingly dangerous hazard in Beverly. The city learned nothing from the disastrous 1961 conflagration in neighboring Bel Air and Brentwood, which destroyed 484 homes and caused $25,000,000 in damage. It was California's worst fire and the fifth costliest in U.S. history.

Catered to in all other matters, the richest residents of Beverly in the hilly north above Sunset Boulevard have the least amount of fire protection. Much the same careless, untreated conditions exist there as those that allowed the Bel Air/Brentwood blaze to rage out of control —uncut brush, shingle rooftops, and narrow streets that have not been widened so that fire trucks can maneuver quickly and without difficulty.

The southern section of the city faces danger, too. By ordinance, apartment houses, all of which are situated in the south, can be no taller than six stories. Commercial buildings, also all located in the south, are limited to ten floors. But, while pressing the City Council for a law that would require owners of buildings to install sprinklers and other safety paraphernalia, Fire Chief Harold Bordner declared that his ladder equipment will only reach to the fifth or sixth floor. He wasn't sure which. But he *was* certain that "people in a ten-story building are beyond any help I could give now." Twenty per cent of the business buildings in Beverly are in that height range.

The Council listened and did nothing except to agree to study the matter further. It did not appropriate a dime for additional ladder equipment. Nor did it pass any legislation to compel landlords to make their buildings as fireproof as possible.

While Bordner repeatedly pleaded for improved, modern protective measures against fire, the Council was not averse to spending money. It allocated $800,000 for an unneeded municipal computer system; $332,338 to a bureaucratic boondoggle called the Building and Planning Department; $25,648 to overhaul a park fountain (about the same amount required for the sorely needed ladder equipment); $21,397 for tennis courts and lockers; and $19,753 for tree replacement. The Council thus exhibited its normal genius for misplaced priorities.

Meanwhile, Bordner continues to warn that, so far as fire protection is concerned, Beverly Hills is "living with a veritable bomb."

5.
"Something Special"

POLITICALLY, BEVERLY HILLS is a strange hybrid. Of the 24,256 who registered to vote in the 1972 Presidential election, 14,372 signed as Democrats, most espousing liberalism. Republicans numbered 7,892, rang-
ing from moderate to somewhere right of Hitler. The radical Peace and
Freedom Party, independents, and those who declined to state any
preference accounted for the other 1,992.

For the voters of Beverly, conflict was built into the Nixon–
McGovern race. The city could claim Nixon as an ex-resident, thereby
owing him a certain loyalty for the three years he had lived in Trousdale Estates. McGovern, however, seemed the perfect candidate for
the town's liberal majority.

The vote was close. With Democrats outnumbering Republicans by
almost two to one, only Beverly Hills joined Massachusetts and
Washington, D.C., in bucking the Nixon landslide. But McGovern's
victory was hardly impressive. The South Dakota senator captured the
city by twelve votes, 8,863 to 8,851—with 6,542 citizens, a hefty 25 per
cent of the eligible electorate, too disinterested to cast a ballot.

Since Democrats running for national office invariably win hands
down in Beverly Hills, McGovern's margin was actually a defeat. A
flock of dinner-table liberals had apparently switched to Nixon. How-

55

ever, with the hindsight of Watergate, Beverly obviously gave its vote to the preferable candidate.

Characteristically, Nixon counted only the numbers, and took his defeat in Beverly with his usual lack of grace. He remarked that that was no way for his former hometown to treat him.

Nixon had further reason to dislike and distrust Beverly Hills. His sojourn in the city had not been happy. Even though he was an ex-Vice President of the United States at the time, Beverly had been alternately indifferent and hostile to him. When he remarked, "This town's too Jewish," Groucho Marx and other Nixon neighbors responded with ridicule. Numerous wisecracks made the party circuit rounds: "Nixon's five o'clock shadow breaks out at two o'clock." "He still looks like a used Edsel salesman." "He'd flunk a political science course at Beverly High." Not famous for his sense of humor, Nixon didn't appreciate the jokes.

Beverly thus lost whatever chance it had of becoming the Western White House when Nixon was elected for his first Presidential term. He chose instead the friendlier, more conservative WASP-ish ground of San Clemente in Orange County.

The sting of defeat and disrespect may also have been the reason Beverly Hills was so well-represented on the "enemies" list prepared by White House counsel John Dean (who now lives in a modest Beverly Hills home). More than fifty Beverlyites made the list, including Norman Lear, producer of *All in the Family*. Lear said he thought he was on the list "because the Nixon Administration finally figured out I was my Bunker's keeper. On the show Archie and Mike have fought a great deal about the Administration and I have known that they (the Administration) have not been pleased."

Making the list, too, was producer-writer Paul Henning, an ardent McGovernite. Henning, who does not live in Beverly, was the creator of *The Beverly Hillbillies* television series, which made no pretense of presenting an accurate portrayal of Beverly but which had the unfortunate result of perpetuating in the popular mind the usual money-mansion view.

Though one out of four Beverly cosmopolites failed to vote for any Presidential candidate, participation in at-home elections plummets far deeper. Indifference by local citizens to local issues is standard.

One of the most divisive and highly publicized issues in recent years was whether or not Beverly should fluoridate its water. It culminated in a special January 1974 election in which a mere 4,830 voters turned out, some 22 per cent of those who were eligible. The pro-fluoridation-ists won by a count of 2,618 to 2,212.

"It's incredible—and a bit scary," the Beverly Hills *Independent* editorialized about citizen apathy. "We scream like wounded eagles when a jet plane flies over our homes, or when a freeway route threatens our parcel of property, yet we go quietly when it comes to fooling around with our drinking-water system. Less than 5,000 people went to the polls to vote on a proposal affecting the health and lives of nearly 34,000 people . . . making it possible for 406 individuals to authorize tampering with the water supply for multiple thousands."

In fact water, the issue that triggered the sovereignty battle in 1923, has remained a continuing bugaboo. The affluent town has possibly the worst water in the nation, so foul-tasting and dirty that many restaurants will serve it only on request, and at the patron's peril. Bottled-water companies do a thriving residential business.

In one more effort to upgrade the water supply, another special election was called in April 1974. Beverly voters were asked to decide if 7.7 million dollars in water bonds should be approved. Also on the ballot were two important seats on the Board of Education.

A four-to-one majority approved the water bonds, and the same majority voted to retain the incumbents on the Board of Education. Total turnout: a scant 4,027 voters, 18.6 per cent of those entitled to vote. In short, the issues of water and schools had no relevance for 81.4 per cent of the city's electorate.

Similar voter turnouts elect the City Council, an unusual quintet that is unpredictable in all things but ineptitude. Considering their individual backgrounds and success in private life, they should govern at a high rate of effectiveness and intelligence, but they do not. And though two-thirds of the population lives in the southern portion of the city, four of the five Council members are from the north. As a group, the Council supposedly has a liberal cast. But in reality, it is reactionary. The Council speaks solely for the selfish interests of a comparative handful of homeowners in the north, a bloc interested only in maintaining the status quo.

No Council member seriously speaks for the impoverished or less wealthy bulk of the populace on the wrong side of the tracks; for senior citizens, who compose 20 per cent of the inhabitants; for the ghetto's discontented young people; for the small number of non-whites who find lonely, uneasy shelter in Beverly; or for the businessmen who largely support the town, paying in excess of 70 per cent of the tax revenue that the city collects. The clout of the Chamber of Commerce turns marshmallow-soft when it comes to arranging a fair shake from the Council for its businessmen members.

The merchants of Beverly complain bitterly that they pay a vastly disproportionate amount of taxes in comparison with homeowners. At the same time, they are severely shortchanged in the quality and quantity of services that flow from City Hall. The situation exists because the majority of Beverly's businessmen do not live in town, and cannot punish the Council members at the polls. The most politically aware Beverlyites, and those who turn out most consistently at elections, are northern householders. Since the votes are in the north, it follows that the town's largesse goes there.

Because of the Council's punitive taxes against its merchant class, not only is business turnover heavy, but few new prestige establishments have moved into Beverly in recent years. In 1975, the town lost branches of two important department stores, Neiman-Marcus and Bullock's. High taxes and restrictive parking codes made it impossible for them to operate profitably. Though the Council is a tool of the wealthier homeowners, it fails to serve even that constituency well. As a governing body, it is a prime example of the American upper bourgeoisie at its most inefficient and incompetent.

Shrewdly, Council members pay themselves only a nominal $200 a month, which effectively freezes out of its chambers any potential candidate who does not have an independent income. Each of the well-fixed lawgivers is elected for a four-year term. There is no direct election of the mayor. Among themselves, Council members pass the mayor's post around each year like a tray of caviar.

Though service on the Council is a part-time job, its meetings are nevertheless notorious for a high rate of absenteeism. Many sessions are postponed. Some never get off the ground. On one occasion the mayor was vacationing in Acapulco, the vice mayor was reportedly ill, and a third member was at a board of directors meeting. The two remaining solons gazed haplessly at each other and adjourned official city business until the following week.

On another occasion, the Council saw fit to meet out of town. Bill Reeder, editor of the *Independent*, noted: "Beverly Hills City Hall's unlisted telephone number last weekend was in the balmy Palm Springs area, thanks to an unprecedented exodus of top echelon personnel—at taxpayers' expense—to the resort city. Our compliments, by the way, to the magician at City Hall who arranged a two-day, two-night spa junket for sixteen people, including lodging, transportation, food and partying."

Reeder soon had further complaints. The first five years of the 1970s, he wrote, "will be recorded in Beverly Hills history as the PGP—the Period of the Great Procrastinators, the time when City Councilmen put off, and put off and put off.

"Our elected officials log more study time than all of Beverly Hills High School; they postpone more often than you do with your dentist; they dally and haggle more than the U.S. Congress. They're long on going to outside consultants; they're short on fuse. They spend a lot of time, too, in executive sessions (both the press and general public are barred from such gatherings)."

As befits its self-declared aristocratic status, the Council—prior to its weekly meetings at the outmoded, wedding-cake City Hall—gathers for dinner at La Scala or another gourmet Beverly Hills restaurant and bills the city for "official business." Council members also use the local police as errand boys, to deliver their mail and paperwork from City Hall to their homes.

The Council's attitude toward city government is casual, sloppy, and frequently incomprehensible. The body has consistently and loftily rejected a solid offer of 25.7 million dollars from Standard Oil for the right to drill two wells in a non-residential area. Beverly sits on an oil site that geologists say is part of a 52-billion barrel reserve sloshing beneath Los Angeles.

Despite climbing taxes, a shortage of municipal funds, the energy crisis, and the oft-expressed desire of a majority of Beverlyites who want the wells drilled, the Council has concluded that removal of the oil would be "ecologically inadvisable." Yet acceptance of the offer would pour 8 million dollars into the tax coffers of the city, add 2.7 million dollars in funds to the school system, and give 15 million dollars to residents in lease and royalty payments.

The construction of a hospital in neighboring Century City, which employs 11,000 people and houses 5,000 in high-rent apartments and condominiums, presented Beverly Hills with a traffic problem. Instead of simply okaying a surface freeway or providing a no-red-light automobile corridor through the city, the Council concluded that the solution was a lawsuit to close down the skyscraper complex, hospital and all. The suit was not pressed only because the Council, after long debate, finally reached the conclusion that the courts wouldn't sustain Beverly's addled case. The Council had moved razor-close to Longfellow's observation, "Whom the gods would destroy, they first make mad."

The Council spends an inordinate amount of time on minutiae, deciding on the maximum number of cats that should be allowed per household (five, it finally decided), if a dentist can practice from his home (no, it decreed at last), or if one citizen could add a second tennis court to his property (yes, they ruled after discussing it for seven sessions).

Even on minor issues, there is an interminable amount of argument. The Council's habitual querulousness is reflected in the predominance of three-to-two votes or two-to-one decisions with abstentions. Lack of rubber-stamp agreement is healthy if and when there are honest clashes in philosophy, if there is reasoned debate, or if there are intelligent alternatives under consideration. But such situations seldom occur. What does occur is petty squabbling and verbal pyrotechnics, often personal in nature.

The Council itself is the best argument for the direct election of a strong, imaginative, independent, well-paid mayor—one invested with real power—to serve a four-year term, giving him time to implement his programs. The mayor, to be effective, should have veto power over the Council. The prime difficulties of the current setup are that untrained people are chosen to govern, that they govern in their spare time, that they aren't interested in governing (only in getting elected), that they aren't qualified to govern, and that it can cost as much as $30,000 to win a Council seat, which excludes those without a great deal of income from running for office. As a city, Beverly Hills is not a democracy but a slovenly oligarchy of the wealthy.

An excellent example of mediocre stewardship was the term of Mrs. Phyllis Seaton as mayor. In April 1973, she became the first woman mayor in the history of Beverly Hills. However, this, unfortunately, was not a victory for women's lib or for Beverly Hills. Mrs. Seaton spent her year as mayor in befuddlement. Her highest level of competence was as a mediator, her lowest as a proponent of government by cliché.

"I don't have a program," the grandmotherly Mrs. Seaton promptly announced when the Council handed her the mayorship like a watercress sandwich. Mayor Seaton was correct—she indeed had no program. She failed to whip the Council into action in behalf of the aged, the young, the poor, the city's employees, or its minorities; she did not attack, much less resolve, Beverly's unabated traffic problems.

Mrs. Seaton, the wife of the gifted producer-director-writer George Seaton (who earned Academy Awards for *Miracle on 34th Street* and *The Country Girl*), considered herself apolitical. She was much given, in her public pronouncements, to such banalities as: "If I've learned anything over the years, it's that words mean very little. I, as a person, and we, the Council, must try to show you by our deeds." . . . "Power is the ability to achieve purpose." . . . "It is important that we support what seems best for the people of the city." . . . "The Council's job is to listen." . . . "The world says Beverly Hills is unique. The talent of our citizens makes it unique and without the participation of the community, none of the Council can do anything." . . . "If the chain of command works well the mayor is the lead horse."

The only shred of wit surrounding Mrs. Seaton's elevation at City Hall came from her husband. Asked for his reaction at becoming a mayor's spouse, Seaton replied, "I've always felt that behind every successful woman is a husband who is exhausted."

At the conclusion of Mrs. Seaton's do-nothing term as mayor, March Schwartz, editor-publisher of the Beverly Hills *Courier*, leaned over backwards to be generous. He said: "She hasn't really had a chance. A bickering City Council, whose members were more concerned with politicizing than with accomplishment, has robbed Phyllis Seaton of the brilliance that could have marked her term as mayor of Beverly Hills. . . . The City Council has done her in with a lack of co-operation so blatant that it would have disheartened even the thickest-skinned politician, let alone a fine lady." Schwartz, however, left open the question of how such presumed brilliance could manifest itself from a woman who, on assuming office, seemed to find it a plus that she had no program for the city.

Upon her retirement, Mrs. Seaton asked a friend, Mrs. Donna Ellman, the wife of an orthopedic surgeon, to run for her seat. Apparently, the Council needed a token woman member, regardless of ability and regardless of the fact that Mrs. Ellman had no previous political experience. More from boredom than any other reason, Mrs. Ellman entered the race and won.

A feisty, brown-eyed brunette, she acknowledges that Beverly has imperfections. "This golden ghetto," she says, "has peroxide wings, meaning it's not always gold that glitters. There are kids on the *north* side who can't afford to buy a new suit for graduation from grade school. And they aren't children of maids. I suppose they're from divorced homes, I don't really know who they are."

Mrs. Ellman lives north of Santa Monica Boulevard and, like all her Council colleagues, when the chips are down, she votes the interests of Beverly's homeowners.

Asked if she's a feminist, Mrs. Ellman spins out a glib cliché of her own. "I'm an individualist. I believe in people." She says, too, "I'm not a liberal or a conservative. I'm some place right in the middle."

Mrs. Ellman's contribution to the well-being of the city has been insubstantial. Impervious to the difficulties of Beverly's have-nots, she has initiated no significant legislation. "Our biggest problem," she maintains, "is traffic."

The four other members of the Council are a doctor, two attorneys, and a retired industrialist. All are driving, ambitious achievers—except when it comes to governing the city.

Councilman George Slaff is a New Jersey–born lawyer, a Harvard graduate who held several pre-World War II jobs in Washington. He was special counsel to the Securities and Exchange Commission, worked for the Federal Power Commission, and also worked for several months with Supreme Court Associate Justice Abe Fortas, whose appointment as chief justice was blocked by the U.S. Senate in 1968. A year later, disclosure of Fortas's link to an industrialist convicted of selling unregistered securities led to his resignation from the Court.

Before forming his own law firm, Slaff was chief counsel for Goldwyn Studios. Persistent and thorough as a lawyer, he fought one case, an anti-trust suit, for sixteen years until he finally won it. Slaff is a liberal, a long-time member of the American Civil Liberties Union and has been a councilman since 1966.

"I'm proud of several things I've done since becoming a member of the Council," he says. "I'm proud of having brought ex-Chief (Joseph) Kimble here to oversee our police department." (The controversial Kimble was quickly fired.) Adds Slaff, in a statement that is open to debate, "I'm proud of having been a part of a community that has changed over these past ten years from a conservatively oriented city to a liberally oriented one."

Dr. Charles Aronberg is described by one of his Council colleagues as an "ecological fanatic." Chicago-born and raised in Los Angeles, he once sold newspapers on Wilshire Boulevard to people who are now his patients and constituents. Voted the "Outstanding Medical Student in the Nation" in 1952, Aronberg says "that crowding, noise, and pollution must be resisted."

Aronberg won his Council seat in 1972 by spending $11,000 of his own money and $8,000 in contributions from supporters. He is the first Council member ever elected from the southern tier of the city. However, he has accomplished nothing significant for his underprivileged constituency. In spirit, if not in precise fact, he is a minion of the north. His fashionable office is on fashionable North Roxbury Drive.

Jake Stuchen is probably the richest of the councilmen. A millionaire businessman, originally from Toronto, Canada, he is a political conservative, a blustery, outspoken oratorical hip-shooter.

Says one of his fellow Council members, "Jake is seventy-two years old, retired, and it is very important to him that he be a member of the Council. This is his primary reason for being. He is devoted to the city and feels that the city has meant a lot to him and he has given a lot over the years." Stuchen undoubtedly spent more than any councilman in Beverly Hills history to win his seat the last time he ran. He reported an outlay of $28,000. According to his colleague, "I know that isn't accurate."

Stuchen says he settled with his family in Beverly Hills "because the area is certainly one of the nicest in southern California," and "because there was a well-established Jewish neighborhood."

"In the last twenty-five years," Stuchen said, "probably the most striking single change I've seen take place in Beverly is the people. The people who started this town really had dedication. They wanted the best possible city. Later on, more and more people moved to Beverly who seemed more interested in economics than in esthetic values."

Stuchen himself has not been immune to even small-change economic considerations—especially when the small change comes from his own pocket. After voters approved the 7.7-million-dollar water-bond issue, the Beverly Hills Water Department announced that customers' bills would increase 20 to 40 per cent, depending on the location of their homes. The department also said it would impose a small charge for lifting water to homes situated above the city's treatment plant. Stuchen's Trousdale Estates pad would be one of those affected. He promptly cried foul, although he and his upper-class neighbors could most easily afford to pay the bagatelle. The average monthly water bill in Beverly Hills is $11.35, and Stuchen and his northern cohorts would suffer a maximum projected increase of 38 per cent, $4.31 a month more. Nevertheless, he branded the extra charge "grossly unfair."

The glaring split between north and south is a subject rarely discussed by the Council, which prefers to convey the impression that there is no social, political, or financial dichotomy in the city. But Stuchen, a few years ago, participated in an unseemly "debate" on the north-south issue with Councilman Aronberg, who felt it was his duty to defend his below-the-tracks power base. Mayor Seaton, caught in the middle, reacted with exasperation. Onlookers were amused, and unsurprised, by the verbal free-for-all. Highlights of the wrangle between the two gentlemen of the Council follow.

Aronberg: "I've sat here for a year and a half . . . and heard speakers both from the Council and speakers before the Council make disparaging remarks about certain sections of the city, particularly the southern part of the city, how it's blighted, how it's populated largely by winos, drunks and alcoholics—and tonight I've heard it called a ghetto. . . . I object strenuously to these remarks. . . . I would request members of the Council and speakers before the Council to refrain from insulting people who live in various parts of the city, particularly the southern area. . . ."

Stuchen: "Madame Mayor, a word about Dr. Aronberg's last remark."

Seaton: "You will be, I am sure, delicate."

Stuchen: "I'll try to be delicate. I have my daughter living in the south end of the city. She's neither a drunk nor an alcoholic. She's a perfect lady. Hundreds and thousands of perfect ladies are living on the south side. But there has been attracted to the south side a number of drunks and alcoholics—and worse. . . ."

Seaton (*interjecting*): "And on the north side?"

Stuchen: "And on the north side, too, living not far from me. (*Audience laughter.*) But . . . the type of housing that's developed there [in the south]—a tract where you find nine people living in a small apartment, all drunks, what are you going to do about that? . . . I don't want Dr. Aronberg to tell me about protecting the south side. I've been doing it for forty years. My whole purpose . . . is to build up the south side to what it was and what it should be. . . . But I do say this, Dr. Aronberg, that my daughter is just as dear to me as your children are to you or your friends are to you."

Aronberg: "Well, I'm sure she is. I've met her and she's a very fine person. I wish you would refrain from insulting her neighbors." (*Heavy laughter.*)

Stuchen: "I'm not insulting her neighbors. The only person here I've insulted so far is you. (*Laughter.*) There are no drunks around her house, incidentally."

Pickfair, the $500,000 home of Mary Pickford and Douglas Fairbanks, initiated the stellar colonization of Beverly Hills. When the fairy-tale marriage ended and the couple was divorced, Miss Pickford retained the mansion.

Aerial view of Pickfair and its majestic grounds. There was more water in the swimming pool than there was on two tracts of neighboring land.

Neither the Depression nor divorce dimmed the glitter of Beverly Hills. In the early 1930s, Mary Pickford decorated her Pickfair Christmas tree with the aid of a young friend.

Will Rogers, one of America's best-loved humorists, dispensed his home-spun philosophy and trenchant political observations in 350 daily newspapers and over the NBC radio network. He also dispensed advice on the Beverly Hills annexation controversy.

Marion Davies, upon whom William Randolph Hearst lavished millions, and Mary Pickford attended extravagant soirées at Hearst's palatial San Simeon estate.

While estranged from Mary Pickford, Douglas Fairbanks spent fourteen months in Europe and was interviewed by curious newspapermen upon his return to Hollywood in 1934. He later married Lady Sylvia Ashley.

Film idol Rudolph Valentino had a brief, scandal-ridden career.

A monument honors Rogers, Pickford, Fairbanks, and five other Beverly Hills' independence fighters, who led the battle against annexation.

Will Rogers *in* LIGHTNIN' Mary Pickford *in* TESS OF THE STORM COUNTRY Douglas Fairbanks *in* THE IRON MASK

IN TRIBUTE TO THOSE CELEBRITIES OF THE MOTION PICTURE INDUSTRY WHO WORKED SO VALIANTLY FOR THE PRESERVATION OF BEVERLY HILLS AS A SEPARATE MUNICIPALITY — ERECTED 1959

—Diane Wagner

Screen comedian Harold Lloyd amused his fans with offbeat movie antics in such scenes as this one. His latter-day, offscreen antics were less amusing.

In 1921, Roscoe (Fatty) Arbuckle was held on a murder charge in the death of starlet Virginia Rappe, but was released on $5,000 bail when the charge was reduced to manslaughter.

Mrs. Nagel, Conrad Nagel and daughter. Nagel was one of the Beverly Hills celebrities who led the anti-annexation campaign.

It girl Clara Bow testified against her former secretary, Daisy DeVoe, who was charged with taking $16,000 from the actress's bank account to buy jewels, clothing, and cars. Miss DeVoe also published accounts of Clara's sexual exploits.

Will H. Hays, president of Motion Picture Producers and Distributors of America, was paid $100,000 a year to eliminate sin.

Pennsylvania-born cowboy Tom Mix was reported to be near death following an emergency appendectomy in 1931. He survived that crisis but was killed in a 1940 automobile crash.

Buster Keaton knew how to make people laugh—until the talkies arrived in 1927.

Still a legend, Gloria Swanson now lives in New York.

*Gloria Swanson began her movie career
in the mid-1920s.*

In the 1920s, Beverly's most renowned thoroughfare was Wilshire Boulevard, named for an enterprising con man.

Seaton: "As much as I feel we need a little comedy in Council chambers . . . I would hope that we would try to restrain ourselves and not have it at the expense of either members of our community or members of our Council."

Aronberg: "Madame Mayor, I'm very serious about this. . . ."

Seaton (*cutting in sharply*): "So am I, Dr. Aronberg."

Aronberg: "Well, I will repeat my request that members of the Council and speakers before the Council do not insult people who live on the south side of the city."

Seaton (*shouting and pounding gavel*): "Dr. Aronberg, that's exactly what I have just said and I will be angry for one moment and you will please be quiet!"

Stuchen (*shouting*): "Why don't you keep quiet, Aronberg! Who are you to. . ."

Seaton: "Now stop it, will you please stop it!"

Stuchen (*to Aronberg*): "Who the hell are you to tell me what to do?"

(*Confusion of shouting voices.*)

(*Brief silence.*)

Seaton (*to Aronberg*): "Will you please take the chair? I would like to talk to it."

Mayor Seaton stepped to the microphone, ordinarily used by members of the public addressing the Council, and delivered an impassioned plea for order and decorum.

Councilman Richard Stone, a former mayor, is perhaps as articulate an Establishment spokesman as can be found in Beverly. He's considered one of the strongest mayors ever to serve Beverly Hills.

As with most successful men who reside in the city, Stone was not born there. Originally from the Bronx, he lived in New York until his graduation from high school. The Bronx of the Depression years was an Irish-Italian-Jewish ghetto of the poor, a hustling borough filled with kids who grew up tough and street-wise. Does Stone feel he's exchanged one ghetto for another?

"I think we all live in ghettos of a sort. Most people tend to be more comfortable with people who think alike, attend the same church or synagogue. There's a great tendency on the part of most of us to try to live in a neighborhood compatible with our own thinking and where our families will be more comfortable."

Stone, his wife Lona, and their three children enjoy a comfortable existence in a quarter-million-dollar Mediterranean on North Linden

Drive between Santa Monica and Sunset Boulevards. A councilman since 1968, Stone derives his income as a busy corporate attorney. He works out of an eighth-floor suite in a Wilshire Boulevard building and is one of those who would be out of reach of local fire-ladder equipment.

Modishly mustached, chug-a-lugging black coffee in his casually furnished den, Stone exhibits a breezy confidence and the attitudes of many have-nots turned haves. He is the archetypical new Beverly Hills man—self-made, highly motivated, an up-from-nowhere elitist with a social conscience, who tends to be liberal in national politics (he voted for McGovern) and conservative in Beverly Hills politics.

Smiling readily, he concedes that Beverly has an identity problem. "The world-wide image of Beverly Hills is a movie town, or an adjunctive movie town. I don't know how many entertainers or stars live in Beverly Hills now. But they certainly have very, very little to do with the community as a community. Some of them, though, are pretty well integrated. I spent many years going through Little League with my sons, and stars such as Sammy Davis, Carl Reiner and Martin Landau came out to watch their kids play ball."

On local issues, he says, there are some very conservative people in Beverly Hills. "I'm one of them, in economic matters particularly. I don't regard Beverly Hills as a liberal community. The so-called liberal dictatorship in Beverly Hills is a myth."

The charge is frequently made that Beverly Hills seems to be a plaything for five rich individuals. How much time does the Council actually devote to the city?

"We have two council members, Stuchen and Mrs. Ellman, who spend a great deal of time working on the Council. But they are not employed, and they have the time available and that is their thing. I'm a practicing attorney and have to continue to practice in order to make a living. I presume that George Slaff and Charles Aronberg also have to keep working to make a living. When I was mayor, I put in three or four times the amount of hours that I do as a councilman. Counting ceremonial things and night work, I spent fifteen to eighteen hours a week at the mayor's job, which is a lot for a fully employed person. It cost me money. You can't really spare the hours that you put in."

Then why not have a full-time, well-paid mayor who would be elected directly by the voters?

"You couldn't pay enough. How much could you pay in such a small community?"

The city manager of Beverly Hills receives more than $37,000 for his services to only 33,416 people. Why not pay a mayor the city manager's salary?

"The city manager is a professional public administrator. You could change the setup so that the mayor occupies the same role as the city manager. But that would be a complete changeover. Nobody to my knowledge has ever seriously considered an elected mayor who would be the chief executive of the community, and I think that's good because anyone who is elected mayor is involved in politics. How can you get elected if you're not? But you have to separate politics and management. If you're worrying about politics all the time, you're not going to be managing your people properly."

Stone's reasoning is difficult to follow in view of the bruising politics for which the Beverly Hills City Council is noted.

"Historically," continues Stone, "the Council, not the population at large, has selected the mayor. The mayor was always a rotating position. Whoever hadn't been mayor, became mayor. Whoever had been mayor twice had to wait his turn until someone else became mayor once. That type of stuff. However, that's somewhat changed now. If you have the power, you become mayor. If you don't have the power, you don't become mayor."

What kind of power?

"It takes three votes to become mayor. That is power on a five-man body."

Why isn't the mayor allowed to serve at least a minimum of two years? It would seem that in a one-year term, the mayor is just beginning to learn his job. Then he has to leave office.

"That's right. A two-year term would be preferable. But you have five councilmen who are elected for four years and being mayor is prestigious. It's a plum. That's essentially why it's been passed around each year."

Are most residents of Beverly Hills happy or unhappy with what transpires at City Hall?

"Most of our people don't even know there is a city hall. I would say a majority of the people who have any knowledge of what is going on are unhappy."

What are they unhappy about?

"You have a north-south split in this community at Santa Monica Boulevard. And you have a southeast-southwest split. Southeast being south of Santa Monica and east of, say, Rexford. And southwest being west of Rexford. As far as the south is concerned, the problem that arises is that the people there, the majority in the community, feel that the greater part of community services and benefits goes to the north, where the homes are larger and the people generally have more money. Historically, the elected officials have come from the north. Because of that, the north has been favored in many areas over the south."

Does that include police protection?

"I don't think police protection is any different between the north and south. But there are more people of importance and power who live in the north, and people of importance and power will tend to get better and faster service than people of less importance and power, because that's the way things are in the world."

How does Stone view his own term as mayor in terms of prestige —and accomplishment?

"Everybody who is human enjoys being the top figure in anything in which he's involved. The mayor is the number-one elected official in Beverly Hills. He sets the agenda, although we are very loose about that. Anyone who wants something on the agenda gets it. The mayor controls the gavel, and that has a little more meaning. But even more than that, the mayor tends to be the spokesman for the Council.

"A forceful mayor, someone who wants to use the job to accomplish something, can push things through the Council. You still need three votes, but it's harder to buck a mayor on an issue than it is another councilman. The mayor spends more time at his job, works more closely with the city manager and frequently has a better grasp of the particular issue that is involved. Knowledge is power.

"Speaking personally, I felt that I accomplished things as mayor that I could never have accomplished as a councilman. And I got some things moving that had been standing still for years."

As one of his principal achievements, Stone cites his housemothering through the Council of an ordinance that reduced the density in commercial structures from a site ratio of 4:1 to 3:1.

"That means that any new building erected in the commercial area will be one-fourth less dense in terms of office space, people, and cars." Stone, however, is quick to hedge on the effect of the new measure. "I don't know what effect this change alone will have ten years from now. But it will manifest itself. At the present time, it has no meaning whatsoever except that one building that was going up now has to be redesigned.

"I am not a believer in development, in progress per se," he says. "I'm not looking for taller buildings. I don't want Beverly Hills emulating Century City. I think we have something special in Beverly Hills for the people who live here. Part of that is derived from the fact that we haven't allowed our growth to get out of hand. But lately, with all the buildings that have been built near our city limits, with all the traffic that flows through Beverly Hills, our streets are getting clogged to the point where we can't move freely through them. We were never rural, but the change in density will help alleviate that a little bit. It will start a movement toward doing something about traffic, which is something that we have talked about for twenty-five years."

Then why doesn't the Council approve a freeway along Santa Monica Boulevard?

"Only if it's underground!"

Despite the traffic that is choking you?

"Absolutely! Despite the traffic that is choking us, which is generated primarily from Century City. Why should we put something in that will hurt us? So that Century City can continue to build bigger and bigger buildings and attract more and more people?"

Wasn't Beverly Hills against a freeway before there was a Century City?

"We've never been against a freeway. We simply said it had to be underground."

Is there any place in California that has an underground freeway?

"Nope. Not that I'm aware of, except for short distances."

Why should Beverly Hills be an exception?

"Because if the state wants to put a freeway through here, it must accommodate the needs and desires of this community. That's why. We don't want it."

A great many other cities in Los Angeles county have felt the same way about freeways, yet they were built.

"But other communities in Los Angeles don't control their own destinies. We do, not totally, but to a large extent. As long as we control our destiny, we aren't going to allow a freeway to cut a gouge right through the center of Beverly Hills to help everybody around us. And that is all it does."

Still a freeway would help the traffic problem.

"It would help the through-traffic problem, except that the history of freeways in southern California indicates that, within thirty days after a freeway is built, it hits its maximum capacity. In other words, a freeway is an attractor. Put a freeway in Beverly Hills with a capacity of 120,000 cars and it will reach that in a month. Right now we have about 40,000 to 50,000 cars a day traversing Santa Monica."

Would Beverly Hills be willing to pay for an underground freeway?

"No! Absolutely not! Why should we pay for something we don't want? Something that would accomplish very little for us, a little but very little."

Besides his having done his utmost to keep a freeway from permeating Beverly Hills, and besides his having lowered the density rate, Stone cites one other achievement as mayor, a rather vague and murky "upgrading of various city commissions, especially the planning and traffic commissions, from a housekeeping to a planning role."

Since Stone also failed to attack, much less ameliorate, any of Beverly's gut problems, it is puzzling to explain his billing as one of the city's strongest-ever mayors. Essentially he played the traditional mayor's role, caretaker rather than creative innovator.

"I think this community has lived off capital for too long," says City Manager George Morgan, who has the unenviable job of reporting to and serving the contentious City Council.

Seated at the conference table in his City Hall office, his dapper, brown suit matching the paneling on the walls, Morgan declares, "The biggest single problem facing Beverly Hills is a lack of community. Beverly Hills is a world community rather than a local community. Many of its prominent citizens are world citizens rather than citizens of Beverly Hills. There are probably better lines of communication outside the community than within.

"I think this is due to a number of things. Frankly, the faith of many people in the community and the close relationship they have to Israel is a factor. Their affluence and their involvement with the problems of major corporations and their high-level political associations with both parties tend to broaden their base of operation so that living in Beverly Hills for them is like starring on Broadway and then going down to play Greenwich Village in an off-Broadway production."

Morgan became Beverly Hills' first city manager in 1971. He was appointed unenthusiastically by the Council, when problems in the city began to mount precipitously. But Morgan has found rough sledding in Beverly. Jealous of its prerogatives, the Council has given him anything but a blank check in his efforts to streamline the city and its institutions. With a salary of $37,400 a year, he may be the highest-paid office boy in the nation. His compensation by itself exceeds the total paid in salaries and expenses to the entire City Council, an aggregate of about $33,000 a year.

Though he earns more than all the Council members combined, he has no real power. He may advise but not consent. He has no vote on the Council. He reigns over all city employees in routine administrative matters but at the bottom line all he can do is implement, no matter how idiotic or vague, the decisions of the Council.

A handsome forty-nine, with neat, geometric features, Morgan is Presbyterian and Republican, born in Malden, Massachusetts, outside Boston. He received his bachelor's degree from Dartmouth, his master's in higher education from Stanford. Father of three daughters, he lives on South Bedford Drive. Habitation on the wrong side of the tracks counts heavily against him in the scale of values in the city he yearns to "preserve, protect and enhance."

Morgan came to Beverly from Palo Alto, in northern California. He was that community's city manager for six years and remembers the experience fondly.

"I was able to be effective there because we had some extremely competent people on the City Council and the city staff," he says. "We had people interested in the community. We had resources that allowed us a tremendous range of opportunity, municipal ownership of all city utilities, and a governmental affluence that permitted us to do everything from building animal-control centers to a medical complex in conjunction with Stanford University."

Morgan didn't seek the job in Beverly Hills. "Beverly Hills came to me," he says. At first he was reluctant to accept the post. "Among professional city managers, Beverly Hills was considered a high-risk city. The manager plan had never been tried. The Council had a historical record of not giving up authority or really intending to give up authority.

"I know a great many career city managers who wouldn't touch a high-risk situation like Beverly Hills with a ten-foot pole. They like to know the ground rules. They like to have established institutions, precedents, a firm and orderly chain of command. I accepted because Beverly Hills offered a challenge, an opportunity to find out what, if anything, I could do here."

Morgan claims he hasn't been intimidated by Beverly's surface reputation. He appears unimpressed by the city's fame and supposed riches.

"More than anything else I feel encumbered by a series of constraints that were written at a time when it must have been important to keep anybody from doing anything wrong. There are so many fake gods in Beverly Hills which protect everybody from everybody else that it's almost impossible to get from here to there in some ways.

"The record clearly shows that Beverly Hills has 'solved' its problems by undertaking consultant studies that were never implemented. The problems were studied until hell froze over. Then the Council got tired of the particular subject under review and moved on to the next problem without solving the previous one."

Caught between a City Council that has yet to yield an ounce of its power to him and an indifferent constituency, it is questionable how effective Morgan can be. He has devised a three-year plan to rescue Beverly Hills from what he says is governmental and environmental decay. He's tightened administrative machinery, upgraded city employee efficiency somewhat, consolidated "fragmentary" functions by department heads, employed an industrial engineer to recommend which properties owned by the city should be kept and developed and which should be sold. He has attempted to improve traffic, parking, and law enforcement. He has made himself available to city employees and the citizenry at large. But he must still put everything before the Council, and there the system and his effectiveness bog down.

Morgan can do little more than view with alarm. Already, he says with a sad shake of his head, there are too many sections of Beverly Hills that are beginning to look like Los Angeles. "You wonder what the difference is between Los Angeles and Beverly Hills when you enter the city on Sunset, Santa Monica or Olympic Boulevards. As soon as the difference disappears, then that which is Beverly Hills has been seriously challenged."

He readily subscribes to the official city policy of an underground freeway. But in the absence of a freeway or any fast-moving channel to relieve automobile congestion, he admits he has no interim solution. "Neither policy-wise nor traffic engineering-wise."

Pulling out a series of charts, Morgan says, "We are looking at a storm-drain program that shows us that, within the next five years, everything in the southeast section has to be replaced because it is obsolete and inadequate, even though it happens to be buried and invisible. Other than the library, we built our first new public facility in thirty-two years in 1972, a new fire station. That means only one thing, that the other two fire stations are over thirty-two years old. As you go down the list it's the same with everything else."

Morgan says the City Hall itself is outmoded, and his aides suffer from a lack of office space. "I had a visitor the other day who is in the sprinkler business. As soon as he walked into my office, he said, 'My God, George, you still have the same sprinkler system that I sold the city back in 1931.' Merely because it's buried, it isn't supposed to be there. Patch it. Maintain it by fixing leaks. But we have to water the grass in our parks by providing additional staff to keep it green with old equipment. The guts of the system won't be long with us. These are the kinds of situations I worry about.

"When you see these signs of deterioration and you look at some of the older segments of the community, that simply isn't good enough for what people in Beverly Hills say they want. You look at the alleys in our community and they are a disgrace as they relate to the front yards. We have to rehabilitate, rejuvenate, rebuild. That's the real challenge. But it won't happen until we get community participation and real involvement on the part of Beverly Hills citizens.

"What we have is a façade. There's still enough Hollywood left in Beverly Hills so that people can talk glibly and superficially about the stars who live here and the supposed glamor of the city. But what happens, what is left when you wipe the make-up off?

"Our primary objective has to be the preservation and enhancement of the residential interests of this community. But to do that we are going to have to compromise, make unpopular decisions with regard to parking, traffic, land use, zoning density, and so on. Then we can improve what unique qualities we have selected to preserve and protect."

But Morgan isn't optimistic about Beverly's future. He pauses and gazes despondently out the window.

"The name of the game in Beverly Hills is schizophrenia. A liberal community with an essentially conservative city government. We are finding that there are no convenient, simple remedies to traffic, parking, airplane noise disturbances, and the intrusion of one land use at the expense of another."

Finally, he says, you must ask the question: "Why a Beverly Hills at all?" His answer: "Because our people want something special, and can afford it. Yet affluence brings its own problems. In the last analysis, there are no remedies money can buy."

6.
"I Lift My Lamp Beside the Golden Door"

IT IS TAKEN for granted by everyone, including those in Beverly Hills, that a majority of the city's residents are of Jewish extraction. Estimates by the Chamber of Commerce and City Hall run as high as 85 per cent. Richard Nixon mistakenly cast a "too-Jewish" label on the town, and many would-be, Christian residents have refused to move to Beverly because of its erroneous reputation as a predominantly Jewish town.

In fact there hasn't been a Jewish majority in Beverly since 1960, and even then it was slight, 52.6 per cent. Since that time, there has been a considerable exodus of Jews from the city.

According to official federal census data, affirmed by Jack Provost of the Research Service Bureau of the Jewish Federal Council of Greater Los Angeles, 46.6 per cent of the population of Beverly Hills, as of 1970, was of Jewish ancestry. However, the current Jewish population is 40 to 42 per cent and declining rapidly.

Why the exodus?

Dr. Norton Stern, a Los Angeles–based Jewish historian, believes one reason is that Jews have found the nearby San Fernando Valley increasingly attractive. (The Valley has a population of more than 1,000,000, with Jews numbering 100,000.)

"In the 1940s, before the Valley became important," says Dr. Stern, "Beverly Hills was *the* place. Large numbers of Jews were attracted to

Beverly Hills because of the movie industry. The Jews were the founders of the multimillion-dollar sportswear industry in Los Angeles. Beverly Hills wasn't far from the studios or the downtown garment center.

"There was also the snob appeal of Beverly Hills as a fine place to live, the image of Beverly Hills as a desirable place to live—perhaps the most desirable place to live for Jews active in business and, after World War II, for Jews in the professions, particularly law and medicine."

Dr. Stern adds that Beverly Hills is no longer an attraction because of the diminished movie industry and the post-war emergence of Jews into every area of economic life in southern California. He also cites the "general downgrading of Beverly Hills at all levels" as another vital factor.

Despite the minority status of Jews, all five members of the City Council are Jewish. Explaining that phenomenon, Councilwoman Donna Ellman says: "Let's face it, we come on pretty strong. The Christians in the city have either abandoned their public-service responsibility or they're satisfied with the way things are being run."

Councilman Richard Stone, asked what it says to the outside world that the entire Council is composed of Jews, replied: "That Beverly Hills is a Jewish-controlled community, that's what it says."

Is that good or bad?

Stone's answer: "That's the fact. Would it be better to have two non-Jews sitting on the Council just so that there are non-Jews sitting there? I don't believe in representation by race or religion. The most active people in the community are Jewish. That doesn't mean that there are not non-Jews who aren't active.* But in terms of numbers of active people, the most active are Jewish. And it would tend to follow that they would end up running the largest number of candidates for public office. Not because they are Jewish but simply because they are involved somewhere along the line. They have the desire or urge to run for office."

During his tenure as mayor, Stone received hate mail with a decided anti-Semitic flavor. "Usually unsigned," he said. "In the election to determine whether or not we would fluoridate our water, I got a couple of letters that tied fluoridation in with Jewishness and Communism. But that comes with the job. I didn't worry about letters like that. They used fluoridation as some form of Jewish plot. If a Baptist were mayor

*Former mayor Phyllis Seaton is Presbyterian.

of Beverly Hills, I think he'd get the same kind of letters from this type of person. Regardless of who was sitting in the mayor's chair, fluoridation would still be a Jewish plot."

Publicly, the Jewish citizens of Beverly are proud of their heritage and generous in their moral and financial support of Israel. But, for the most part, they ignore the spiritual inspiration available in the city's two synagogues. Figures from the synagogues themselves indicate the baleful turnout. At orthodox Beth Jacob, the congregation numbers 1,200 and at reform Temple Emanuel, worshipers total 850.

Both *shuls* provide every possible inducement for attendance. Beth Jacob has classes for retarded children, religious instruction for young people from kindergarten to high school, a busy Sisterhood and Men's Club, study groups for married couples, Sunday school, a nursery, and the Hillel Home Summer Camp. The synagogue is charity-oriented, supporting the drives of the United Crusade, Heart Fund, United Jewish Welfare Fund, and Bonds for Israel. Temple Emanuel has a nursery school, a bridal room, an auditorium, a special meeting room for its board of directors, and sleek rabbinical offices. Its most conspicuous adjunct is a modern two-story religious school, replete with an extensive Judaic library, a theater, and an underground parking lot.

The drift away from formal faith among Beverly's older and middle-aged Jews is ascribed to an emphasis on secularization and materialism. Among younger Jews in Beverly, large-scale interfaith marriage has winnowed the ranks of the synagogues. "The evidence is overwhelming that children of mixed marriages will end up as non-Jews," says Rabbi Roland B. Gittelsohn. Erosion of synagogue attendance among young Jews in Beverly has also been caused via conversion by evangelical Christian denominations, especially by such fundamentalist denominations as the Baptists and the Pentecostals, neither of whom are represented in Beverly though they are very much in evidence in surrounding communities.

Among the Jewish population of Beverly, one of the most hallowed customs of Judaism is in disfavor. Fewer *bar mitzvahs* are being held each year. To reverse this trend, two innovations—one not very successful, the other gaining in popularity—are being tried. A companion to the *bar mitzvah* rite (celebrating a Jewish youngster's initiation into adulthood) has been introduced for girls, but these *bat mitzvahs* have not caught on noticeably. The other innovation has had more impact; many *bar* and *bat mitzvahs* are being enlivened by the performance of a belly dancer. At best, belly dancing is a debatable art form, but it has two non-debatable aspects, both in conflict with Jewish tradition. It is an Arabic dance, and its most alluring feature is sensual, a voyeuristic stimulant designed more for adults than thirteen-year-olds.

For position-conscious Jews in Beverly Hills, neither of the local synagogues is considered fashionable. The fashionable one is Rabbi Edgar Magnin's Wilshire Temple, which is not in Beverly Hills, though the rabbi lives in Beverly, on Walden Drive, a short street just north of Santa Monica Boulevard.

Says one of the rabbis on the staff of Wilshire Temple, which has been in existence for more than one hundred years, *"Anybody* who would go to temple from Beverly Hills would come to *our* place. *We* had Jack Benny. Until he became very ill, we had Jack Warner. We have Milton Berle and Red Buttons!" The congregation, he adds, is 2,600, with about 500 from Beverly Hills, a Blue Book 500 apparently.

In contrast with the synagogues, the five Christian churches in Beverly have much larger per capita congregations, though they, too, are losing membership swiftly, contrary to religious trends in the rest of America.*

The sole Catholic sanctuary, located north of Santa Monica, is the Church of the Good Shepherd, known by the less reverent as "Our Lady of the Cadillacs."

"We aren't a dying parish," maintains Monsignor Daniel Sullivan, who has the largest congregation in Beverly—4,500. But he worries about the future. "We're stable, more or less. The majority of our members are in the upper-age brackets. Many of our young people, when they marry, leave us because they can't afford to live in Beverly Hills."

The lack of young married couples is also due to the Church's anti-abortion stand. Many object to Rome's position on the issue. So apparently do their elders. Otherwise, Catholics would constitute a majority instead of 30 per cent of Beverly's population. Local Catholic couples are either lucky or practicing forbidden contraception. The average number of children in Catholic families in Beverly Hills is two, which conforms to the zero population growth in the rest of the city.

Good Shepherd worshipers (not all of whom live in Beverly) include: Rosalind Russell, Jane Wyman, Jane Wyatt, Jimmy Durante,

*The authoritative *Yearbook of American Churches 1975* notes a minuscule drop, 0.14 per cent, in church attendance in the United States since 1970. The comparative figure for Beverly Hills is 15 per cent.

Loretta Young, Irene Dunne, Ricardo Montalban, Gene Kelly, Bob Newhart, and the superpious Danny Thomas.

All Saints' Episcopal Church, which has a choice location on North Camden Drive, is headed by the Reverend Doctor Kermit Castellanos. Its parishioners are not demonstrably generous. The 3,000 members of the congregation contribute $300,000 yearly, $100 per worshiper. Past faithful ("but not every Sunday," according to Reverend Castellanos) were Humphrey Bogart, Dick Powell, and Agnes Moorehead. Van Johnson and James Mason attended the church before they left Beverly Hills. Present celebrities who show up with some degree of regularity are Fred Astaire, Randolph Scott, Raymond Massey, Dorothy Lamour, and Robert Young. But nothing approaching the full membership is ever apparent at the church, not even on Easter Sunday or at Christmas. No more than one-third of the claimed congregation is on the premises for any service.

The two Presbyterian churches in Beverly found themselves between a rock and a hard place in 1972. Attendance was down, expenses up. There was no choice but to amalgamate. This event emerges in a Chamber of Commerce brochure as: "A unique spiritual happening. The Beverly Hills Community Church and the Beverly Vista Church, both landmarks of service in the city since 1921 and 1927 respectively, have chosen to join hands and facilities to strengthen their forces and more effectively meet the challenges and needs of today's world." Reverend David Rees, pastor of the surviving 1,000-member entity, the Beverly Hills Presbyterian Church, puts the merger into succinct perspective. "There wasn't room for two churches."

Television's Ralph Edwards is an elder in the church. Reverend Rees praises Greer Garson, who is married to millionaire Texas oilman Buddy Fogelson, for her considerable financial support. Jimmy Stewart "is no longer active, but I imagine he attends church somewhere," says the reverend.

The cleric with the best sense of humor in Beverly Hills is the Reverend R. John Perling, pastor of Mount Calvary Lutheran Church. "We're in the slum section of Beverly Hills," he says. "Someone's called us a hole in a Jewish doughnut. Now they're attempting to make us into a bagel." The church is located south of Olympic Boulevard, where there is a heavy Jewish population.

"Eight or nine Protestant churches have been phased out in Beverly Hills and the Beverly Hills area in the last seven to ten years, including three Lutheran churches," says Reverend Perling. "Connie Stevens came by the other day to serve as godmother at a baptism, but she isn't a member. Red Skelton and Bob Hope have visited us, but they're not members either. We have some TV writers, cameramen, and sound-men from the Hollywood colony." The church, which has been in Beverly Hills since 1940, has a congregation of 155.

Who is or isn't worshiping at the sacred premises of the First Church of Christ, Scientist, Beverly Hills, is a matter of considerable secrecy. Founder Mary Baker Eddy decreed that names of members and the size of Christian Science congregations should be available only to God. Clerk of the church is Joyce Lotta, who concedes, "We're not a rich church. The cost of upkeep is high—gardeners, water, electricity. We have an auditorium seating over 900 people. No, it's not com-pletely filled at our Wednesday testimony meetings or at the two Sunday services. Doris Day used to come, but no longer. Carol Chan-ning attends the church when she's in Beverly Hills." For Miss Chan-ning, one of the strong points of Christian Science is that members do not celebrate birthdays. "Isn't that marvelous, darling?" she once told an interviewer.

Of the 11,000 on the rolls of Beverly's seven houses of worship, including some 500 who attend the Christian Science tabernacle, at least one-third do not live in the golden ghetto. Counting the 500 select who flock to Rabbi Magnin's temple, there are about 8,000 in Beverly who are formally religious, less than one-fourth the population. The remaining 24,000 living in God's greenest acres are un-churched and un-templed. They presumably worship in private, are atheists, or by their indifference to spiritual matters, exhibit—with a lack of hypocrisy rare in Beverly Hills—their honest allegiance to Mammon, the city's one true deity.

God isn't the only minority in Beverly Hills.

There is a permanent Japanese population of only seventy-nine. All are live-in gardeners except for less than a dozen who've achieved professional or managerial rank and can afford to live in town, though they are discouraged from buying or renting. Discrimination against the Japanese in Beverly hasn't changed much since World War II. They are still *persona non grata,* except behind a lawn mower. (Virtually all of Beverly's 721 gardeners are of Japanese descent. They earn from $25 to $200 a month and commute to and from town in rickety pickups.)

Besides the sprinkling of Japanese, other minorities number: 14 American Indians, 31 Filipinos, 130 Chinese, and 293 Mexican-Americans. Most are servants.

The 348 blacks are the largest non-white minority living in Beverly. Again, most are servants. Because they are more readily employable as domestics and work cheaper, black women are preferred and are more visible. As servants, they outnumber black men two to one.

To be black and young in Beverly Hills is tantamount to solitary confinement. There are 201 white infants less than one year old in the city. Not a single black child in that age bracket lives in Beverly Hills. There are only 36 black children under eighteen residing in the entire town as against 6,380 in the same age group for whites.

Since the 1965 Watts riot, in which thirty-four were killed and forty million dollars' worth of property was destroyed, the fear of blacks in Beverly Hills has been pervasive.

"I have to be honest," says Irwin Zucker. "In case of a very severe economic crisis, in case of another Watts riot, where do you think a lot of anti-Establishment blacks are going to run and burn down homes? They are going to run to wealthy areas. They are going to run and burn down Beverly Hills. It sounds ridiculous, doesn't it? Yet I'm convinced it could happen."

Zucker, and many others in Beverly Hills who share his fear, may or may not be paranoid. But a wave of unease sweep through the city during the six days of rioting in Watts. A small indication was that dozens of once-fashionable statues of Negro jockeys outside some of the town's most expensive homes, Ann Rutherford's among them, were hastily removed or painted white. One was painted green. The Irish householder said, "Now it looks like a leprechaun." A more significant indication of fear was that the Beverly Hills Police Department was on stand-by alert until several days after the Watts riot subsided.

At the height of the disorder, newspapers quoted a number of militant blacks in Watts who pointed out it was self-destructive to destroy their own city. To make their protest as dramatic as possible, they repeatedly urged that the torch be put to Beverly Hills, since it seemed the most obvious symbol of Establishment wealth.

As to discrimination, the blacks have a Grade-A case against Beverly Hills, not only because so few are permitted to live there or because they are treated so shabbily. A great deal of the property that was gutted in Watts—supermarkets, liquor and appliance stores—was owned by absentee Beverly Hills businessmen who were charging blacks *more* for merchandise of *lesser* quality than was paid in Beverly Hills itself. In many instances, the cost of living in Watts was higher than in Beverly Hills. A wilted head of lettuce in Watts, to cite but one example, was and is fifteen to thirty cents more than the same field-fresh produce sold in a Beverly Hills market. With only one unreliable bus line providing transportation out of town, and with a large segment who can't afford cars, the citizens of Watts were and are consumer captives. Watts is not a city that has the opportunity to comparison-shop. To this day, there is still much Beverly Hills money invested in Watts, and it is earning healthy returns.

Despite the pretense that Beverly Hills is an open city, and despite fair-housing laws, which supposedly prevent discrimination, the black is the tenant of last resort for even those landlords who charge as little as $135 a month for a southside apartment. The black will occasionally get an apartment only if a white renter cannot be found. Most landlords, however, won't rent to blacks even if a white tenant is impossible to come by.

To a large extent, it is the blacks themselves who've boycotted Beverly Hills. It's not only difficult for them to get in but they are the first pedestrians and drivers to be hassled by the police. Any black not in a maid or chauffeur's uniform is automatically considered "suspicious" by the local gendarmes.

The token black royalty living in Beverly Hills is made up of a fistful of doctors, attorneys, businessmen, and such show-business stars as Ella Fitzgerald, Diana Ross, Greg Morris, and Sammy Davis, Jr. (The late comedian, Ernie Kovacs, once ribbed Davis: "You're colored, you're Jewish, you have one eye. The only thing you've got going for you is that you live in Beverly Hills.")

Acceptance of even rich and famous blacks in Beverly is rather recent and still tentative. For years prior to his death, Nat King Cole tried without success to buy a home above Sunset Boulevard. He met stone-wall resistance. Cole died in 1965, shortly before the peak of the civil-rights movement, which compelled Beverly's real-estate brokers and homeowners into taking a more circumspect stance. But the black, no matter how prominent, is also the homeowner of last resort. This attitude is tempered only when the discriminatory white Establishment is confronted with important blacks who can make newspaper noise and can afford attorneys to press their cause.

There are still less than fifty non-servant blacks living in Beverly

Hills. Other blacks are kept at bay by the conspiratorial policy that makes them "last-resort" renters and buyers. Landlords inform a would-be black tenant that an empty apartment was rented yesterday or an hour ago. The vacancy sign? The landlord simply forgot to take it down. Wealthy blacks who want to buy homes are stalled as long as possible. They are falsely informed by brokers that several other clients are interested in whatever home they may want to buy. Usually a white purchaser does turn up.

Says a spokesman at the Beverly Hills–Hollywood branch of the NAACP, "This is the toughest and most frustrating kind of discrimination we have to face in Beverly Hills—the hypocrisy of public liberals and do-gooders who are private nigger-haters."

There is a good deal of civil-rights chic in Beverly Hills. Millions have been raised at society parties for the NAACP and other black organizations. White entertainers from Beverly Hills have donated their time and talent at endless money-raising benefits for blacks. In national elections, the city votes liberal Democratic. George Wallace would receive a rude welcome in Beverly Hills and Sammy Davis or Greg Morris, if either chose to run, would be elected to the City Council hands down. That's the sham public posture. Beverly Hills believes in freedom, equality, and dignity for blacks in Chicago, Illinois; Jackson, Mississippi; Montgomery, Alabama; and in Archie Bunker's Queens, New York. But Beverly Hills, long after the fair-housing battles were supposedly fought and won in the courts, does not believe in constitutional guarantees or human rights for blacks in their ghetto.

Aside from the real-estate freeze-out, Beverly Hills' two-faced racial policy was aptly illustrated in 1973, when the California League of City Employee Associations filed an official protest against the city with the state Fair Employment Practices Commission.

The move was initiated as a result of a petition signed by nineteen black employees in the parks department, who objected to their identification by race in disciplinary reports. League President Philip A. Bowers, Jr., thought the incident serious enough to ask (unsuccessfully) for the resignations of the two management men responsible.

Looming in the background of Bowers' protest were other unpalatable realities. Though 35 per cent of city workers were black or Mexican, management was overwhelmingly white. Of the sixty-seven men in the parks department, more than half black or Mexican, supervisory personnel was exclusively white. Of the forty-six men in the city government of Beverly Hills who had high-salaried management jobs, only four were members of minority groups. (Two had been promptly appointed forty-eight hours after the complaint to the FEPC.) Other city divisions, including the library and the police and fire departments, had little or no minority representation.

"We feel that the situation has now reached the critical stage," Bowers told the FECP in a bristling letter. "We have both an economic and a moral problem that can no longer be subjected to inordinate delay." A series of incidents had occurred over a period of years, the letter charged, "that indicates to us that a degree of racial prejudice may exist that is unacceptable to a majority of minority employees. We have attempted through endless meetings and discussions, and through the issuance of stringent demands, to get the city to move to correct this problem. At this point, we have received only a token acknowledgment and token action by the city."

Two city officials responded unconvincingly. City Manager Morgan said steps would be taken to improve the lot of minority employees. Steve Graubard, assistant city manager in charge of personnel, asserted that Beverly Hills was "trying to recognize talent . . . regardless of who has it, whether a minority person, a woman or a man. When we go outside for people, we utilize all the resources at our disposal. It's tough to find minority management people. Private industry offers more money, so they go there, or to a city that pays more than Beverly Hills."

The complaint to the FECP did not provoke any retaliatory action; however, neither did it inspire reform. The City Council has not taken any steps to lessen prejudice in hiring. Beverly's policy of tokenism in employing non-white managerial personnel is still in force.

Another exploited minority in Beverly are the 620 municipal employees. From top to bottom, all are extremely restive, for financial and other reasons. The employees, too, are prisoners of the image of boundless wealth. Each year, employee demands for salary increases and improved fringe benefits escalate—the workers feel that Beverly can well afford to give them a larger slice of its purported wealth.

So much rumbling dissatisfaction was heard from the troops that Dr. Edward Glaser, who runs a Wilshire Boulevard firm of consulting psychologists, was hired by the City Council to probe the attitudes of workers toward the city and the Council itself. Dr. Glaser turned in an eye-opening white paper. His report was based on "personal interviews with a stratified sample of the city's personnel and upon data from an employee opinion survey."

He pointed out: "We have elicited more brickbats than bouquets. A survey of this sort tends to over-focus on 'what's wrong' rather than 'what's right' by the very nature of the questions about how things might be improved." Despite the disclaimer, the City Council was jolted by how much was wrong.

Proceeding objectively, Dr. Glaser's team of interviewers gathered a harvest of complaints from those who work for the city. "A persistent charge leveled at the City Council is 'penny-pinching,' that it fails to pay fair wages except where it has been forced to do so under pressure from organized employee groups," the Glaser report said. "Although wages have been raised for certain employee groups at the lower level, salary increases have not been accorded to a comparable degree for individuals at the higher administration levels. These people feel that they are being exploited."

But lower-level employees didn't agree that they were being paid fairly, or that their fringe benefits were sufficient. And both upper-level personnel and rank-and-file workers were dissatisfied with the City Council's antics.

"The Council's behavior is unbecoming for this type of city and causes a great deal of distress among employees who feel that the Council doesn't care about them and that they want good service for nothing," the report said.

Among those who answered Dr. Glaser's questions, there was resentment that the city paid so little that few employees could afford to live in Beverly Hills. Hence, Dr. Glaser concluded, employees had little loyalty to the city.

There were complaints from members of the fire and police departments that, since they were "necessary evils and not a source of revenue," they were "largely unappreciated." Living conditions in the fire department were described as "deplorable," not conducive to good morale, and "indicative of the belief that the City Council and management don't care about the safety of employees."

Revealing, too, were write-in remarks by employees to the "opinion survey" section of the Glaser report. The level of disenchantment evident in the responses to ten statements is representative.

All in all, I am reasonably well-satisfied with the working conditions in the city of Beverly Hills.

Working conditions are OK—living conditions in the fire station do not begin to compare with other fire departments.

I would appreciate a greater spirit of teamwork and co-operation among department heads.

Poor hours.

Combination of badly overworked staff and shoddy administration creates a peculiar condition in morale only to be equaled in Camarillo [a state mental institution].

An eight-hour day is passé!

Inter-department communications should be improved.

Good; however, could have better equipment and training.

Wage and other benefits lacking.

The location is convenient. The salary is considerably lower than cities in the adjacent areas with less demanding clientele but similar cost of living.

This is a city run by power politics; appointments are sometimes made as political footballs, not on merit.

I am reasonably well-satisfied with the working conditions in my Division-Department.

Room for improvement.

"Reasonably" is the key word.

Physical conditions—yes. Mental conditions—no!

There is a serious problem among the secretarial staff. There has been a tremendous turnover of staff in the past, and I think there will be in the future.

Recently the tree-trimmers were forced to work under dangerous conditions!

Too much discrimination. Give my superintendent a bull-whip and he will be in his glory.

Management could be better.

Work every Saturday.

Unrealistic demands by administration to perform herculean tasks without sufficient staff, equipment, space or time.

Disorganized; poor communications; no one will accept any responsibility.

There is no consideration at times for relief help and sometimes one person is left alone during lunch hours.

Except for the administrative area—that is intolerable.

Except for equipment, training, and shortage of personnel strength.

Lack of sufficient personnel.

There is considerable harassment for minor infringements considering the high professional caliber of the staff.

Only if this question pertains to my immediate department. If it pertains to the library as a whole, it has an aura of deceit.

Beverly Hills compares favorably with other places to work that I know about.

Wages and benefits are below par. Living quarters at (fire) stations are disgraceful.

I am sick and tired of the mayor reminding the city employees that it is a privilege to work for Beverly Hills. It is indeed an attractive city, but bread is what it's all about.

Employees are looked down upon. Employees are just a number in "B.H."

Beverly Hills is always at, or near, the bottom in salaries and benefits.

Unreasonable stringency.

As a municipality yes, as a division no.

Except for salary of professionals. Most libraries pay more.

Pay and working conditions superior elsewhere.

This is my first experience in a municipal system; it is difficult to compare this to private industry.

Except in equipment, budget.

Negative in matters of wages and benefits.

Salary range is less than neighboring libraries.

The location is convenient. The physical surroundings are pleasant. There is a good book budget. There is not nearly enough money for adequate staff, supplies, and equipment and community enrichment.

In my present job, I feel there is adequate opportunity for me to grow and advance.

Grow, yes. Advance, no.

Very limited.

The city will not accept the fact that there is a definite need for a larger department. It decreases in size rather than increases.

Too little emphasis on day-to-day work habits and far too much emphasis on ten-minute oral interview for promotion.

There is really no place for me to promote to.

The present senior secretary has been there twenty years and will be probably another ten years.

No opportunity whatsoever.

Unless the foreman dies there is none.

If management acts honestly, yes; if they act as usual, never.

I think I have advanced as far as I ever can in this library.

Only in knowledge—no advancement possible.

There is limited personal growth in my present job—I am looking for promotion.

Small city, promotions too infrequent.

There are not enough higher positions toward which to advance. There are no opportunities for acceleration if an outstanding job is done.

I expect to stick with my job rather than look for a better one, at least for the next two years.

If I could start over again, I'd go to a larger fire department.

I'm too old to go to Los Angeles.

If the opportunity arises for advancement, I will work for another city. Unless there is a change.

If I were young enough, I would leave here immediately for another fire department.

Who would hire me?

Plan to leave shortly.

A job is a job.

There are too many unemployed just now.

I don't have a college education so I am limited—also, women don't have as many opportunities.

Unless supervisor becomes too much for me.

If I get a promotion.

I have the opportunity to talk freely with my immediate supervisor as much as I want to about problems affecting my work.

This is a problem since conversation can be overheard.

Providing the problems are significant.

He will listen, but his hands are tied.

But it gains nothing.

I can, and he is always courteous, but there is no action.

I can talk all I want but that is about as far as it goes.

Nothing is done.

My immediate supervisor successfully avoids the temptation to act in a needlessly dictatorial manner.

> Some are definitely dictatorial.
> My supervisor acts only in a dictatorial manner.
> He lets you know who's in charge and won't listen to you.
> He used to say that he'd fire anyone who didn't agree with him.
> Constantly chews people out in front of others.

I am pleased with the extent to which salary increases and advancements are based on actual merit.

> Merit has nothing to do with it. Salary increases, if any, are automatic.
> I don't believe this is the case at all. A merit increase is practically unheard of.
> I have had no experience with this so far.
> This concept has received lip-service only and is getting no better.
> I have seven years' experience and must start on the bottom of a pay scale that takes three years to get to the top.
> Salary benefits given only on whim of top (ivory tower) personnel.

I take pride in being an employee of the city of Beverly Hills.

> Disagree strongly. But I do take pride in being in the fire service and being a member of the Beverly Hills Fire Department.
> I used to, but not anymore.
> Most citizens in Beverly Hills think we are compensated on a par with Los Angeles and surrounding cities. The City Council knows we are not, and doesn't give a damn.
> I don't really care.
> I take pride in doing a good job anywhere! Not just in Beverly Hills.
> It's a job.

The City Council is interested in the rights and benefits of its employees.

> Council seldom makes feelings known.
> Their only interest is how much it's going to cost.

Council is not interested in employees.

They represent very affluent population and are only interested in getting the most and giving the least. They don't represent the worker who lives outside Beverly Hills and has no political voice.

I believe their only interest is themselves.

Since the Glaser revelations in the early 1970s, little has been improved between the Council and city jobholders. The same dissatisfactions exist today. Asked his opinion of the highly critical report, Councilman Stone said:

"One thing the Glaser report pointed out was that our city government hadn't created paradise in Beverly Hills. We have the same problems most communities have. We have dissatisfied people. Racial attitudes contribute to that. Bullying foremen contribute to that. So does poor leadership. I don't think we realized all this. Maybe we didn't want to realize it until the Glaser report.

"It pointed out a lot of things that perhaps, to a certain extent, the Council had closed its eyes to. The Council is relatively remote from lower-level employees. We have no real contact with those who clean the streets or the garbage people or the gardeners who clean the parks. We have more of a relationship with the police but even there the lower-level patrolman doesn't come in contact with the Council."

Despite the Glaser report, the Council further alienated non-management personnel by hiring a controversial outfit to aid in its last negotiations with the city's unions. Brought in by the paper liberals at a cost of $1,100 a month was William Hamilton and Associates. Homebase for the company is the city of Orange in Orange County, the most conservative county in California, perhaps in the nation.

"That particular firm has a notorious record of breeding disunity, discontent, and lack of accord in every city [in which we] have had experience," said Philip Bowers, Jr., whose California League of Employee Associations represents all municipal unions in Beverly Hills except the police, firemen, and teachers.

After extensive negotiations, not much was given away to Beverly employees. City gardeners, tree-trimmers, secretaries, clerks, recreation personnel, janitors, librarians, and sanitation workers were offered a 2.7 per cent pay hike. They eventually settled for 5.02 per cent, which still put their salaries below those paid for equal jobs in such poorer communities in the county as Burbank, Culver City, Glendale, Los Angeles, Manhattan Beach, Redondo Beach, and Santa Monica.

The raise failed to meet the surge in inflation, although none of the employees covered in the settlement was earning more than $150 a week. Some, particularly in the parks department, were taking home as little as $80 a week after deductions. None were happy with the outcome of the negotiations, and employee discontent against the well-fixed Council members continued.

Another commodity in minority supply in Beverly Hills is patriotism.

When Harry Truman died on December 26, 1972, Governor Ronald Reagan proclaimed a state-wide day of mourning. Reagan, as staunch a Republican as Truman was a Democrat, quickly gave state employees a day off as a tribute to the fallen ex-President. The Los Angeles City Council voted to give its 27,000 employees the day off. So did the city councils of Santa Monica and Culver City. Beverly Hills, reportedly, was the only city in the nation where it was business as usual. City Hall remained open and city employees stayed at their jobs. Responding to criticism by employees and many residents that the "open city" policy was tasteless, Councilman Stuchen said the town had saved $13,000 by not declaring an official holiday in the wake of Truman's passing.

When former President Lyndon Johnson died soon after Truman, on January 22, 1973, Beverly Hills was in a bind. Again the rest of the country officially mourned the death of a President, and again Beverly Hills was the sole reported exception. Richard Stone, who was mayor at the time, explains: "I was out of town when Truman died. Had I been here, we would have closed City Hall for him. Truman was one of my heroes. We should have closed City Hall for him. But I wasn't going to do it for Johnson when it hadn't been done for Truman. That would have looked like Truman was singled out as a target. We failed to honor him and so we couldn't honor Johnson."

Who made the decision not to honor Truman?

"Vice Mayor George Slaff talked to the other councilmen on the telephone, and I guess the mutual decision was not to. I don't know what their reasoning was. It could have been nothing more simple than how do you mourn the death of a man. Is it necessary to give city employees a day off so that they can go out and frolic and do what they want in order to express a feeling of mourning. I don't know that it is."

In late March and early April 1973, President Nixon was in town to attend a dinner at the Beverly Hills Hotel and meet with Nguyen Van Thieu, president of South Vietnam, who was staying at the Beverly

Wilshire Hotel. The Beverly Hills Police Department joined with the Los Angeles County Sheriff's Department and a phalanx of Los Angeles city police officers in helping the Secret Service provide the customary tight security at the two hotels.

Cost of protecting Nixon and Thieu, mostly police overtime, was $50,000. Beverly Hills promptly complained about paying its share of the tab—$20,000. The amount was hardly excessive, particularly since Beverly Hills was the host city and should have quietly and generously offered its hospitality.

But City Manager Morgan asked the Council to send letters of objection to the Secret Service and Governor Reagan. "The cost involved in offering adequate police protection is a heavy drain on city funds," Morgan contended. He said the letters "should suggest that the state and federal governments make provisions for some form of financial assistance." The more he thought about it, the more emphatic Morgan became. "Federal financing should be mandatory!"

Beverly Hills could easily and graciously have absorbed the $20,000 into its annual $1,750,736 police budget. Or it could have written the sum off against the yearly $124,000 that the U.S. government supplies Beverly under the federal revenue-sharing plan for cities. It was a squalid, cheapskate performance by a city that bathes in its perfumed reputation for affluence.

The lack of instinct for doing the right thing at the right moment, in regard to the deaths of Truman and Johnson, and the disrespect, in Nixon's case, for the office of the Presidency, proved Beverly Hills a town without class or style.

An even more shameful dereliction of national responsibility and duty concerns Beverly Hills' participation in the Vietnam War.

The city was the draft-dodging capital of the nation.

According to official U.S. Department of Labor Manpower Administration figures, over 9,000 Beverly Hills young men turned draft age in the course of America's twelve-year involvement in Vietnam. But Vietnam veterans in Beverly Hills number only 333.

To cite but one contrast, the city of Azusa in Los Angeles County has a population of 25,312. That is 8,104 *less* than Beverly Hills. Yet 1,731 of its sons served in Vietnam, *more than five times* the number who participated from Beverly. Azusa is a mere thirty-five miles from Beverly Hills but, in terms of influence (none) and affluence (average family income is $9,651), it is light-years away. The often-voiced charge that the Vietnam War was fought by the poorer echelon of American manhood is nowhere more starkly demonstrated than in comparing the circumstances of the two cities.

What is even more to be condemned is that Vietnam left the young nobles of north Beverly almost untouched. Of the 333 Vietnam veterans in the city, only 37 came from the north although it had 30 per cent of the town's draftable males. Throughout the Vietnam hostilities, conscientious objectors were thick north of Santa Monica Boulevard. Many who should have gone boasted openly about how much their fathers had paid for deferments and how connections had been used to keep them out of service. Beverly Hills doctors certified their own sons and sons of important friends as drug addicts and homosexuals, both grounds for deferment. The richer parents of Beverly paid endless college bills so that their offspring could remain in school as long as possible, earning them exemptions. Other exemptions were obtained via a mass of early weddings and swift pregnancies. At least 2,000 potential Beverly Hills servicemen were kept out of uniform through hasty but convenient marriage and fatherhood.

Less than the fingers of one hand are needed to count how many sons of stars served in Vietnam. Comedian Jerry Lewis, who is commended for very little by those in Beverly Hills who know him best, deserves commendation in that he didn't try to prevent a Vietnam tour of duty for his son Gary. Superstar James Stewart, who is roundly commended for much by his Beverly Hills intimates, including his service in World War II as a bomber pilot and his unpublicized bombing mission over North Vietnam in 1966, lost his twenty-four-year-old stepson Ronald, who was killed while leading a patrol near the DMZ.

Asked if his son's death in Vietnam was needless, Stewart, gray-haired but still handsome and youthful, replied, "No. I never thought he was wasted. I did think, and will always think, that the war was mismanaged, that the utilization of power was mismanaged, but my wife and I never think of our boy's death as tragic. We think of him as a man who gave his life for his country."

As a brigadier general in the U.S. Air Force Reserve, it would have been easy for Stewart to make a phone call or use his clout in order to exempt his son. That he never did so, that Stewart and his late son exhibited uncomplicated patriotism, was viewed by the sharpshooters and angle-benders of Beverly Hills as naive.

Finally, it is worthy of note—and considerable thought—that when some 20,000 Vietnamese swarmed into Camp Pendleton in 1975, following the Communist take-over of Saigon, not one family in the golden ghetto offered to act as a sponsor for a refugee. The camp is a ninety-minute drive from Beverly.

For the Vietnamese, just as for the non-white minorities who live or work in Beverly Hills, the promise chiseled into the Statue of Liberty—"I Lift My Lamp Beside the Golden Door"—is an ironic joke.

7.
To Have...

INSOFAR AS IT can be weighed, measured, observed, and interpreted, society in Beverly Hills numbers four loosely knit, fluctuating, and overlapping categories—the idle rich, the do-gooder rich, the getting-on-in years movie-star rich, and the nouveaux riches.

In what passes for society in Beverly Hills, there are status symbols and then there are status symbols. It is no longer enough to drop names (save one) or to have a chauffeur-driven Rolls, Tiffany diamonds, a closet stuffed with $800 nightgowns, breakfast in bed on Porthault linen, and a home so large that you can say, "Darling, I've never counted the rooms." Points are now scored by having a one-of-a-kind status symbol or as nearly a one-of-a-kind status symbol as possible.

Examples: Department-store heiress Virginia Robinson says—with aristocratic stoicism—that she's down to "just six servants." Sybil Brand, the town's most triumphant do-gooder, has a jail named for her. And retired screen star Ann Rutherford, who was Andy Hardy's pristine girl friend, has a complement of Chinese employees whom she jokingly refers to as her own tong.

The most impressive status symbol of all accrues to any woman who can lay claim to having slept with John F. Kennedy. At least five local swingers have publicly crowed the distinction.

94

As both a naval officer and a senator, Kennedy was a familiar poolside figure at the Beverly Hills Hotel. Even when he was President (though the trysts had to be arranged more discreetly), Kennedy could spot a compliant political groupie with the same acumen as Henry Kissinger, his successor as Washington's ambassador of sex. Until his marriage, Kissinger visited Beverly as often as possible and dated half the actresses in town.

Of the five women in Beverly who claim intimacy with Kennedy, only one, a leggy actress, is telling the verifiable truth. Kennedy's rumored affair with Marilyn Monroe is still a matter of vigorous disagreement along the social treadmill. One of Miss Monroe's psychiatrists and several of her intimates swear it never happened. Others all but swear they saw them sandwiched between the sheets.

Society in Beverly Hills is the province of women. Only they have the time, the inclination, and the bank account to indulge in upper-crust trivia.

A large segment of the population of Beverly, 31 per cent, consists of separated, divorced, or widowed females. Add in the married women and females outnumber males three to two. The bulk of them live in the south, hoping for an entrée into the minority ranks of the brassy belles who dictate who's who in Beverly society. Few from down under make it.

Somebody named Denise Hale, a dimly known, meddlesome, and not universally admired doyenne, was quoted by Rex Reed in *Harper's Bazaar* as saying that top-rung social standing in Beverly is attainable through "a combination of money, power, achievement, savoir-faire, great connections throughout the world, wit, talent and charm." If those were truly the yardsticks, perhaps only Cary Grant would qualify. The list would certainly exclude Mrs. Hale, whose references for elevating herself as the arbiter of Beverly Hills society are that she's married two highly successful men. Her ex-husband was director Vincente Minnelli, who made a string of hit musicals at MGM, won an Academy Award for *Gigi,* and fathered Liza Minnelli while he was married to Judy Garland. Denise is now the wife of Prentice Cobb Hale, who owns Neiman-Marcus and Bergdorf Goodman. If Mrs. Hale, the self-proclaimed leader of the Beverly Hills upper crust, has exhibited any of her own admittance standards to society, displayed a talent for anything except marrying rich men, she has kept the details a well-guarded secret.

But, for the most part, Beverly Hills society is a "meritocracy," which is the best thing that can be said for it. Since there is little money around that stretches back more than a generation, it is the men and women who've succeeded on their own who are sought after and who constitute Beverly society.

The "meritocracy" of Beverly Hills society is unparalleled among all the social centers of the world. From the Côte d'Azur to Palm Beach, society is made up of coupon-clippers pointlessly lolling their lives away with inherited money. These useless types feel uncomfortable and guilt-ridden in the presence of the self-made. Those who rate at the top of their A-list are deposed kings who—before they were thrown out of their palaces—swiped enough from the local treasury to keep themselves in villas for the rest of their lives.

Egypt's ex-King Farouk, who read comic books and had one of the world's largest private collections of pornography, was a hero to the coupon-clippers. So was the late Duke of Windsor, who was almost given a ticket for double-parking outside the Beverly Hills Hotel in 1959. Police Chief Clinton Anderson intervened, winning a nod of appreciation from the Duke and protests from non-titled Beverly Hills citizens who had been forced to pay fines for the same offense.

Some say the Duke perfected the science of freeloading. At any rate, there isn't anyone who can recall his ever having picked up a check. Nonetheless, socialites (including a few, but not many, in Beverly Hills) fell over each other to wine and dine the Duke and his Duchess.

The Duke and Duchess of Windsor weren't a big hit in Beverly Hills. They were greeted with passing curiosity, a pair of shooting stars that dazzled for a moment and then, mercifully, disappeared. At the half-dozen or so parties they attended, they had little to say that was worth hearing. Nobody gave a damn anyway except a handful of hostesses who were thrilled to boast that they had entertained the royal couple. The local consensus was that the Duke and Duchess were superficially charming and totally vacuous.

The summa cum laude for a Beverly Hills hostess with party pathology is to snag John Wayne, Frank Sinatra, Katharine Hepburn, or Loretta Young—none of them accept many of the bas-relief invitations to the so-called right parties. The aging movie superstars are the royalty who matter in Beverly Hills, the aristocrats Beverly Hills thrives on and understands.

It is interesting to consider the competition between Beverly Hills and Palm Beach and the clashing life-styles among the socialites in the two towns. Each is quietly contemptuous of the other, each expresses cordial hatred toward one another, each puts the other down.

The Florida compound, with a population of 9,086, is more exclusive. It has more money than the golden ghetto, a median income of $40,000 to $50,000 a year. Acre for acre it has more millionaires than Beverly. The average age in Palm Beach is fifty-eight, which qualifies it as the world's richest senior citizens' colony. The average age in Beverly is forty-seven. The pedigrees of many in Palm Beach yawn back to the *Mayflower*. Precisely the reverse is true in Beverly, where the ancestries of the French poodles are usually more distinguished than those of their owners.

The standard in Palm Beach is money without merit, and scruffy royalty makes far more of an impact there than in Beverly Hills. So do pure socialites. Barbara Hutton ranks higher in Palm Beach than does Cary Grant. But it was Beverly Hills' Cary Grant, a kid from a Bristol, England, slum who junked the Woolworth memsahib, the classic poor little rich girl who has only one Palm Beach–approved distinction—she's never done a lick of labor in her life.

Even a minor star such as Polly Bergen, who can light up a Beverly Hills gazebo in red silk hostess pajamas like an old-fashioned July Fourth fireworks sky, is more estimable than Palm Beach habitués who have never achieved anything on their own and likely never will—the fortune-inheriting Phippses, Shevlins, Munns, Guinnesses, Bakers, Drexels, and the late queen bee of the lot, Post Toasties heiress Majorie Merriweather Post, whose only accomplishment of note was contributing her daughter, Dina Merrill, to Hollywood and Beverly Hills. Dina, in spite of her mother's $250 million, had the grit and stamina to carve out a respectable career as an extremely competent actress.

The sole Palm Beach green blood with any style, with some achievement frosting her wealth, is Rose Kennedy, who rarely goes to parties, preferring to devote her time to her family and charity.

On a dullness scale of one to ten, Palm Beach society rates a lackluster five, Beverly Hills a shaky two. In Palm Beach, it's party all night and sleep in the next day. In Beverly Hills, the parties seldom last beyond midnight, and it's work the next morning. Important social events are rarely scheduled in Beverly from Sunday to Thursday. In Palm Beach, the action may occur any night of the week, since no one has much to do the following day.

Of the two principalities, Beverly Hills is preferable because it is livelier, more diverse, less snobbish. It takes but one hit film, television series, record, or book to be accepted.

In Beverly, the latest fad is low-key informality. The era of the formal, home-catered party is past. Most large parties now take place in a hired hall. The most fashionable is Upstairs at the Bistro, above a babbling, day-long crowd of famous drunks hugging the bar, sometimes six-deep. The water hole on North Canon Drive was founded in 1963 by sixty movie-colony investors, each of whom put up $3,000. The backers included Tony Curtis, Louis Jourdan, Jack Lemmon, Dean Martin, Merle Oberon, Otto Preminger, Frank Sinatra, producer Sam Spiegel, Robert Stack, Jack Warner, and director Billy Wilder.

Downstairs at the Bistro the decibel level is so high that it's close to impossible to talk without shouting. The room has no booths, and the tables are jammed together. It is a place to be seen, not heard. As it is very important to be seen in Beverly, the Bistro is extremely popular, so much so that Kurt Niklas—the German-born, forty-eight-year-old, gray-haired owner, who bought out the original backers—says it's worth "in excess of one million dollars."

Other favored party spots are any of the twenty-one country clubs within easy reach of Beverly. The Los Angeles Country Club, possibly the most exclusive, bars actors. When retired movie cowboy Randolph Scott, married to a Du Pont heiress, applied for membership, he was informed of the policy. "If you've seen any of my pictures," he said, "you'd realize I'm not an actor." Scott's application was accepted.

The most-favored and most-used party sites are three of Beverly's thirteen hotels. Only on their grounds would a self-respecting $25,000 Mercedes allow itself to be parked. Among the trio, the competition is fierce to land the huge social shindigs. The bill for one of these brawls, depending on the number of guests and whether the champagne is imported or domestic, can run a host, a sponsoring charity, or a corporation as much as $100,000 for a one-night celebration.

The most prominent of the three is the Beverly Hills Hotel, a massive brown stucco building on Sunset Boulevard. Its eminence is undeserved, but myth replaces fact too often in Beverly, and its patrons, especially show-biz names, pay luxury rates for decay. The green lobby carpet is frayed and badly in need of replacement. The plumbing rumbles and the tennis courts are clumsily squeezed into an odd corner of the grounds. The location is inconvenient to everything, and a car is necessary to go anywhere. Both room service and delivery of patrons' automobiles are slovenly. It perhaps owes its drawing power to the adventurous tales that have flowed from its private bungalows and to the literally billions of dollars in deals that have been spawned at its pseudo-svelte Polo Lounge bar and restaurant.

The Beverly Hilton is the flagship of that imperfect chain of expensive plaster cages. It has long been the meeting place for the Writers Guild of America, as well as other organizations. The film and television writers arrive in everything from Volkswagens and Toyotas to Jaguars and Bentleys. But celebrities generally prefer to avoid the Hilton's chain atmosphere, and major names troop in only to attend the latest good-cause banquet, an event such as the Ladies of Charity St. Louise de Marillac get-together, which brings out Bob Hope, Ronald Reagan, Irene Dunne, and Ann Blyth. The Hilton's only advantage is that it is within walking distance of the Wilshire Boulevard shopping area.

Even more advantageously situated for shopping is the Beverly Wilshire, the elegant, yellow-awninged concrete ranchero of Hernando Courtright, the bushy-eyebrowed proprietor who unhesitatingly declares, "We operate the best hotel in Los Angeles. It is a European-style, personalized hotel. We deal with people who are spoiled and I don't mean that slightingly—they are merely people who have the money to call their own shots."

Since he took over the hotel in 1961—buying it from fast-fading real-estate tycoon Bill Zeckendorf, who owned it for ten days —Courtright has restored the reputation of the Beverly Wilshire. He also expanded the once-intimate Oak Room into a larger restaurant renamed El Padrino—Spanish-Mexican in decor, with silver horseshoes nailed to the heavy oak doors. There, table captains bow humbly before such diners as Robert Mitchum, Warren Beatty, Doris Day, and Richard Harris.

Local society in Beverly Hills can be traced to the arrival of Mr. and Mrs. Henry Winchester Robinson on February 4, 1911, eight years before Douglas Fairbanks, Sr., bought and refurbished his hunting lodge. The Robinsons purchased fifteen acres on what is now a cul-de-sac at the highest point of Elden Way on the hilly, terraced terrain above the Beverly Hills Hotel.

Now, the high, gray wall surrounding their Roman mansion is chipped and neglected, crying for a paint job. Entrance is navigated through a grilled iron gate 142 feet from the front door. A visitor is ushered in by Ivo, a tall, slick-haired man with dark, flitting eyes. In a Bulgarian accent aburst with pride, Ivo describes himself, not as a butler, but as Mrs. Robinson's "major-domo."

The ninety-seven-year-old mistress of the mansion, wearing a purple wool dress on a warm summer evening, is white-haired, blue-eyed, five-four, and petite.

The living room is glutted with antiques. In the sun-speckled sitting room, Mrs. Robinson sits on the throne of a gold velvet sofa that appears well-worn and slightly frayed at the edges. A musty aura permeates the house.

"I was a spoiled child," she says. "Oh, it was so funny when we came out here. I was three or four years old. There was no place to stay. We couldn't get a room, so my father rented Nan's boardinghouse in downtown Los Angeles. He rented the whole boardinghouse. It was quite large. We stayed there for a month or two."

Virginia and Harry Robinson were married in 1903. "Harry and I grew up together. He was a fat boy and I thought, 'Pouff, I'm not going to marry him.' I had many other suitors. But I changed my mind. I never liked weddings and refused to wear a wedding veil. My gown was a cream-colored one the dressmaker made for me with a crumpled-out skirt.

"We went on a three-year honeymoon and stayed at the Waldorf in New York and then traveled from Europe to Kashmir. When we returned, everyone was talking about the new Los Angeles Country Club; so one evening we started out to find it. We never did find the club, but we found this piece of land. Just like that, my husband said, 'This is where we're going to live.'

"This Burton Green had built Beverly Hills. But there wasn't one house here. There wasn't a single thing out here. Just a little bit of a real-estate office, kind of a shed, on Santa Monica Boulevard."

The Robinsons traveled to Japan and then lived at the Los Angeles Country Club until Mrs. Robinson's father, Nathaniel Dryden, a wealthy architect who'd inherited a Texas sheep ranch, built Beverly's initial mansion.

"We moved into the house, staffed it, and gave our first dinner party a short time later."

Mrs. Robinson's husband died on September 11, 1932. "I don't like to talk about it."

The Robinson department-store empire was begun by her late

husband's father. It's now a chain of twelve whose label is almost but not quite as tony as Saks' or Magnin's. The first of them was called the Boston Store in honor of the founder's hometown.

"One of the first things I remember was having five dollars and somebody taking me to the Boston Store. I bought five dollars' worth of handkerchiefs. I've used them practically all my life. They were little cheap ones, with flowers on them."

No, Mrs. Robinson doesn't know how many rooms are in the two-story house.

"I've never counted because I never knew which was a room and which was a closet. I can't tell them apart. There are all these rooms downstairs, storerooms and closets everywhere. My clothes are all kept downstairs, you know, that sort of thing.

"I always kept a larger staff than most people. John, one of my butlers, killed himself here in the house. When the Depression came, he said I was going to become poor. I think he was just frightened for me and everything. He talked about boarding up the swimming pool. He said we couldn't even afford water, silly things.

"But the Depression didn't matter in Beverly Hills. I guess it was a dreadful thing for the country. It was nothing to us. But you would hear so much talk about it. People talked, talked, talked about the Depression. And I suppose that made John depressed. He'd bought a lot on Camden and things in Bel Air and paid $32,000 down, and then he couldn't sell any of it. I helped him all I could, but I couldn't do much. He shot himself in his room. He was a dear person. He'd lived with us twenty years.

"I'm down to just the six servants now. Two butlers who serve and do everything. It's very nice. I have one that's very, very beautifully trained [Ivo]. Sometimes I think he should have a vacation, but he hasn't taken one in the five years he's been with me. I have a cook and a kitchen maid, a housemaid and a chauffeur.

"I always used to have at least four butlers. I always kept four men in the house. But, you see, it's hard to get help, get the good people that you want. They get so much money from the government, you know, they just think, 'Why work?' "

Though she doesn't number them among her staff, Mrs. Robinson employs twelve full-time gardeners, augmented by as many as are needed in the summer when her grounds require more attention.

"You know, Mary Pickford's been here. Oh yes, she's quite a friend of mine. Poor dear, she's so sick these days. I don't see her now but Buddy Rogers comes around a great deal. He is a dear person, so nice, and so loyal to Mary.

"I know an awful lot of people. I guess everybody in Beverly Hills has been here. People ask me how it feels to be the First Lady of Beverly Hills and I tell them that I don't think I am. I think Mary is.

"My back lawn takes enormous parties. It was built for parties. Once I had a party and I didn't know who anybody was. It was very funny. When I came into the garden, Mary Pickford came over and told me, 'Goodness, this is disgraceful. No one has the slightest idea who you are.'

"I said that was all right, that I'd just go back to my room, but Mary wouldn't hear of it.

"She said to one of the butlers, 'I want two chairs placed here very prominently for Mrs. Robinson and myself. We will sit here and everybody is to be introduced to us when they come in.' That was very nice of Mary. She knew how to manage so well."

Years before he became the chief of police, Clinton Anderson lived in Mrs. Robinson's house for two months.

"The police department felt I was in some kind of danger, so they had him come out and he stayed in the servants' quarters. He was so nice. I don't know if he ate in the kitchen or what he did. He just sat all day long on a chair up on the balcony, protecting me."

Mrs. Robinson's favorite charities are the California Institute of Technology, a refuge in Pasadena for bright students majoring in the physical sciences, and the Hollywood Bowl.

"I like music so much. I just used to give money away to the symphony. But I've stopped it now. I don't like the new Music Center. I don't like where it is, all the way downtown in Los Angeles. It's so far. And everything is underground. They want you to leave the car downstairs, you know. Well, I don't want to do that. I don't like the fumes. It takes the chauffeur so long to get the car out of there. It's just an unfriendly place."

Mrs. Robinson recalls a brief fling at entrepreneurship.

"I bought the whole nine acres where the Beverly Hills store is, where the Hilton Hotel is. When I started the store, I had different architects and all, but then everybody died. We had eight million dollars to start with and it got up to where it was going to cost nineteen million. I wanted to have a children's department, a playground and soda fountains, those kind of things. And make a lot of money, too. I went to New York and the banks kind of discouraged me. I said, 'Oh well, it's just too much for a woman.' So I sold. I could have taken stock, but I just took money. I don't own one thing in the stores now, but they all think I do."

How has Beverly Hills changed since the days of Burton Green? "Sometimes I'm shocked at the changes. You come down the streets and it seems as if you've never seen them before. I don't drive, you know. I've never driven so I don't know where I am very much of the time. I don't know the names of the streets. One day I said to the chauffeur after we got back from Santa Barbara, 'I like this way you came. It's so nice. I hope we come this way again.' And he said, 'This is the way we always come.' I couldn't believe it. It just suddenly seemed that there were so many new houses and streets, changes, you know."

Mrs. Robinson voted for Nixon because she was "frightened" of McGovern.

"He had terrible ideas. I thought he was going to give everybody one thousand dollars to start with, give one thousand dollars to hundreds of thousands of people. What would happen then? I couldn't understand *The New York Times* going for him. I just can't understand why people do such strange things."

Despite her age, Mrs. Robinson is still in the social whirl. She goes out almost every evening.

"I like to be active, but now I'm not so good on walking. And I don't dance as much as I used to. You have to give up in some ways. Everybody says I don't look my age. I do lead a young life.

"I still enjoy entertaining. The last party is always the best. The secret of a successful party is to enjoy yourself. If you don't enjoy yourself, how is anybody else going to have a good time? You mustn't invite people indiscriminately. Lists, the butler has the lists of people I should invite.

"When I'm not giving a party or I'm not invited out, I play bridge. Then I always have a Wednesday lunch for ninety. I still do that, though it seems silly to have so many people.

"I play bridge with the best players I can find. Eddie Cantor was a great player. Fred Astaire was here, and I played with him, too. I play for small stakes. I don't like to play like some people do, for blood: five, six, ten dollars is the most I lose or win. One time I did play in a big stakes game. It got to be one hundred dollars. But I didn't like it. I don't like losing money."

Is money still important in Mrs. Robinson's life?

"I would take some more. I could use it."

She pauses as her two dogs—Bobo, a poodle, and Monet, a greyhound—bound into the room. Ivo appears with candy, which Mrs. Robinson feeds the dogs. "The darlings have a sweet tooth, you know." Ivo pours a glass of champagne and Mrs. Robinson tells her major-domo, "I think our guest will be going home soon."

On the subject of money, she adds, "I'm really not a money woman. I don't care about money. It's hard for me to think much about money, but I always liked to have lovely things. I get my clothes in Europe and I travel a lot and I have a very nice life."

To what does Mrs. Robinson attribute her longevity?

"Everybody asks me that. It's very funny because even fifteen years ago, the doctors said they would like to talk to me, find out what I do and don't do. I played tennis and dived off the board into the pool and did thirty-two laps twice a day until I was eighty-five."

And now, three years short of a century of life, what is Mrs. Robinson looking forward to?

"Why, I don't know. Tomorrow, I suppose. Yes, tomorrow. That's the answer."

Her will, she says, provides for her home and park-like grounds to be deeded to the city of Beverly Hills as an arboretum and botanical garden. She is also leaving one million dollars for upkeep.

Polite good-bys are said. The door of the Roman-style mansion is quietly shut, leaving Beverly's chatelaine to her tomorrow.

"There are so many rich women in Beverly Hills who do nothing. I don't understand how they live. They must be bored to death. I could never live that way."

Sybil Brand, the crusading matriarch of Beverly Hills, has made certain she's never lived that way.

The daughter of Chicago stockbroker A. W. Morris, Sybil arrived in Los Angeles more than sixty years ago at the age of two-and-a-half. By the time she was twelve, she was into the humanitarian work that has been the keynote of her entire life.

Through a client, Mr. Morris learned there was a shortage of diapers at Los Angeles' Children's Hospital. Young Sybil rounded up a group of schoolgirl friends and they hem-stitched diapers non-stop for three days, donating them without fuss.

Sybil married Harry Brand in 1936, and they moved to Beverly Hills the same year. George, their only child, is a film cutter. Harry Brand has retired after more than forty years as head of publicity for Twentieth Century-Fox. He was there throughout the salty, glittering, eventful years of taskmasters Joe Schenck and Darryl Zanuck.

Walking with the aid of a cane, Harry Brand is on his way out the door to exercise the family chihuahua. "The last time I saw Sybil was a week ago," he says, smiling. "She's a pip. Always busy. If there's a committee she isn't on, let me know."

Under a halo of reddish-gray hair, Sybil, a trim woman with square features, somehow creates the impression she's at a gallop, even though she's sitting on a white couch in the living room of her unpretentious, stucco home on North Rexford Drive. Impatient with interviewers, Sybil Brand has no interest in personal publicity. She will resort to flackery, and expertly so, only to assure the success of one of her pet projects.

At the moment, the living room resembles a small liquor store. Cases of booze are scattered along the floor, on chairs and on tables. The donated Scotch, bourbon, vodka, and gin are leftovers from the previous night's $125-a-plate premiere that Sybil masterminded for *Lost Horizon*. The swells from the Shangri-La of Beverly Hills naturally had turned out for the movie version of Shangri-La. (Produced by Ross Hunter, Sybil Brand's neighbor, the picture was subsequently roasted by critics. Roger Ebert, of the Chicago *Sun-Times* called it one of the worst films he'd ever seen. In fiction as well as fact, the inhabitants of Beverly Hills failed at creating Shangri-La.) But the premiere raised $135,000 for the Motion Picture Country Home and Hospital.

For Sybil Brand, however, $135,000 is not enough. She's been on the phone all morning selling the remaining booze at $5 per bottle and trying to find a wealthy donor to pick up the tab for the rent on the hotel ballroom and the other incidental expenses of the premiere. She watches the charity money she raises like a kid guarding a piggy bank. Only $25 of each $125 paid per person, she explains, goes for overhead—and she clearly begrudges the overhead charges.

"Some of the richest people in Beverly Hills are among the cheapest in the world," says Sybil Brand, scowling. "Most of those who come to my affairs don't have a great deal of money. As a rule, millionaires won't buy tickets to a premiere if they can't be there themselves. It never occurs to them that they could give the tickets to friends, or simply send a donation they can easily afford."

She shakes her head indignantly. "I've seen some of the wealthiest people in Beverly Hills actually steal liquor at the galas I've organized.

Many of them walk out with full bottles. Sometimes they even take bottles of soda mix. To me, that is stealing money from the needy. I can sell that liquor. Every penny counts."

She says that no one can do anything alone. "I have wonderful friends. It's like a circle. They pitch in and help. I always try to get girls on my committees with whom I've worked before—the ones that will actually work. There are some who will always sign up. But they don't always work.

"When it comes to invitations, I don't send out a lot. It's crazy to waste beautiful invitations. I only invite people I think will buy."

By her own estimate, she's raised between 15 and 20 million dollars for good works. The figure is undoubtedly higher. Sybil Brand, who's been called the Golda Meir of Beverly Hills, is too busy to keep a tally.

Bob Hope once cracked, "There's no disease left for me to sponsor. Sybil Brand has taken them all."

Seemingly, she has. In over forty-five years, she's raised money for leukemia victims; the Reiss-Davis clinic, which provides treatment and therapy for emotionally disturbed children; a new pediatrics admittance room in the children's pavilion at Cedars of Lebanon Hospital, which was dedicated to the memory of Sybil's father, mother, and brother; the American Cancer Society; the Braille Institute; the Spastic Children's Guild; the Los Angeles Jewish Home for the Aged; Mount St. Mary's College; and a forest of other organizations. She's worked with paralyzed veterans at Long Beach Hospital and has been a member of Presidential Committees for the Handicapped under Eisenhower, Johnson, and Nixon.

She's also been extremely active in civic endeavors, spending six years as president of the Los Angeles County Public Welfare Commission, and eight years as chairwoman of Los Angeles' Vocational Training and Advisory Committee, an adjunct of the city's probation department. She has also been on the Beverly Hills Chamber of Commerce, was a founding member of the board of governors of SERVE (Servicemen's Emergency Recreational Volunteer Events), and served on the National Council of Christians and Jews.

"I spend comparatively little time doing things for the people of Beverly Hills," she says. "It isn't that they don't need help, but people outside Beverly Hills need more help than people inside Beverly Hills."

Though she's been warned for years by her doctor to slow down,

Sybil has ignored the advice. She's out virtually every evening, and often her escort is the still-dashing actor Cesar Romero. "Harry has a bad leg," she says. "Besides, he rarely goes to these things."

Sometimes Sybil is so harried that she isn't quite sure where she's going when she leaves the house with Romero or other friends. She is also capable of an occasional display of delightful eccentricity.

While Sybil was attending a friend's party one evening—with her husband present on this occasion—a woman came up and embraced her warmly. They talked animatedly for thirty-five minutes.

"Who was that?" Harry asked when the woman had gone.

"One of my best friends."

"I never heard you mention her name. I'll bet you haven't seen her in twenty years."

"So what? I haven't seen a lot of my best friends in twenty years."

Sybil made a mental note to mark down the name of the recovered "friend," who had recently moved to Beverly, as a potential guest at a future gala.

"I love to work," she says in explanation of her hectic schedule. "And it helps if you don't sleep much."

Sybil and her husband have a house in Palm Springs, but it's rare for them to spend two weeks a year there.

She describes herself as "not a religious person as such. I go to temple on the important holidays, and I have a profound belief in God."

She's a registered Democrat, but worked for Nixon in his 1972 re-election campaign.

"I asked Mr. Nixon cold-turkey if he thought I should change my registration to Republican," she recalls. " 'No,' Nixon replied, 'stay a Democrat. That's the best thing that can happen to me. I need all the Democrats I can get.' "

She also worked for the re-election of then-Senator George Murphy, one of her Beverly Hills neighbors.

"I told Murphy he had the wrong people around him, that he was taking the wrong appointments, the wrong engagements. I predicted he would lose unless he started taking the right engagements. He also needed to get rid of some of the people around him." If Murphy had drafted Sybil Brand as his campaign manager, possibly he would not have been defeated.

The triumph that Sybil Brand views as her most lasting and satisfactory occurred while she was a member of the Public Welfare Commission. She volunteered to serve on the Commission's jail committee "because no one else wanted the job."

Through the early 1960s, female prisoners in Los Angeles were huddled into the downtown Hall of Justice building. There were 2,500 inmates in a lockup meant to house 1,200.

"It was a disgrace," says Sybil, "overcrowding, danger of epidemics, juveniles in with adults, unbearable visiting conditions. Imagine thirty people crowded into one small room, with prisoners and relatives trying to talk privately through a net screen."

Sybil Brand began her crusade. She got down on her hands and knees and laid carpet to brighten several of the cells. She obtained telephones for the visitors' room so that inmates could talk privately with their families. She arranged for hardened prostitutes and drug addicts to be quarantined from teen-agers.

But there was a clear and present need for a new women's prison. There was also a highly unlikely chance of obtaining it. Indifferent Los Angeles voters had previously refused to approve a bond proposal to fund the proposed institution. Moreover, a two-thirds majority at the ballot box was necessary for passage. The question was how to convince the electorate to spend 8 million dollars for the facility.

Sybil had learned a thing or two from her husband's professionalism as a publicist. The need was to dramatize the issue to the public, and in order to do that she had to get inside the existing jail with a camera crew.

The sheriff turned her down. That only made Sybil more determined. She waited until the sheriff left town, and then went to a judge, a family friend, and received special permission to photograph the jail. She had a fifteen-minute film assembled and—with Harry's help—it was exhibited in every major theater in Los Angeles and Orange counties.

Media people were invited to screenings, and the campaign caught fire. At the time, there were four newspapers in metropolitan Los Angeles, and they all featured the story of the abysmal jail on their front pages. Television, radio, and newspaper commentators joined in. So did a forgiving sheriff, the police department, and the county Board of Supervisors.

At the next election, the bond proposal passed handily. Construction of the jail, located near the harbor city of San Pedro, was completed in 1963. The facility has pursued a policy of emphasizing rehabilitation through job training rather than punishment. Its graduates have one of the lowest recidivism rates of any prison in California.

There was no difficulty finding a name for the facility. It was christened the Sybil Brand Institute for Women.

When Sybil toured the jail for the first time, the grapevine passed the word she was inside the institution. Up and down the cells and dormitory corridors the women prisoners—some veterans of the old jail—cheered lustily as she walked past.

"It was the greatest tribute I've ever received," says the woman who has been paid homage by presidents, governors, and scores of local politicians.

Sybil Brand has spent her life remembering the injunction of her father: "Never let a day pass without doing something for those less fortunate than yourself."

Sybil Brand has never been movie-star beautiful. She doesn't have Ava Gardner's nose or Raquel Welch's figure, or anything approaching Virginia Robinson's money. Nevertheless, she is the richest, most beautiful woman in Beverly Hills.

Ann Rutherford played Scarlett O'Hara's sister in *Gone With the Wind*, as well as the virginal Polly Benedict in fifteen Andy Hardy movies. Her screen image across a panorama of seventy-eight films was purer-than-pure. It is a minor shock to discover, therefore, that today Ann Rutherford is as sophisticated a lady as Polly Benedict was demure and naive.

At fifty-five, and looking twenty years younger, Miss Rutherford is among the elite of Beverly Hills, busily and somewhat gropingly trying to live happily ever after. She and her second husband, Bill Dozier, producer of television shows from *Playhouse 90* to *Batman*, have been married for twenty-one years.

Their home is a handsome $500,000 Georgian-style mansion replete with sauna. While her husband was an active producer, she built a projection room on the site of her World War II victory garden, so that he could watch rushes in comfort. The expansive house is on Greenway Drive, considered the most desirable and exclusive street in Beverly Hills. The entire block has less than fifteen homes and the view from the front lawns is the golf course of the Los Angeles Country Club.

According to Miss Rutherford, she and her husband are now dabblers in the Beverly Hills social scene. They refuse more invitations than they accept. Declares Miss Rutherford, "So-called Beverly Hills society isn't really part of our lives. Anyway, it's such an iffy thing and lacks permanence. It changes with the winds of fashion, with the winds of *Vogue* magazine and *Women's Wear Daily*.

"We are a transient community. We take and lose from all the stages of the world. When you boil it all down, what matters are the few people you know whom, if you get your tail in a wringer, you can call at three o'clock in the morning and they'll talk to you."

Miss Rutherford has retained her beauty. Her face is still cameo-like; her hair is streaked fashionably with two horizontal lines of gray. For an interview, she wore a white turtleneck sweater and tailored, white-and-brown striped, bib-front overalls, whose right strap, having a mind of its own, kept falling provocatively after each adjustment.

She lights a filtered cigarette and toys with a heavy Steuben bowl on a table in the yellow-and-brown living room. Through a nimbus of blue smoke, her voice chimes gaily. "Parties in Beverly Hills have improved enormously. Parties are lovely now. No longer do you have to go through that agony of surveying your closet, wondering who hasn't seen what or where is there a good designer who'll do something perfectly smashing for you.

"I don't truly think there is a Beverly Hills society," she says. "There was, some years ago, what they called the Hollywood 400, but even that was an ersatz thing. It consisted of people who gave lots of tent parties, people who were very large stars, but I don't think they believed in it themselves.

"Most parties now are in the home, and when I say in the home I don't mean in the tent. There was a time from perhaps 1936 to 1966 when, if you gave a party worthy of being called a party, it had to be under a tent. You not only sent out invitations, but wall-to-wall reminders, the little engraved dillies that said, 'Don't forget, we're giving a party on the such and such and we're expecting you at so and so o'clock.' A proper party then was much like the early days in Boston. After you sent your invitations and reminders up front, you met with your caterer and tent man to plan everything. Those are very few and far between now, and I think it's a blessing.

"If you want to have a fun party in this town, you'll have somebody from New York, somebody from London, from Greece, someone from a totally different walk of life. People should inspire each other chemically to better conversation. The main thing is getting the right people together.

"If you're going to have a party and invite only the top producers, there is nothing for anybody to call and thank you for the next day. They've all been to that party. All the wives know exactly what the other wives are going to wear. The whole secret is having a good blend. If you invite only actors, it's going to be a foot race to the mirror to see if the lipstick and the toupees are on straight. If you have all lawyers or insurance people, it's going to be a bleak, dreary thing with all the women in one room and the men in another.

"You must have a mixture of bright, articulate people and, of course, that isn't always easy, because most couples are like a phonograph record—you have the hit side and you have the flip side."

In the last few years, she's not only attended fewer parties, but those she's given have been smaller and far more informal.

"If the men want to wear a caftan, or an open shirt with a scarf, and the ladies don't want to rush out and buy something new, then bless them, they shouldn't. Let them wear Levis and just come and enjoy themselves.

"I've finally decided we could roll up the rest of the house and just keep the sunroom going. Because of the scaled-down level of our entertaining, and since our children have grown and left home, we really use the dining room and buffet only for those dinners at Christmas time."

Miss Rutherford contends that the Beverly Hills social set is no longer as insular as it was previously. Too, publicity counts for little and the day of the debutante has had it.

"You used to be graded on how many pictures of your party appeared two months later in *Life, Photoplay, Movie Week,* and whatever those other magazines were called. Or you sat under the hair dryer and scanned the society pages of the newspapers to see how much was written about your *soirée* and how many pictures were run. But press coverage of a party is no longer important, influential, or sought after.

"Both our daughters went to private girls' schools and they couldn't have cared less about coming-out parties, being debutantes and all that stuff, which is predicated on values set at least twenty or thirty years ago. I think young people today want to make their own way. They want to make their own mistakes, and bless them for it. The only lessons you retain are the ones you teach yourself.

"My generation and the young people in Beverly Hills are no longer climbing in that direction. None of us cares much, if at all, about society, whatever society is supposed to be."

Among the definable local life-styles observed by Miss Rutherford, who has lived in Beverly Hills since 1942, are the country-club style and the swinger style.

"Those are the people who are totally destroyed if they're not seen at absolutely every party and opening. They are the professional partygoers, and that's ridiculous. It's a crock. But those are lonely people, I'm quite sure. I think the happiest people are those who have their own inner resources even if the children have spread their wings and moved away. People who can be content by themselves."

Further subcultures, she elaborates, are the gin-rummy hounds, or the women who play backgammon all afternoon. There are also the tennis buffs and the ski buffs. Finally, there is, she says, the chic style.

"The cult of ladies who go to the Bistro, then shop for something to wear tomorrow at the Bistro. They have ladies who come to their homes and put funny fingernails on them if, God forbid, they break one.

"The real doers in Beverly Hills are the ladies who are flexible, who are malleable, who travel, who keep themselves in shape without being slaves to Marvin Hart. I adore him, he's a marvelous man, a fabulous masseur, the *in* masseur. He is the gentleman who will look at an Ann-Margret or a Jennifer Jones or someone else in impeccable shape and say, 'You need an eighth of an inch off your left thigh.' Then he'll give them punishing exercises; but some people require this kind of discipline. Some ladies can afford this and have the time for it and this can be their be-all and end-all."

Miss Rutherford knows whereof she speaks, since she's a self-proclaimed dropout from the chic set.

"It isn't that I don't approve, because at one time I did it. Then I sat down and had a period of self-examination, and thought, 'What has become of the last two or three years?' By the time I got up and pulled myself together of a morning, it was time for Romanoff's. One would scurry to lunch or maybe first you went to an early fashion show at Adrian's. Then you met your luncheon chums, and you would consult your watch rather hastily and think, 'Oh, my God, I am lunching again tomorrow. What in God's name will I wear?' You'd streak off to Adrian's or Saks or Magnin's and brainwash someone into altering something very quickly so you could wear it tomorrow.

"I suddenly realized that life must hold more than this for me; there had to be a great deal more than this to the business of living. So I knocked it all off and started taking up hobbies. Then I found some of the hobbies consuming my life. One of them, painting, kept me up until five o'clock in the morning for about a year and a half. So I had to kick painting. I went into gentler things that didn't require quite as much time, particularly coquillage."

Coquillage, the art of decorating objects with shells and coral in rich floral patterns, proved a successful venture for Miss Rutherford. She began by embellishing a clock housing she'd purchased for two dollars on a trip to Italy. Then she graduated to adding her deft touch to mirrors. The finished products were sold at Neiman-Marcus and at several exclusive stores in New York, each piece retailing for upwards of $1,100.

"I did extremely well with them. Now I've tapered off and currently I'm up to my ears with five hundred pounds of white shells and five hundred pounds of white coral." (Several half-finished examples of her work repose in her dining room.) "But coquillage was a marvelous escape and, I suppose, creative. Anybody who's ever acted likes to be creative. I didn't realize as I was growing up that I liked to create things. I just knew I enjoyed acting because it was an escape."

Since her withdrawal from the unfulfilling world of chic and the non-sustaining pastimes of painting and coquillage, Miss Rutherford has contented herself with devoting part of her time to charity and the rest to the comfortable role of Mrs. Chips.

"I've been very active with the Reiss-Davis clinic. We went to the Liza Minnelli thing. Liza did a benefit for the clinic and we raised $198,000. And I'm helping to raise money for The Visionaires, which aids blind children. It's a very small organization and few people know about it. This sounds so wild, but someone once said, 'All the good diseases are taken.' Almost every Sunday on television a star will raise bales of money for whatever the *in* disease is. But there is something totally irresistible to me about a blind child."

She expresses delight that her husband has retired from show business. "It's a man-killer. I've seen it kill many favorite friends of ours. But I don't think a man should retire *from* a business. He should retire *to* something. When Bill quit, the first years weren't what we'd call a smashing success. Now it's marvelous. He's retired to teaching. He lectures one night a week at Mount St. Mary's Doheny campus and five afternoons at UCLA. He teaches drama and the nuts and bolts of network TV.

"Now Bill is Mr. Chips and I'm Mrs. Chips and it's great fun. It's a whole new world for him. People must touch new life at new points. It can be very stultifying living in the past. I will definitely not mention names, but some people I've known for many, many years, people who were terribly important in their day, are making love to the past. I adore them and like to spend time with them, but when I meet them I say inwardly, 'Oh dear, he's going back to that story about Greta Garbo or Pickford or Clark Gable.' That's yesterday. It isn't today. You can't look back. Something might be catching up to you. That's why I don't even keep scrapbooks."

Concerning the image of Beverly Hills as El Dorado, she says it isn't so. "The *business* has been an El Dorado for me. It's opened doors in my life I'm sure wouldn't otherwise have been ajar. I would have ended up either a schoolteacher or just a housewife. I'm just a housewife now and as happy as if I had good sense."

Ann Rutherford Dozier performs her housewifely duties with the aid of what she jestingly calls "our tong," a Chinese family whose five members live in the Doziers' mansion. Her tong is a subject she obviously enjoys discussing.

The parents, Tsai and Ah Yiang Tuck, have been an indispensable part of the Dozier household since 1966. They were hired via mail, and it took a year and a half of red tape—endless forms to be filled out and correspondence with immigration and customs authorities—before they reached Beverly Hills by way of Peking, Shanghai, and Hong Kong.

She had fired all her previous servants, Miss Rutherford recalls, telling them, "I can cook better than you! I can clean better! And I don't break things! Everybody out!" Then, until the Tucks arrived, she and her husband handled the household chores.

"Bill and I discovered we both liked to cook. We watched Julia Child and just cooked up a storm. We did the housecleaning ourselves and had a marvelous time until the coming of Tsai and Ah Yiang."

The evening prior to the couple's arrival, Miss Rutherford was busy sorting clothes in the laundry room. "I was throwing things into the dryer," she says, "knowing this was going to be my last true washing until I taught the servants how to run the machine. I encountered three pair of Bill's jockey shorts that really needed throwing into the rag bag. But I was going to a party and here I was in my robe, with my slip on under it, and I had my hair all done. I thought I'd wreck my manicure if I ripped the elastics off the waists. I decided I would fish them out another time. Then I forgot all about them.

"The next day Tsai and Ah Yiang arrived and I tried to give them two or three days rest. They'd had a long journey from Hong Kong but by six o'clock the following morning Tsai was dusting the cars and before we knew it they were handling our whole house.

"A week later I happened to go through the kitchen and the dearest domestic sight met my eyes. At the stove, Tsai was turning bacon with his chopsticks, and at the kitchen table was this dainty little Ah Yiang—who looked like a court maid from the days of Napoleon—with a teeny, tiny embroidery hoop. Firmly ensconced in the hoop was the butt of a pair of my husband's $1.39 jockey shorts that should have been thrown away four years ago. Ah Yiang was weaving stitches like a blind nun under water, the most beautiful work I'd ever seen. She'd already done the two other pair. I couldn't tell her I'd planned to throw them out, for her not to waste her time. I thanked her and made signs of appreciation. She speaks no English at all, but her husband is very articulate.

"I took the shorts upstairs and showed them to Bill and there were tears in his eyes. He said he hoped he got into an accident so that when they undressed him on the emergency table the doctor would look at his shorts and say, 'Somebody sure loves this guy.' He was so touched he wouldn't part with those jockey shorts; they became his dearest treasures for at least three more years, until finally the elastics got shot and he had to toss them away.

"Tsai and Ah Yiang care. They are dear, lovely and loving human beings. There is something about them. I've never felt such an affinity for any people in my life as I have for them. We've done our best to spoil them because we love them so genuinely. But they are totally unspoilable."

Tsai and Ah Yiang are less than four feet eight inches tall. "If we'd seen full-size photographs of them we would have thought we were hiring midgets. They looked like they couldn't lift an option. But all we saw were these marvelous faces, people who stood on their ability and talent, and to this day they are the tallest people I know."

When the Doziers began giving smaller dinner parties, Tsai, who had studied under a Cantonese banquet master, began to shine. He prepared what Miss Rutherford describes as "Chinese chow like you've never tasted." But Tsai can only conjure his delicacies for a maximum of ten people.

"He does crisp duck that comes right out of your ears. He does a dessert called Peking Dust where he works over fresh chestnuts like for four days. He boils, fries, bakes, and then mixes them with whipped cream. They are incredible.

"It's very tough to have a Caucasian dinner for ten people that can last four or five hours. But there's something languorous about Oriental food. Each guest is dignified by having his own particular course. That means that for ten people there are ten main courses. That doesn't count the soup, noodles, the rice, the dessert, or any other little odds and ends that may come in from the kitchen. You learn to pace yourself, you learn to relax and just enjoy sitting at the table and eating.

"We've streamlined things a little by putting a Lazy Susan on the table and it's almost like an audience participation show. People love twirling the Lazy Susan."

Among those who imbibe Chinese chow at the Dozier home are Jennifer Jones, who is married to Norton Simon, the publishing and food-products multimillionaire and noted art collector.

"I'm sure Jennifer and Norton are accustomed to a footman on every toe, but they are so dear and so ingenuous. They so enjoy Tsai's lovely meals."

Virtually every dime earned by Tsai and Ah Yiang after their arrival was sent back to Hong Kong to support their three teen-age sons and keep them in English-speaking schools. Soon there was enough money to bring the sons to Beverly Hills.

"The boys spoke proper English but they understood quite slowly, articulated carefully, and would drop the articles in their sentences," says Miss Rutherford. "I took a deep breath and slammed the two youngest into Beverly Hills High School, and the eldest I put into Santa Monica College. They all went out and got full-time jobs. One even worked in a laundry. Within six months each had paid outright for an automobile and one has a Honda besides. They all get A grades. Bill and I can go to a party and come home at three o'clock in the morning and see lights burning in their rooms. Here are these youngsters putting in sixteen hours, eight at school and eight at work. And then they do their homework until three and four in the morning.

"They've made me impatient with some members of our younger generation. I remember getting in my car and driving down Sunset Boulevard and hitting hippie heaven. Some youngster would thrust a dreadful newspaper in the window and ask me for fifty cents to buy some bread. I'd break into my bag and give the money to the poor slob. But after seeing our Chinese youngsters, I'd find myself hissing at hippies like a viper, 'You're lazy. Get out and work for it like our kids at home work.'

"Because Tsai and Ah Yiang's children were born and reared after the war and all the trouble, they evidently had wheat products in their diet. They are so much taller than their parents. One son is about five feet eleven. But his father, this tiny little whisper of a man, perhaps he weighs ninety-two pounds, just has to look at him with a gleam in his eye and the son goes hup, two, three, four—and does what he's told instantly.

"The sons are so considerate of their parents, and the older the parents the more the children revere them. To me that's what it's all about. You're over the hill in this country at thirty. But the Orientals for thousands of years have had the right idea. They make growing older more worthwhile. The older you get, the more they put you on a pedestal.

"They are the most incredible and the most memorable people. If I could write, I would write an article about them for the *Reader's Digest*. They have wisdom and respect. They call my mother, who is pushing eighty, 'Old Missy.' Each of our daughters is referred to as 'Little Missy.' When my mother comes over, no matter what they're doing, they'll stop and line up and help her out of the car.

"They care about people. They will put their lives on the line for you. That's a tacky phrase, strike that. But they do care and they want to make you comfortable. They want to earn whatever it is that you are paying them. It's really very touching."

Is there a feeling of guilt about having five servants for two people?

"We don't have five servants," Miss Rutherford replies. "We have two servants and three houseguests. The three children live here as our guests. We pay their entire keep. I mean we house them, we feed them. They have provided their own cars. They are educating themselves and we are as inordinately proud of them as we are of our own children. The only ones that work for us are their father and mother, but their mother has been unable to work for the past few years. Ah Yiang had an operation on her vertebra. She lives with us, of course, but she is unable to work.

"When we need the kids to wait on table they are paid exactly as we would pay any other help. They are exemplary. And I fully expect one of them to be president of General Motors.

"All I know is that we have the most enchanting family in the world living with us. The only one I see chronically is Tsai. Ah Yiang is back there doing her exercises. Hopefully, it will make her vertebra better. The kids are still holding down their full-time jobs."

The Doziers have two daughters. The oldest, Gloria, is twenty-eight.

"As a treat after she graduated from high school I took her on a seven-week trip around the world," says Miss Rutherford. "The incredible thing to me was the child I took with me was so different from the one I brought back. The kid I took with me was going to go to college to do us a favor, because we expected it. Then she made a deal with her father. The deal was that, if she completed college in three years, she could take another trip abroad. She did graduate in three years and this time she wanted to take in Russia. Then she changed her mind and went to Australia. After that trip, she asked her father, 'If I get my master's degree, will you let me go again?' And her father said, 'You bet I will.' She received her master's and Gloria took a trip to Europe with a friend. Bill picked up the tab; he treated them. It's been so rewarding for Gloria, Gloria's father, and me."

Gloria is married and lives in Denver. Her husband is a buyer for a department store associated with the huge May Company chain. "No children yet, but three dogs," says Miss Rutherford. "She's out of our smog and into everything in Denver worth being into. She takes tennis lessons, and she helped keep the Olympic Games out of there. *She belongs!*"

The younger daughter, Debbie, is twenty-five. Her ambition is to be an actress. "She is super-talented, super-bright. The world is going to hear from her, mark my words."

Both daughters are by previous marriages. Debbie's mother is Bill Dozier's ex-wife, actress Joan Fontaine. Gloria's father is Miss Rutherford's former husband, David May, who is heir to the department store complex that employs Gloria's husband.

Of her ex-mate, Miss Rutherford says, "David May is a very special man, a lovely man. He lives about eight blocks away, and he now has his third or fourth crop of kids, and well he should because he's a wonderful, marvelous and sensational father. And Bill is a marvelous father. David and Bill are very firm and staunch friends. In fact, we're all very close. We spend Christmas and New Year's Eves together."

8.
...and Have Not

No GALAS ARE sponsored for Beverly Hills' senior citizens. There's no need, according to some spokesmen for the town.

"We have something in Beverly Hills for everyone, from the tiny tot to the retired elder citizen," avers Bill Reeder of the *Independent*. "And that's the way it should be in 'The Garden Spot of the World.' "

"All our elderly people belong to country clubs and drive Cadillacs," says one member of the City Council.

Hardly.

Better than three-fourths of the aged, most impoverished, live south of Santa Monica Boulevard. For most of them, Beverly Hills is anything but the world's garden spot. In fact, only a small percentage of Beverly's senior citizens have ever been inside a country club or owned a Cadillac.

The following brief sketches of Beverly Hills' senior discards are similar to those found in any American city—yet they are especially incongruous and particularly poignant in a town that prides itself on its wealth, a town that raises upwards of $100,000,000 a year for outside charities.

She was eighty-one and lived in a down-at-the-heels hotel less than a hundred feet from City Hall. Her sole income was a $200-a-month check from her son. The City Council could peer through the window

119

of its chamber and watch the bent figure with toothpick legs out for her daily stroll. "She'd take a walk every day," the clerk at her hotel recalls. "It was a walk to nowhere." Almost every day in the course of her walk this harmless, shabbily dressed Presbyterian lady would be accosted by the same Beverly Hills policeman, who'd send her back to the barren prison of her room. "Dreadful treatment," adds the clerk. "Taking that walk was her only recreation. She told me the officer said she was 'cluttering up the streets.' " The woman died in 1975, victim of a stroke and neglect. No one gave much of a damn, not even her son, an airline executive. He sent the money to bury his mother, but didn't attend the funeral. He didn't wish to interrupt his Biarritz vacation. When he was home, the son also lived in Beverly Hills, ten minutes away from his mother, on North Foothill Drive, in a $375,000 house.

The future is bleak for two Beverly Hills senior citizens, both in their seventies, as they sit in their tiny Burton Way apartment, waiting for the imminent death of the husband. "My husband's going to die. He's just had his fourth heart attack. Where am I going to get the money to bury him?" A visitor hesitantly suggests the wife ask the county about a pauper's burial for the man, to whom she's been married for fifty-two years. After three phone calls, she locates the proper agency. When she hangs up, it's hard to read whether her expression is relief or pain. "The lady said it would be very dignified and practical. They have free cremations."

According to figures compiled by the U.S. Census Bureau, Beverly Hills has one of the most mature populations in the nation. Close to 50 per cent of its 33,416 citizens, exactly 14,948 are sixty-two and over. The senior citizen tally includes 1,997 who are seventy to seventy-four; 1,243 in the seventy-five to seventy-nine range; 629 between eighty and eighty-four; and 329 who are eighty-five and beyond.

Awareness of the poverty and problems of an estimated twenty million senior citizens has surfaced only recently in America. But in Beverly Hills, that awareness has yet to manifest itself.

"One of the revelations of the last census was that . . . certain neighborhoods of West Los Angeles (including Beverly Hills) generally pictured as wealthy have many nearly destitute people," wrote Los Angeles *Times* reporter Doug Smith. "These are people who have lived many years in houses or apartments on fixed incomes from pensions or Social Security payments and have lost pace in the race with inflation. Property taxes and rents in particular have gone beyond their ability to pay. . . . The surprising fact was that 20 per cent of these elderly were living on less than $2,300 a year, the figure used to determine eligibility for public low-rent housing."

Joseph Schechter, who has spent fourteen years as a volunteer at the West Side Jewish Community Center for senior citizens, which serves two hundred of Beverly Hills' aged, says, "These people must have a roof and they just can't find a place cheap enough. They pay up to $125 for rent and then, after medical expenses, they hardly have enough left for a proper diet."

The unstated but nevertheless official policy of the Beverly Hills City Council toward its aged amounts to an up-raised middle finger. To the Council, the solution would be for them to all go away. And that is what is happening. By steadfastly refusing to meet any of the real needs of the un-moneyed seniors, the Council *is* slowly driving them out.

What the Council calls "undesirable, unsightly, or unsafe structures" in the southeastern portion of the city are being condemned, and developers are being invited to replace them with high-rent luxury apartment buildings. If that policy continues, there won't be a poor elderly citizen in Beverly Hills in another decade—hardly a humanitarian solution to dealing with the impoverished aged.

But, because the elderly do vote, the Council has had to make a gesture of some sort, especially after a small band of Beverly's aged, who do not have a formal organization or lobby, began turning up at Council meetings, applying what verbal and moral pressure they could. The Council did not come forth with a plan for low-cost housing, the prime need of most Beverly seniors. Nor did it give thought to programs for manpower retraining, job placement, or asking the city's rich doctors to treat the city's seniors at no cost or at minimum fees. The humanitarians on the Council, after hemming and hawing for more than six years, finally turned the problem over to the City Planning Commission, which found a "solution"—a plan to spend $110,000 to build a twelve-hundred-square-foot senior citizens meeting place in a city park. Twelve hundred square feet is less than the size of many living rooms and back yards in Beverly Hills.

Small as the concession was, it was still clouded by the usual graceless, acrimonious Council debate.

The proposal for the senior citizens center, nothing more than a meeting room with a small kitchen and a john, came before the Council in March 1973. Richard Stone, then the mayor, supported it. Councilmen Charles Aronberg and Jake Stuchen were opposed.

Aronberg, ever the fanatical environmentalist, wasn't ready to concede an inch of green space to senior citizens.

Stone declared: "There are times when we must consider the needs of the citizen and sacrifice a few blades of grass for them."

"I cannot support any proposal that puts a building on open land," retorted Aronberg, "and I resent this being turned into a political issue of park versus seniors."

"You said it, I didn't," Stone countered.

"Well, you implied it, Mayor," Aronberg exploded. "You want this because you want to show the seniors you're for them."

Denying Aronberg's charge, Stone pounded his gavel angrily.

Aronberg maintained that he was in favor of a senior citizens facility. "The only problem," he said, "is land use. The present proposal would eliminate valuable park land, and such land is an irreplaceable community resource." Aronberg proposed that the facility be built at an unspecified location, that the $110,000 limitation be removed and no maximum placed on the cost of the building.

Roared Councilman Stuchen: "I object more to that than the original idea. If we say the sky's the limit, we'll go bankrupt."

The Council adjourned amid confusion and bitterness.

"Part of Hitler's program was *Lebensraum*, more land," said an eighty-one-year-old Jewish man with a white beard and darting blue eyes, after witnessing the debate. "That's the way he justified Nazi aggression. It is rather interesting that I see the same battle going on in my own little city. They are fighting over land, these Jewish councilmen of ours. Instead of giving the land to the people, they tell us about *Lebensraum* for flowers and grass. How sad and disgusting and disappointing. At least Hitler said he wanted land for people."

The following month, a compromise was worked out among the councilmen. They unanimously approved the center on Aronberg's condition that 5,000 feet of previously undeveloped park land be seeded with grass.

Peter Schroeder, the only man in Beverly Hills who works with the elderly on a day-to-day basis, has bittersweet memories of the hassle over the senior center. Pleased at the small step in the right direction, he feels it's too little, too late, that much more is needed to supply the present and future needs of the aged in Beverly Hills.

"Whoever thought there was a need for a senior citizens center in this town?" he asks. "A center where the elderly could go daily to participate in programs designed specifically for them. Millions of people still believe everybody in Beverly Hills is a millionaire. When you say 'Beverly Hills' in Kansas City, their reaction is wow! Beverly Hills to them is the epitome of the good life. But if you were to tell them in Kansas City that there were impoverished elderly living in Beverly Hills, they wouldn't believe you. They'd think you were putting them on. They wouldn't believe that there are a tremendous number of people here living on welfare, food stamps, or only a Social Security check. I know senior citizens in this town who can't afford bus fare, literally can't afford to ride the bus, people who worry about where their next meal is coming from.

"The center was overdue. I don't think I've heard of another important community in the country that doesn't have such a center. Beverly Hills has come into the game in the ninth inning."

His voice filled with conviction, sounding neither maudlin nor florid, he says of the center: "Think of that building. Think what it's going to manufacture. It won't be a factory making bullets, a building sending pollutants into the air from its chimney. Its chimney will send up rays of happiness, love and enjoyment, interpersonal relationships between the lonely, the poor and the forgotten. That's the product that will emanate from that building."

Schroeder's voice is refreshing. If there is a bit of the preacher in him, he comes by the inheritance naturally and honestly. His grandfather was a Lutheran minister and his father was also a staunch Lutheran, who died when Schroeder was seven. After his marriage to a Catholic girl, Schroeder converted.

He is thirty-nine years old, and good works have consumed much of his life since his birth in Syracuse, New York. His background includes stints as an administrator for the Boy Scouts, the Little League, the YMCA, Community Chest, and boys' counselor for the Kiwanis Club. He came to Beverly Hills in November 1971, competing successfully against a number of other applicants for his job. Ideally and sensibly, Schroeder should have headed up an independent agency for senior citizens. Instead he's buried in the bureaucracy of the recreation department, though the scope of his work far exceeds the narrow confines of that city agency. Schroeder's formal title is Senior Citizen Liaison. He *is* that and more.

Valentino-handsome, the man doesn't seem to fit his mission. He's narrow-waisted, five feet ten, the father of two teen-agers. In a red-striped tie, blue shirt, and carefully pressed dark suit, he is, even at the end of his customary twelve-hour day, immaculate.

"A lot of people have asked me how I came to work with the elderly. They say, 'You're a nice-looking guy and the women must be after you, and you must be quite a swinger.' But that's not me. As a matter of fact, I'm very, very shy with women and that's one reason I've been married seventeen years and will be married only one time in my life."

He considers his involvement with senior citizens in Beverly Hills part of a pioneer endeavor. Basically, he says, it's a brand-new movement in the city.

More than anybody else in town, Schroeder understands the ice-floe psychology of City Hall and the attitudes of Beverly's richer residents. He reckons that he's reached only a handful of Beverly's needy elderly, those who are troubled both financially and emotionally and are particularly vulnerable.

At his office in Roxbury Park on South La Cienega, Schroeder works at a battered desk, a hand-me-down from the police department. He doesn't even have a typewriter to call his own. He has been using an old Royal typewriter loaned by a Beverly Hills television writer.

"I've had it repaired," he says, showing a bill for $25.15. "The writer hasn't asked for its return, but I think it's a question of ethics. It was loaned to us on a temporary basis, for a month. We've had it more than a year. So I think it's time to send it back. I put a request in the budget last year for a secondhand manual, but didn't get it."

Schroeder has no secretary and no staff except ten part-time, unpaid senior citizen volunteers he has trained himself. While running a shoestring operation, he has managed to initiate a number of helpful programs, notably the Senior Citizens Information and Referral Center, which is manned by volunteers and located on the mezzanine floor of City Hall. The Council would not provide an office for the service. Its only bounty, besides the installation of one telephone line, and the presentation of an old picnic table as a desk, was the approval of an expense voucher of $89.99 for two screens Schroeder purchased at a hardware store, to allow seniors who wish to discuss their economic and psychological problems in person a speck of privacy.

A shortage of money and manpower has allowed the service to operate only two hours a day, three days a week. The rest of the time, the calls come directly into Schroeder's office.

His phone rings incessantly with seniors requesting information on convalescent homes and hospitals, legal matters, leisure activities, educational opportunities, housing, and employment. Says Schroeder: "We've had a tremendous number of calls concerning Project Find." Project Find is the federal Food Stamp Program.

"Referral and information," Schroeder points out, "are very important services to the elderly. Helping the aged is more than providing games like bridge and lawn bowling.

"For scores of our seniors, my phone is their only lifeline to the outside. Some are so lonely they fabricate problems. A lady who told me she was sixty-eight kept me on the line for more than an hour complaining that her garbage hadn't been collected. I referred her to the sanitation department. But then she moved on to other subjects, everything you can imagine. A nice lady. A nice lonely lady. Such calls are a cry in the night. They are calls of human concern." Schroeder hopes eventually for a seven-day, round-the-clock hot line for any senior citizen who's lonely or depressed or just wants to talk.

When he first came to town, the Beverly Hills Adult Club was faltering with a small membership. He talked the club up to seniors, got some newspaper publicity for it, and increased its size to more than six hundred members.

"With the larger membership, we had to find another place to meet. We were evicted from the library. The fire department said the auditorium there could only legally hold one hundred and twenty-eight. We surveyed this community from top to bottom, looking for another place to meet, everywhere from the American Legion Hall to All Saints' Episcopal Church to Mount Calvary Lutheran and the synagogues. We finally made a deal with Beth Jacob. We had to negotiate. For a donation of thirty dollars a week, they allowed us to meet there, which is where the club will stay, hopefully, until the center is completed here in Roxbury Park."

Schroeder has also set up a reduced-fare bus program for oldsters. He originated Operation Grandparents for shut-ins. Volunteers help the helpless by doing their shopping, checking books out of the library for them, writing their letters, telephoning them daily for chatter and reassurance, taking them for walks if they are ambulatory, and providing companionship.

Operation Gap is another Schroeder brain child. Under that program, senior volunteers work as tutorial aids at Beverly Hills High School on a one-to-one basis with students lagging in their studies and with those for whom English is a second language, primarily the children of live-in Mexican servants.

For Schroeder, Beverly Hills is a four-rung society: the ultra-affluent, the affluent, the middle class, and the poverty stricken.

"Never mind Kansas City, most people in Los Angeles and in Beverly Hills itself aren't aware how many poor people there are in this town. It has come as a shock to the Council to realize that there are a great number of elderly citizens who have little money, who do not even have sustenance, who are on welfare.

"And yet the Council for the most part treats senior citizens as adversaries. *What is this enemy doing in our midst?* The councilmen are prisoners of their own myths and publicity. By the same token, some of the aged poor also believe the mythology. You wonder why they even want to live in Beverly Hills. In another community, it would be much less expensive for them to manage on their fixed incomes. But whether you live east, south, north, or west in Beverly Hills, that seems to be the pinnacle of the American Dream. In many, many cases our seniors have sacrificed greatly, and too much, for the Beverly Hills address. They've fantasized themselves into believing they are part of the American Dream as represented by Beverly Hills."

He says he hasn't found any expression of outward resentment from the poor in south Beverly Hills against the rich in the north. "It is something they don't seem willing to express. But you can read their eyes. There is some resentment that life was not as good to them as to those in the north. I've never heard it expressed openly, although you can sort of feel the vibes of resentment."

Schroeder has never had a single call from anyone above the tracks. Yet he wonders: "There must be lonely people up there. Why shouldn't a wealthy woman in the north—one, say, who is seventy years old—avail herself of our services? Why don't we have a single volunteer from the north? The south relates to the south very well, and the north relates to the north very well. But the south and north do not relate at all to each other. Still my phone is going to ring someday and there's going to be a call from somebody in the north who needs help. Someday perhaps there will be a lot of calls and volunteers from the north."

Why should Beverly Hills, or any other American community, care about the elderly in the first place?

"When you bring a child into the world, you have an obligation, a lifelong commitment," Schroeder answers. "Parents have that obligation from the day of birth to the end of life. In a society that calls itself civilized," he continues, "the obligation is one of humanitarianism.

That's why you, me, the City Council, everybody has to care."

At the hundreds of charity balls and fund-raising events held in Beverly Hills each year, money is garnered for almost every conceivable cause. An Yves Saint Laurent fashion show featuring diamond-studded movie-star models Anne Baxter and Susan Strasberg accumulated $400,000 for the United Jewish Welfare Fund. At one annual Beastly Ball, Jimmy Stewart paid $4,600 to become the "adoptive father" of an orangutan. The ball was sponsored by the Greater Los Angeles Zoo Association. Financier Mark Taper outbid Henry Fonda, snagging a zebra for $2,300. Other well-heeled Beverly residents paid $2,000 for a cape buffalo, $1,400 for a red kangaroo, $1,300 for a Galápagos tortoise, and $750 for a baboon.

Does Schroeder find it ironic, if not heartless, that money can be so easily raised for animals but not the senior poor of Beverly?

"Of course, but obviously these people are unaware of conditions in the south. Or they are aware and don't care. Then there are some people who don't like to hear certain things. That's the mythology of Beverly Hills at work again. Possibly there's a communications gap. Maybe the problem simply is that they aren't informed. Maybe if the people in the north were informed of conditions here on poverty row, they might have a slight seizure, they might faint. Perhaps they need that kind of awakening."

Schroeder says there's a job to be done in Beverly Hills for the elderly that simply isn't being done.

"We're not going to be able to do the job until the entire community and the entire municipal government realize that our elderly are in trouble. Until the myth is destroyed that in Beverly Hills all senior citizens own yachts, go on fishing trips to the Bahamas, and travel to Europe and Israel twice a year. Until it is realized that the aged do not all belong to country clubs. Until it is realized that there are people here who are screaming quietly for help. The picture of the elderly in Beverly Hills as rich, comfortable, and happy is an outright lie. It is rather aggravating to watch the trustees of the people refuse to accept and deal realistically with the problems of senior citizens."

Outside Schroeder's office are several tennis courts—and his remarks are punctuated with the exclamation points of racket pinging against ball. "This city cares more for tennis courts than people. They have 'over-prioritized' tennis. I know there's a demand for tennis courts, but how many can you put up?"

The city, he says, gives the affluent what they want, but those who aren't affluent do not get what they want, much less what they need. "Senior citizens get only what the city wants to give them when they want to give it to them."

Despite the record of neglect, Schroeder remains sanguine about the future.

"What I'm trying to do is stir the Council and the north out of their own mythology. I can only deduce that it wasn't done in the past because they didn't want to face up to the reality that there are people starving in Beverly Hills. But there's no reason why, from this point on, with the data and knowledge that we now have, that we can't move forward and deal with the elderly population in this community on a respectful, helpful, and dignified basis."

A new hunger has been gnawing inside Peter Schroeder. A great many senior citizens have asked him to run for a seat on the City Council. His is the voice they want to speak for them. The seniors feel they are unrepresented on the Council. Given the large bloc of elderly poor and near-poor, Schroeder would probably be a shoo-in winner. However, he lives in a spacious apartment in Hollywood, and the Beverly Hills municipal code requires that a councilman reside in the city.

Even if Schroeder could find comparable accommodations at a comparable rent in Beverly, he would have to resign his job in order to serve on the Council. Under a "conflict of interest" stricture in the code, no one who is employed by the city can be a councilman. Unless he found other employment, Schroeder's income would be confined to a councilman's $200 monthly. As it is, he finds it difficult making ends meet. He is paid less than the $10,285 median income in America. He is paid less than it normally costs merely to make the race for a Council seat. His salary is $9,100 a year, and he's probably the most underpaid man in Beverly Hills.

9.
Alma Mater

OF THE LONG list of imbecilities that exemplify the thinking of Beverly Hills Establishmentarians, their approach to education takes first place.

The myth of the city's superior schools has persisted from the outset. As far back as the 1930s, Pierce Benedict, in his *History of Beverly Hills*, unabashedly claimed, citing no evidence, "Without exception the schools in Beverly Hills, the four public grammar schools, the two denominational schools, and the high school, are unexcelled in the state."

Beverly still has the same number of schools and is still racking up fulsome praise for the quality of its education. *Newsweek* called the city's school system "probably the best in the West . . . in a class by itself." Charles S. Benson, Professor of Education at the Berkeley branch of the University of California and a consultant on educational finance to the Senate of the California legislature, calls the Beverly Hills school district "one of the jewels of our educational system."

Such praise is not predicated on the scholarship of Beverly's students, but on the amount that is spent for each pupil's education.

Since 1968, because of pressure by educators and parents, there has been a nationwide, confusing swirl of judicial and legislative action to "equalize" education through the illusory panacea of money. In California, Beverly Hills became target number one of the equalizers.

The fire storm began with a lawsuit initiated by a group of parents in the name of twelve-year-old John Serano, Jr., of blue-collar Baldwin Park in Los Angeles County. Young Serano was presumed to be educationally handicapped because his district was spending under six hundred dollars a year for his schooling while Beverly Hills was ladling out more than twelve hundred dollars for each of its students.

In effect, two questions were being asked: Shouldn't society afford the same opportunity to a poor man's son like John Serano, Jr., as it does to Desi Arnaz, Jr., scion of Beverly Hills millionaires? Why not spend the same amount on the education of Serano and Arnaz?

The Serano champions were challenging the traditional, bedrock basis of school financing—the property tax. Beverly Hills, with a high assessed property valuation, could allot considerably more money per student than could such poorer districts as Baldwin Park. This, it was charged, constituted a violation of equal protection under the Constitution's Fourteenth Amendment.

As a "friend of the court," Beverly Hills fought the case for three years in a series of legal battles, arguing that, rather than forcing Beverly to spend less per pupil, there should be an injection of more federal and state money into those school districts considered less fortunate. The schools should "level up, not down."

The issue reached the California Supreme Court in August 1971, and its decision triggered a battle royal around the country—a battle that instigated some changes in school financing and wild disorder in the American educational system.

The California court voted 6 to 1 that differences in property taxes did indeed lead to vastly unequal educational opportunities between rich and poor in the state's 1,076 school districts. The property-tax underpinning for school financing was, no doubt about it, unconstitutional.

"We cannot agree," said the court, "that Baldwin Park residents care less about education than those in Beverly Hills solely because Baldwin Park spends less than six hundred dollars per child while Beverly Hills spends over twelve hundred dollars. To allot more educational dollars to the children of one district than those of another merely because of the fortuitous presence of [higher valued] property is to make the quality of a child's education dependent upon the location of private, commercial, and industrial establishments. Surely, this is to rely on the most irrelevant of factors as the basis for educational financing."

In ruling the property-tax base for school funding unconstitutional, the California Supreme Court suggested no alternative. The search for an alternative became the problem of the state legislature, which in December 1972 finally came up with a two-pronged bill that it felt complied with the spirit of the Serano decision. The measure did not abolish the property levy as the principal source for funding the schools, but it did put an unspecified ceiling on how much local communities could tax property owners in the name of education. The bill also provided 2.1 billion dollars in fresh money for poorer school districts over a three-year period.

Neither section of the bill accomplished its stated purpose—to equalize educational spending and improve the opportunities of all the John Serano, Jr.'s, in California.

The new money had the temporary effect in Baldwin Park of nearly doubling the amount that the city had at its disposal for student education. In practice, most of the additional money was eaten up by inflation and by increased salaries for administrators and teachers.

Educational expert Paul Holmes, a consultant to the legislature's Assembly Education Committee, was soon estimating that as little as ten to fifteen dollars was being assigned to the improvement of the curriculum in Baldwin Park schools. He was skeptical that equalization was possible. "It's like walking halfway across a room and then halfway again and so on," Holmes noted. "You never get there."

But the egalitarians thought they had another way to get there. They asserted that equalization was possible by taxing all California property uniformly, the proceeds to be distributed even-handedly to each school district. Such a system would provide every California pupil, including those in Beverly Hills, with an $800-per-year education. Beverly was in shock. To the city's Establishment that obviously meant leveling down, not up. The equalization concept was written into a bill introduced in the legislature. It was narrowly defeated—but it may still re-emerge as the wave of the future. Hawaii already has such a system in operation.

To further complicate matters, the United States Supreme Court, in March 1973, ruled in *San Antonio Independent School District* v. *Demetrio P. Rodriquez* that funding education through unequal property-tax rates *was* constitutional. The $594 spent per pupil in one Anglo school in San Antonio, Texas, even when compared with the $356 allotted to a school in the same district attended primarily by Mexican-Americans, did *not* discriminate against the poor.

The vote was 5 to 4, and the majority opinion, written by Justice Lewis F. Powell, Jr., asserted that education is "not among the rights afforded explicit protection under the Federal Constitution"—nor, he said, did it afford implicit protection. Powell also said that there had never been a consensus that "the poor, the racial minorities or the children in overburdened core-city school districts would be bene-fited" by switching from local property-tax financing to another sys-tem. The issue, in any case, was legislative, not judicial. The justice added that he was not putting the Court's imprimatur on the present system.

Actually, he was doing exactly that. The status quo had been main-tained. Each state was now free to devise its own formula for financing education. Theoretically, there could be fifty different formulas con-cocted from Maine to Hawaii. Most importantly, the thrust of the ruling was that individual local districts could still determine how much they chose to spend on their schools. The richer districts would continue to spend more; the poorer districts would spend as much as their tax base—buttressed by federal and state aid—allowed.

The Supreme Court's decision and the defeat of the uniform prop-erty tax in the California legislature eased the shock in Beverly. The city would not have to deal with a national or state equalization policy, only with the California statute that provided an unstated property-tax roof and the possible future passage of a parallel property levy.

Since the Serano ruling, when Beverly was spending a little more than $1,200 per pupil, it has found the tax room to increase the indi-vidual student stipend to its current level—$2,000 per pupil, more than twice the average $950 that is spent on pupils in the rest of California. The eight-hundred-dollar increase was managed through an addi-tional levy of three dollars per every hundred dollars of assessed valuation, which Beverlyites, for the most part, approved without complaint.

For a total student enrollment of 5,620, and for upkeep and im-provement of the physical facilities of its schools, Beverly Hills is now spending for education almost two-thirds the amount it spends for all other city-provided services. A total of 13.6 million dollars goes for education compared with the 21.6 million dollars budgeted for every-thing else. In addition, the school system accepts grants from private benefactors. And in concert with the City Council, the independent School Board of Supervisors has made plans to create a foundation to supply more funds when and if needed.

As is the custom of colleges and universities, Beverly will also urge well-fixed individuals to endow a mathematics chair, an economics chair, etc. Such unprecedented money-raising high jinks below the college level are legal unless the state legislature specifically outlaws them, which it is unlikely to do unless there are protests from outside Beverly.

The Beverly Hills school system has such an embarrassment of riches that it is seeking to rid itself of two oil-producing wells on the campus of Beverly High. The wells generate between $1,800 and $2,500 per month in royalties, but the school would prefer to reclaim the acre-and-a-half drill site and utilize it for a playground with additional tennis courts. Despite the fuel famine, administrators have repeatedly petitioned the Beverly Hills Oil Company to pack up its equipment and leave. But the company has a long-term lease and refuses to cancel its contract. Beverly High, therefore, must suffer the burden of the wells until the turn of the century. Complains Mari-Ann Strandwall, a physical education teacher, "It's disgusting. The oil wells stink to the point where you can't breathe any more."

Well-intentioned but misguided equalizers who envy the Beverly Hills school system haven't thrown in the sponge. They believe their cause has been just put aside temporarily. But, before continuing their efforts to obtain the same amount of money for every student, the equalizers would do well to consider the little-realized fact that the Beverly Hills educational system has been a miserable failure. In the last analysis, the amount of money spent per student is irrelevant, and a better case may well be made for spending less rather than more.

Beverly Hills has had more than fifty years to prove that a school district with an open checkbook is capable of educating students into greater achievement and a higher earning capacity. But the supposition that money makes a successful student is another golden-ghetto fairy tale.

It is even money that John Serano, Jr., goaded and stimulated by want, will make a more distinguished contribution to society than Desi Arnaz, Jr., whose only distinctions are a recognizable name and un-earned money. It is also even money that Demetrio P. Rodriquez will make a greater impact during his lifetime than Doris Day's son, Terry Melcher, whose distinctions are similar to those of Arnaz, except that he was a friend of that fine specimen of American manhood, Charles Manson.

The futures of Serano and Rodriquez are already more optimistic than those of Arnaz and Melcher. It is doubtful that the latter pair have much to look forward to. Both have already tried and failed at show-business careers. Privilege has handicapped them. Because they are hungrier, leaner, tougher, the future belongs to the Seranos and the Rodriquezes of America.

The most methodical, surefire way Beverly Hills can further cripple its young men and women is for the city to spend even more on their schooling. Conversely, one of the most effective ways to enhance the lives of Beverly's youngsters would be to spend no more on them than the national average, $700 to $800 a pupil. The millions being wasted on education in Beverly could be diverted to the city's senior citizens, to upgrading the southern portion of town, to giving merchants and homeowners a tax cut, and to raising the pay of municipal workers.

Most sociologists, educators, and politicians ceaselessly point out that poverty leads many young people into lives of crime and non-achievement. Seldom mentioned is the fact that poverty has been the prod that has given the nation most of its stellar achievers, including most of the parents who've made it to northside Beverly Hills.

The youngsters of Beverly are caught in a trap. They are helpless victims of a too richly endowed school system that spoils them and scuttles their ambition.

Texas computer-czar Ross Perot is one of the few contemporary rich men who understands that money does more to manacle than liberate children. "I'm giving my kids," he says, "the opportunity of working their way through school and earning their own fortunes."

Harvard sociologist Christopher Jencks (in a study based on his own research) and Johns Hopkins sociologist James Coleman (who surveyed 4,000 public schools and 645,000 students) both rip apart the cherished American belief that the money spent per pupil makes a difference in subsequent income or happiness. Both Jencks and Coleman reached the same conclusion—that the quality of a school has little or nothing to do with how well its students learn or how well they apply what they've learned.

"The character of a school's output," Jencks says, "depends largely on a single input, namely the characteristics of the entering children. Everything else—the school budget, its policies, the characteristics of the teachers—is either secondary or completely irrelevant." School, he adds, cannot control the factors that lead to achievement, cannot determine who will be rich or poor, successful or a failure, happy or unhappy.

Jencks's conclusions aroused a good deal of comment and controversy. In answering those who criticized Jencks, Daniel Patrick Moynihan, the Harvard urbanologist, former U.S. Ambassador to India, and recent U.S. Ambassador to the United Nations, said, "All new information is thought to be threatening at first."

Columnist James J. Kilpatrick, who also agreed with Jencks, said: "Other factors, most of them beyond the reach of the state, have much more to do with failure or success. We have no idea what these factors are. Home environment is an obvious consideration, but there are others—luck, ambition, natural talent, a child's knack for doing some economically marketable thing better than another child. One boy hits a ball harder than his brother. Who knows why? God knows why."

Declared Edward Zigler of Yale, the former director of the U.S. Office of Child Development: "We've been sold a bill of goods. School people keep saying we should do more, whereas the real wave of the future is for schools to do less and let other social institutions play a larger role."

Even the amiable Kenneth L. Peters, Beverly Hills' Superintendent of Schools, asserts candidly, "There are a lot of factors that are not measurable in education. If somebody would come up with the formula that 'X' number of dollars results in students achieving at maximum levels, I would buy it because the public constantly says to me, 'Show me that spending $2,000 is more than twice as good as spending $950 per child.' And I can't show that."

For some parents in the golden ghetto, it matters little if their children are doing poor or rotten work. At Beverly High, 40 per cent of the expensively educated scholars have C, D, and F grade averages. Parents of such underachieving students are nevertheless heartened because their youngsters are attending an "unsurpassed" high school. A grade of C or D at Beverly High is equal to an A or B at any other school, or so the parents are told.

The noblest boast of Beverly's educators is that nine out of ten of their graduates go on to college. There's the fairy-tale syndrome bobbing up again. The implication is that a college degree means living happily ever after. Even if the suspicious statistic is accepted at face value, higher education is no guarantee of whether the youngster is going to be a success or a failure.

Harvard's Office of Graduate and Career Plans, basing its information on an annual questionnaire study, reports that each year 30 per cent of its graduates cannot find employment and that another 33 per cent are undecided about what kinds of jobs they should look for—and this after obtaining degrees from what is still regarded as the finest university in America.

If it was once true that a college diploma was a passport to prestigious employment and higher income, it is no longer so. Upper Beverly Hills has a herd of alumni from Harvard, Yale, and Vassar, living in $150,000 to $400,000 homes, who earn $90 to $150 a week. Many haven't had a job since graduation. The bulk of Beverly High graduates, however, wind up at UCLA, an academically undistinguished mill with an enrollment of 25,500.*

"Unexcelled" Beverly High has a single distinction. It has its reputation as the most glamorous school in America because of the number of kids with famous names who've marked time there. The school publicly plays down this image, but privately administrators and teachers are impressed by the students who carry the well-known handles. Interestingly, not one of the youngsters has surpassed the fame, professional accomplishment, or earning power of their celebrated fathers and mothers, who attended far more modestly endowed schools.

Among those who have attended or are attending Beverly High are the children of Morey Amsterdam, Gene Barry, Polly Bergen, Joey Bishop, Victor Buono, Sid Caesar, the late Lee J. Cobb, Jackie Cooper, Bob Cummings, Tony Curtis, Ella Fitzgerald, Buddy Hackett, Florence Henderson, Louis Jourdan, Danny Kaye, Don Knotts, Jack Lemmon, Art Linkletter, director Delbert Mann, the late quizmaster Hal March, Dean Martin, Darren McGavin, Corbett Monica, Greg Morris, Jan Murray, Jack Palance, Carl Reiner, Debbie Reynolds, Gloria Swanson, Danny Thomas, and Mel Torme. Diana Ross's brother and the son of jockey Bill Shoemaker are presently enrolled. Phil Ritz, of the Ritz Brothers clan, is a graduate and is pursuing an offbeat career: he is the only alumnus of Beverly High to become a matador.

While it's true that talent, unlike money, cannot be inherited, the odds would favor a better showing among the celebrity kids, most of whom have dreamed of show-business stardom.

Beverly High offers them plush opportunity. It possesses all the equipment necessary for a student to produce a film from beginning to end. It has a 1,700-seat theater, another that accommodates 200 persons, and a 99-seat "community playhouse." The backstage facilities rival anything on Broadway and, in the person of John Ingle, the

---

*Among its alumni are convicted Watergate principals John Ehrlichman and H. R. Haldeman. The latter grew up in Beverly Hills and attended private schools prior to entering the university. He no longer lives in Beverly.

school has an excellent drama coach. Beverly High also has its own closed-circuit television station, with a network-quality studio, and a radio station more powerful than several local FM and AM outlets. With all of that, one would expect it to have graduated at least one Spencer Tracy, one Mary Martin, one Jack Benny. Such is not the case. It has produced no superstars.

Two Beverly High grads have made it big, but no thanks to the school. Composer-conductor André Previn received a D in music, indicating the school did not cultivate, recognize, or encourage his abilities. Maria Tallchief's mastery of ballet was a result of her child-hood on an Oklahoma Osage Indian reservation, where she absorbed and took part in chanting, rhythmic tribal dances. Her talent was honed, not at Beverly High, but in her training after graduation with the Ballet Russe de Monte Carlo.

Where are Beverly High's Katharine Hepburns, Laurence Oliviers, and Marlon Brandos?

In non-entertainment fields, Beverly grads haven't set the world ablaze either. Since its inception, the system has churned out only one Rhodes scholar, who has done nothing since to distinguish himself, and nobody at Beverly High even remembers his name.

From a list of "notable graduates" supplied by Beverly High, the following are the school's top seven: Adrienne Hall, holder of the advertising industry's Woman of the Year award; William Lusk, de-scribed as a "major builder in Orange County"; Admiral William P. Mack, onetime Superintendent of the U.S. Naval Academy; Sherman Melinkoff, dean of the UCLA School of Medicine; Victor Palmeric, board president of the bankrupt Penn Central railroad.

The sixth and seventh positions are held by Max Rafferty and Ed Reineke. Rafferty is the former Superintendent of Education for the state of California whose ultra-conservative views turned off the elec-torate in 1971. After his defeat by Wilson Riles, a black liberal, Rafferty disappeared into the Alabama school system, where he apparently finds George Wallace an admirable superior. "We try to keep the fact that Max Rafferty went here quiet," says one Beverly High adminis-trator.

Reineke served invisibly under Ronald Reagan as California's lieutenant governor. Soon after Reineke entered the 1974 Republican primary to succeed Reagan, a federal grand jury indicted him on three counts of perjury in a Watergate-related episode. He was convicted on one count of perjury and given an eighteen-month suspended sentence. Following his conviction, he resigned from office and dropped out of the race for governor, his public career ruined. Subsequently, his conviction was overturned by a federal appeals court, and he is now a real-estate broker.

The eighth most notable graduate is difficult to determine. The contenders are California State Assemblyman Robert Badham, whose constituency is the yacht-and-catamaran district of Newport Beach, filled with movie-star refugees from Beverly Hills; Alan Sieroty, the assemblyman who represents Beverly Hills in the state legislature; football players Steve Horowitz, Don Long, and Jim Powers; and baseball's Jim Palmer.

It is anything but a distinguished list for rich, highly praised Beverly High, one of the "jewels of our educational system." Not only isn't there a household name among its pre-eminent graduates, but if that is the top of the heap, what has been achieved by all the other grads of Beverly High? The nation is obviously filled with thousands of also-rans with expensive Beverly Hills educations.

By contrast a single unheralded school, Boys High of Brooklyn, New York, has generated a far more eminent and illustrious graduate list than Beverly High. And it has done so with an expenditure of less than one-third of what is spent per student in Beverly Hills.

"Boys High has always been part of a real ghetto, a gutter ghetto," says Irwin Zucker, founder and director of the school's West Coast Alumni Association located in Beverly Hills. Boys High is located in the urban jungle of Bedford-Stuyvesant, where today many residents walk the streets in the company of police dogs. Since World War II, the neighborhood's racial mix has changed from predominantly white to virtually all black. In fact the student body at Boys High is now 97 per cent black. But it is safe to wager—crime, drugs, poverty, and police dogs notwithstanding—that future graduates of Boys High will surpass those of Beverly High.

Beverly High might do well to begin a student exchange program with Boys High. Exposure to hard-core reality would go far in modifying the attitudes of too many Beverly High students who are archetypically overindulged and unmotivated.

"At its so-called peak," recalls Zucker, "the area could most charitably be described as a slum. Most of the parents of my friends were first-generation immigrants from Poland, Russia, Germany, and Italy. English was rarely spoken in any of our homes. My parents were from Poland, and we spoke Yiddish. Nobody came to Boys High in a chauffeured car, or any car. I'd get a nickel for a trolley ride but I'd save it and walk the six miles to school. I used to hide that precious nickel in the sole of my shoe. Word got around about that and frequently some guy would threaten to beat the hell out of me unless I gave him the nickel."

Since the list is so strong, it would be presumptuous to name the top Boys High graduates. Beverly Hills took two months to scrape together its "notables." "We really had to rack our brain," said John Rosemond, director of student activities. In rattling off the prominent grads of Boys High, Irwin Zucker's only problem was that he might omit some noteworthy achievers.

A writer's who's who of Boys High alumni includes: Norman Mailer; Isaac Asimov; Manfred Lee and Frederick Dannay, the creators of Ellery Queen; Norman Podhoretz, the editor of *Commentary* magazine; Jack Newfield, whose last two widely read books were *Robert Kennedy: A Memoir* and *The Populist Manifesto*; and Clifton Fadiman, book editor and critic of *The New Yorker* magazine from 1929 to 1935, former master of ceremonies of radio's literate *Information Please*, author of ten books and more than one hundred essays, member of the selection committee of the Book-of-the-Month Club, and a member of the editorial board of the *Encyclopaedia Britannica*.

Graduates of the Brooklyn school who went into show business are: Frank Yablans, the former president of Paramount Pictures; the late Edward Everett Horton; singer Alfred Drake; critically acclaimed Shakespearean actor Arnold Moss; comedian Alan King; David Dortort, producer of the *Bonanza* television series; Norman Lloyd, producer of *Alfred Hitchcock Presents*; Irving Mansfield, producer of *Talent Scouts* and other shows, and the widower of novelist Jacqueline Susann; Lawrence Spivack, moderator of *Meet the Press*; Oscar Katz, former head of daytime programing for CBS; the late news-commentator Gabriel Heatter; and I. A. L. Diamond, who collaborated with director Billy Wilder on the scripts of *Some Like It Hot, The Apartment*, and *Cactus Flower*.

Boys High graduates who entered the world of medicine: Dr. Albert Wiener, co-discoverer of the Rh factor in human blood and the 1966 recipient of the Joseph P. Kennedy, Jr., International Award for Research Prevention of Mental Retardation; Dr. Robert Samuel Stone, pathologist, cancer researcher, professor of management at Massachusetts Institute of Technology, dean of the medical school at the University of New Mexico, and the former director of the National

Institutes of Health, which *The New York Times* called the "top administrative position in American medical research"; and Dr. Leo Rangell, president of the International Psychoanalytical Association, 1969–71.

Other distinguished Boys High achievers: Sidney Hook, named chairman of the philosophy department at New York University at the age of thirty-two and the author of nine books on philosophy; Dr. Alfred Gottschalk, president of Hebrew Union College of Cincinnati and Los Angeles; famed attorney Louis Nizer; Emanuel Celler, dean of the House of Representatives, who served continuously in Congress from 1922–1972; composer Aaron Copland; William Levitt, founder and builder of Levittown; Rabbi Meyer Heller, of Beverly Hills' Temple Emanuel synagogue; baseball's Tommy Davis; basketball stars Connie Hawkins and Lenny Wilkens; and football's Dave Smith and Allie Sherman.

The record of the golden ghetto versus the gutter ghetto speaks for itself. (Walter J. Muller, Boys High football coach for thirty-five years, was fond of saying, "The reputation of a school is cast by the shadow of its alumni.")

The prime reason given by most parents who move to Beverly—a move relatively few can afford and which therefore entails considerable sacrifice—is the reputation of the school system. The supremacy of education in Beverly is part of the pitch of real-estate brokers when they deal with clients who have school-age children. More often than not, it is *the* deciding factor in closing a sale. The fallacy of top-level schools is perpetuated at every opportunity. A "Parents Guide," published jointly by the school district and the PTA, tells fathers and mothers they are not sacrificing in vain—"The Beverly Hills Board of Education wants the best school system that can be built—a system of education that is second to no other in the country."

The system, nevertheless, is average. However, there are some compensations for students.

In 1974, a group of Beverly High scholars were given a chaperoned five-week summer tour of Europe. The cost was $3,200 for each pupil, exclusive of spending-money for incidentals. In Paris, the night-life scene as well as the standard visit to the Louvre was on the itinerary. "It was a great trip," said one of the scholars after he returned. "The best thing about it," the fifteen-year-old boy confided, "was that I visited my first whorehouse and I got laid for the first time."

In the judgment of the school board, the fledglings who attend two of the city's elementary schools are "recreationally underprivileged."

A choking chunk of cash is being spent to right that presumed wrong. At Beverly Vista, $300,000 is earmarked for the purchase of a pair of apartment houses adjoining the school. The site will be used as a playground, although the present playground is spacious and adequate. For the seven hundred children attending Horace Mann, $235,000 has been budgeted to buy a knot of homes abutting the school. That site will also be used as an unneeded recreation area.

At Beverly Vista, kosher food has been made available in the cafeteria, the result of fervent lobbying by the Hillel Talmud Torah, a private Hebrew school. (Meantime, approximately two hundred elementary-school pupils in Beverly receive free or reduced-price lunches. The funding does not come from the city, but is provided by a special California Department of Education program for needy children. Striplings of parents whose gross income is $204 a month or less are eligible. Mrs. Sylvia Besser, co-ordinator of the program in Beverly, says that to protect these young people from discrimination and humiliation their identities are kept secret. They pass through the same lunch lines with their classmates, who have no way of knowing they are on the program.)

Beverly's pupils are guarded as if Armageddon was scheduled for next Tuesday. John H. Marrow, head of the district's disaster preparedness program, attended a five-day training seminar at Camp Roberts, a northern California military base, to learn how Beverly's students could best be protected from bomb threats, falling aircraft, severe windstorms, explosions, chemical accidents, fires, earthquakes, floods, and war. Also tidal waves. There has never been a tidal wave in Beverly Hills and one is not expected. But if a tidal wave should occur, the splendid offspring of Beverly will presumably survive.

There is an air of the exclusive country club about the Beverly Hills schools. Three full-time investigators, one an ex-FBI agent, are employed to make certain that all students live within the city limits. About one hundred "illegals" are booted out each year and returned to the ignominy of their own neighborhood academies. Parents in Beverly Hills are now required to sign an affidavit of residence under penalty of perjury!

What the school system boils down to is the imposing fifty-million-dollar physical plant. The charm of the architecture, especially at Beverly High, is what impresses mom and dad, who remain blissfully unaware of the threadbare performances of alumni, the pedestrian abilities of most teachers, and the perfunctory level of classroom instruction.

The lovely 26-acre campus of Beverly High is crowded into a pocket off Santa Monica Boulevard. Somehow the beauty of the flowing, stately, and tasteful older buildings isn't spoiled by the heavy, black skyscrapers of Century City looming overhead. The purity of the Norman-style buildings has been compromised to some degree by the intrusion of several new, ungainly, modern structures, but the overall effect is still eye-pleasing.

One of the new structures is a glassy, red brick, five-story 12.5-million-dollar job with elevators, an underground parking lot, a planetarium, an enormous library, a marvel of a science lab—and girls' johns where, one teacher attests, the debutantes do not flush the toilets after use, eat their lunches on the floors of the bathrooms, and smoke marijuana. "You wonder, you really do, what kind of homes they actually come from," says the teacher.

But, parents and educators are quick to point out, there's more to Beverly High than buildings. After all, 60 per cent of the students receive A and B grade averages.

According to figures published in June 1975 by the Los Angeles *Times*, there were twelve other high schools in Los Angeles that had more students than Beverly High with a 3.6 or higher grade average, which is A work. It is worth re-emphasizing that the students in those twelve high schools have less than half the amount of money spent on them than is shelled out for a student in Beverly.

In any case, A and B grades at Beverly High are suspect because of widespread cheating and bribery. During exams, some teachers are masters at looking the other way while students cheat. Often they leave the room while exams are in progress. Crib sheets are common, and in some courses advance copies of tests are passed out, especially to seniors headed for college.

Beverly's teachers also labor under a quota system whereby their competence is questioned if more than half their pupils do not receive A's and B's. Though the quota is unwritten, teachers are made aware of it when they are hired.

Competition for the 325 teaching positions in the Beverly system is considerable. "We have the highest-paid teachers in the state, if not the nation," says Superintendent Peters. Average teacher salary at Beverly High, he states, is close to $17,000 for a nine-month year. A number of instructors, if they take on summer classes and have built up seniority and tenure, can earn as much as $25,000 annually.

As always, averages are misleading—the top brings up the bottom. First-year teachers in the golden ghetto earn $8,305 to $9,529, far less than the cost of many student cars in the parking lots of Beverly High. There were enough dissatisfied teachers in 1975 to demand a healthy salary increase. Among some, there was discussion of a strike. The school board kept the lid on by giving a 5 per cent across-the-board increase and higher allowances for medical and dental insurance.

"Everything is relative in terms of salaries," says Peters. "We put some of our teachers into the $20,000-a-year and more bracket and when the cost of living keeps escalating their relative position in terms of investment in a home, a car, and other costs which they incur are related to their earning power. It's the great American way. Most of us live up to what we make, teachers included."

Peters adds that a "very small percentage" of Beverly's teachers can afford to live in the city. "A handful who are unmarried can find a somewhat competitively priced apartment. We have another handful who are married and in some cases live in the modest areas of Beverly Hills, which means a $60,000 home. And there are a few who are married to husbands with good positions who can well afford to live in Beverly Hills."

Peters is a bespectacled, agreeable man of fifty-seven, low-key and polished, a not completely uncritical partisan of Beverly's schools. After twenty-five years in the system, including a stint as principal of Beverly High, he has become the highest-paid public official in town. As Superintendent of Schools, he earns $43,950 a year, has free use of a Mercury station wagon provided by the city, and possesses that still-lofty status symbol, an English secretary. Among his cardinal worries are land and tennis courts.

"We are a wealthy school district but land poor," says Peters. "All our schools are on substandard sites. None of our elementary schools are over five acres, and the state recommends fifteen acres at minimum. It creates distinct problems relative to running the type of physical education program you would like to run because we just don't have the available land. In several of our primary schools, we are not able to separate the very small children from the seventh- and eighth-graders on the playground.

"Beverly High lacks tennis courts. For a school the size of Beverly

High there should be about eight more courts than the five we have, only three of which are of championship caliber. The other two, because of poor location and lack of space, are substandard."

Academically, however, Beverly Hills schools are anything but substandard, according to Peters.

"We have had the financial wherewithal to employ a staff and conduct a program I think is unusual in any part of the country. This is a community that has a very heavy commitment to public education, and high aspirations for its young people."

Among the courses offered at Beverly High, in addition to such basic subjects as English, Math, History, Home Economics, French, Spanish, and German, are: Hebrew, Latin, Weight Lifting, Body Mechanics, Co-ed Social Dance, Drill Team, Folk and Square Dance, Golf, Paddle Tennis, Spirit, TV Production, Film Production, Archery, Backpacking, Badminton, and Surfing. All are credit courses.

How does Peters answer the oft-expressed charge that Beverly High is a country club for spoiled kids?

"I've been faced with that one for more than twenty years. We have some spoiled kids running around and some overpermissive homes and we have kids that do not take advantage of their opportunities. But there are spoiled kids and spoiled parents in every community and the socio-economic bit isn't really the basic factor."

In what way are Beverly High students spoiled?

"Many of them have learned to expect a great deal from any contact that they have. Sometimes they expect more than they have a right to expect. In some cases, and I am talking about that small segment that would be called spoiled, I think they have a certain dependence on being rescued by their parents in any type of difficulty they encounter. These patterns are rather similar to spoiled kids generally. The spoiled kid in Beverly Hills has the same make-up as the spoiled kid anywhere."

For all the money expended on students, the showing of the alumni indicates that Beverly's schools largely produce underachievers or average students. Why don't they achieve at the level of their parents?

"You have a pattern here that would not be unlike most communities. Possibly it's a little exaggerated here, because there is a concentration of a few more people with wealth regardless of how they achieved that wealth and means. But their attitudes in terms of their youngsters are traditional. They want more for them than they had, whether it is in the field of education, the home they live in, or

Newspaper publisher William Randolph Hearst and Marion Davies at a San Simeon costume party.

Clark Gable and Carole Lombard were among the stars fêted by Hearst.

Even during World War II, the narrow Beverly streets presented a prob-
lem. Unwidened, they still do.
—Beverly Hills Chamber of Commerce

It's still prestigious to be paged via telephone at the Beverly Hills Hotel swimming pool. Generally, the page is arranged in advance to impress others.

—Robert C. Cleveland

Joan Crosly of the Hollywood Women's Press Club stands between Jack Benny and actor Alan Alda at a Beverly Hills Hotel function. The luncheon was Benny's last public appearance before his death a month later.

When Princess Margaret stayed at the Beverly Hills Hotel in 1965, a special suite was redecorated for her.

Entrance area connects new and old wings of Beverly Wilshire Hotel.
—Thelner Hoover; Beverly Wilshire Hotel

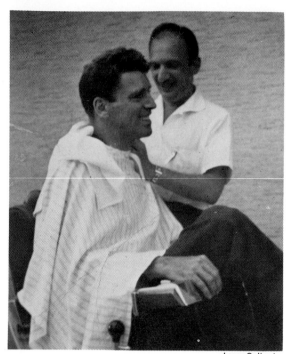

—Larry Gelbart

Morry Mandel cuts Burt Lancaster's hair.

Main façade of oilman E. L. Doheny's Greystone mansion, now rented for one dollar a year to the American Film Institute.

—Keller

The inscription "I Love You Jaynie" still exists at the bottom of the late Jayne Mansfield's pool, part of the "pink palace" she inhabited in Beverly.

—Diane Wagner

—Beverly Hills Chamber of Commerce

At a typical northside Beverly Hills home, it is nearly obligatory to have a Rolls-Royce parked in the driveway.

Oil wells mar the campus of Beverly Hills High. Century City skyscrapers rise in the background.

The underpaid Beverly Hills police in action, handcuffing suspects.

Beverly's top do-gooder, Sybil Brand,
with a favorite escort, actor Cesar
Romero.

—Beverly Hills Chamber of Commerce

The wedding-cake City Hall, where office space and services are in short supply.

Parks for senior citizens can be, and are, as lonely for the oldsters in Beverly Hills as anywhere else.

—Irwin Zucker

Garbage-strewn streets, a major problem in Beverly Hills, are a part of the northside mansion area tourists never see.

recreational opportunities. My dad was a railroad man and he always wanted something better for me. And he knocked himself out so that I wouldn't be a railroad man."

Until the late 1960s there were less than a dozen blacks in Beverly classrooms, the children of a few stars, of live-in servants, of janitors and gardeners employed by the school district. When nationwide demand for wider school integration finally began to be felt in Beverly Hills, the city came to grips with blacks in inimitable Beverly Hills style.

Peters explains: "We instituted a multi-cultural transfer program five years ago in which we brought in one hundred black students to Beverly High under a special arrangement with Los Angeles County. We were very concerned about this, not because of the basic intelligence of blacks, but because their backgrounds wouldn't allow them to compete. You would find them in the slower sections, you would find them in the remedial sections. Ultimately, if they had a long enough stay, they might meet the competition without any problem. But I don't think you can lift a youngster out of the ghetto and thrust him into this type of competitive enterprise and have him surrounded by a different environment for one-third of his day."

That's their code for selective tokenism. The special arrangement with the county meant that only youngsters from the black aristocracy, the wealthiest, and those who'd garnered the best grades, were allowed admittance under the transfer program. Even so, integration hasn't come very far at Beverly High. About 125 of the school's 2,450 students are black. The city's elementary schools are still almost completely white.

In a town where "busing" is as dirty a word as "bankruptcy," most blacks arrive at Beverly High in cars every bit as expensive as those driven by the richest white youngsters. There is, of course, no "multi-cultural transfer program," educationese for pressured integration, compelling white students from Beverly to attend schools in the black ghettos of Los Angeles.

"Most communities seem to rebel at the word 'bus,' " says Peters. "When we announced our multi-cultural transfer program, parents immediately identified it with busing because they were black youngsters. At the outset we held meetings on this so that people would understand exactly what we were doing, that there was no busing involved. Even today, five years after the program began, I have people ask me about that busing program at Beverly High. I say we don't have a busing program."

Have there been any racial incidents?

"None I would call primary incidents. There have been situations where a black and a white have gone at each other with fists. But then we have white after white and black after black doing the same thing. There was one incident, I was a little amused by it at the time, in which some black youngsters put up posters that related to Christmas. Apparently some of the Jewish kids objected to this and tore them all down. There was a confrontation of sorts. It was quickly resolved because the differing parties concerned were brought together. There was absolutely no intent on the part of the black youngsters to thrust Christmas at the Jewish youngsters. It was just a feeling of the season and they were going to display it. I guess the black students hadn't quite been through enough orientation to know there was some objection to the over-emphasis on the Christmas season in a predominantly Jewish high school."

While the Jewish population of the city is under 50 per cent, the number of Jewish students attending Beverly High is estimated by Peters to be 80 per cent. The seeming anomaly occurs because Jews have more children of school age and the bulk of non-Jewish students are sent to private schools, a gauge of how deep the Christian-Jewish breach is in Beverly Hills.

"We have the usual discipline problems," Peters admits. "Students who are verbally aggressive toward teachers or peers. Truancy is a problem. And our theft runs the gamut. We have lost some very expensive electronic equipment from our TV studio. Turntables, stereo systems, and microphones have been bodily lifted out. We have theft of money from lockers and theft of science equipment. Wrist watches and jackets are stolen in the gym while the kids are showering.

"The vandalism starts with the scratching up of the restroom walls, which has been a tradition for nine hundred years at schools. I always tell new principals or assistant principals and teachers that until they've been rapped on the wall of the boys' restroom, why they really haven't made it yet. It's always a shock to a new instructor, one who thinks the kids love and adore him, to walk into a restroom, and see a four-letter word, F-U-C-K *Joe Dokes* or whoever it is.

"We have a lot of broken windows because we have a lot of glass, in the new building particularly. Many of the doors that lead into the patio areas are glass, reinforced but full glass doors. Architecturally, they are very attractive but from a practical point of view not very smart. Kids will kick a glass door in. It doesn't shatter, but it breaks."

Peters declares that 70 per cent of Beverly High students have experimented with drugs! The rate is shockingly high compared with Los Angeles' city schools, where a survey revealed that 51 per cent of students have tried drugs at least once.

"The percentage drops down rather dramatically from the occasional user to the hooked person," Peters says. "We've had some that have been in really bad straits, and have been sent away and haven't recovered as yet.

"We have kids on pills, no question about it. We get kids who manifest the symptoms of being on uppers or downers or something or other. The school physician checks them, and we send them home or have their parents come and get them.

"The biggest share of the cases are kids who don't know what they're on. They have just taken a pill that somebody has given them or something they found in the family medicine cabinet.

"We received pretty good press-coverage here recently right after we submitted a report to the County Superintendent that there had been no arrests of students for the use of drugs on the campus. About two days later, a whole batch of them were picked up and arrested. Most of the kids, we chose to believe, knew they were taking pills but didn't have the slightest idea whether they were taking barbiturates or amphetamines. It turned out some of them were taking LSD."

Does Peters find it incongruous that youngsters, many from affluent homes attending an affluent school should use drugs so profusely?

"I think we have all come to understand a little more clearly that affluence doesn't mean happiness. It's also understandable that a youngster can be surrounded with an exciting educational opportunity and that doesn't solve all his problems, because he has many, many other places in which his problems can be generated. The drug culture springs primarily out of frustration and unhappiness that can occur in any type of community or society."

Yet many would argue that most kids in Beverly Hills have so much more than young people who live elsewhere. A 70 per cent rate of drug use amounts to an epidemic. Why should youngsters living in such affluence be frustrated or unhappy?

"That, of course, is gross oversimplification. The various factors that create frustration and unhappiness can be found in any home, the wealthy as well as the moderate. In Beverly Hills there is the high divorce factor, the absentee parent factor. It's certainly no secret that in the high-income brackets you have, in many cases, what amounts to the absentee father because of the success syndrome we all live in. The more successful the parent is, the more occupied he is. Sometimes both parents are successful and have less time to devote to their children. But I don't think you can restrict these causes only to homes of affluence. We have areas in Beverly Hills, apartments especially, that are quite moderately priced. We have single mothers working like mad to support a family. We have the usual bit of desertion or the husband who refuses to pay alimony. We have all of this in Beverly Hills.

"A lot of people want to look north of the railroad tracks and say, 'This is Beverly Hills.' But Beverly Hills has areas that represent the very moderate type of circumstances that you find in most communities."

Peters is a Presbyterian and lives in the San Fernando Valley suburb of Tarzana. He has three children. As an employee of the city for more than two decades, he's had the option of sending his children to Beverly Hills schools. However, his oldest, who is now twenty-five, attended school in Tarzana, not Beverly. His other two, a seventh-grader and a fifth-grader, are still in Tarzana schools. "We've been very pleased with the quality of their education there."

The superintendent of an educational system theoretically second to none says he doesn't plan to transfer his two youngest children to Beverly elementary schools or have them attend Beverly High.

10.
The Finest Police Force
Money Can Buy

ON A STEAMY August morning in 1925, two attractive, worried young women stood before a Beverly Hills judge waiting for him to mete out the full penalty of the law for their offense. Although they had pleaded guilty to a misdemeanor, they weren't anxious to spend time in jail. The judge's decision spared them that indignity: each was fined seventy-five dollars. But there was a problem. The girls both told the judge they didn't have the price of the fine.

"Then go out and earn it, but *not* in Beverly Hills," His Honor declared. "Case continued for ten days."

The women returned on schedule for their next hearing and were able to pay their fines. Justice, at least as practiced in the golden ghetto, had been served.

The women had been convicted of prostitution within the boundaries of Beverly Hills, and, of course, they had earned their court levies by continuing to ply their trade—but in Los Angeles.

The geographical distinction was of paramount importance to the judge, who had conveniently overlooked the circumstance that the ladies hadn't forced themselves on the squires of Beverly Hills, who were eager to buy what the girls were selling.

The fable had already been established that the honest, God-fearing

149

citizens of Beverly, having achieved Paradise, had no reason to break any statutes.

In dealing with the prostitutes, the judge knew how they were going to earn their fines. He wasn't bothered one whit that he was indirectly acting as a pimp by placing the girls in the position of buying their freedom through a further breach of law. What mattered was that another blow for purity had been struck within Beverly Hills and the maxim upheld that all criminals were outsiders.

The supposition that all or most crime is caused by interlopers is still widely believed in Beverly Hills. The city, after all, came to prominence as a purported crime-free sanctuary.

One of the fundamental assumptions of Beverly's pioneers was that the aristocratic town had no need to deal with the dark side of human nature so far as its own citizens were concerned. The City Council passed the customary laws, but the ordinances were for non-residents. The sole reason for the police force was to guard against the uncivilized barbarians certain to invade. The ruling ethic was that citizens of Beverly who might stray from the straight and narrow were innocent until proven guilty. Non-Beverlyites, however, were guilty until proven innocent.

With orthodox golden-ghetto arrogance and paranoia, Pierce Benedict wrote in 1934: "Beverly Hills is composed of wealthy, law-abiding residents, automatically making it the cynosure of the criminal element of the country." The implication was and still is: if that exterior criminal element could somehow be kept out of the city, Beverly wouldn't need a police force or a jail.

The reality, from the beginning, has been otherwise. Citizens of Beverly Hills have been murdered, raped, robbed, and mugged in Beverly Hills by other Beverly residents as well as by outsiders. Every day of the week, Beverlyites victimize each other. More than half of those arrested in the city are locals accused of crimes against fellow citizens.

For its size and population, Beverly Hills has always been one of the most lawless cities in the nation.

Most Beverlyites assume there hasn't been a killing in town since Bugsy Siegel was mowed down in 1947. Unless the victim is prominent, few in Beverly take note of "routine" homicides. Actually, murder in Beverly is relatively common, far more common than most of its citizens realize. The city has a higher murder rate than Los Angeles and most cities of approximately the same size and population.

According to FBI statistics covering 475 cities in the 25,000 to 50,000 population range, there are nearly 900 murders a year, an average of less than two per city. Beverly exceeds the average with three or more killings a year, and unless the cases are open-and-shut, the culprits are never caught.

Beverly spends little time or money unraveling murder cases. The Bugsy Siegel murder is still unsolved. So is the 1969 case of a Mexican maid who allegedly killed her son and her sister. Beverly's Police Chief B. L. Cork says a warrant for the maid's apprehension was issued, but "the suspect is evading arrest by living somewhere in Mexico." And there it rests. Yet Cork, when he was a detective, was sent on an extensive manhunt for three thieves who'd heisted $50,000 in gems from a Beverly Hills VIP. Cork investigated the case in Corpus Christi and Houston, Texas, Shreveport, Louisiana, and *Mexico*, where he caught the suspects and returned them for prosecution. Obviously, recovering diamonds is more important to the Beverly Police Department than the apprehension of a suspected killer of two people.

The wonder is that there haven't been more killings. There are more than six hundred burglaries and robberies a year in Beverly, and it is little short of miraculous that someone isn't gunned to death every day in the course of all that thievery. Particularly in the north, someone —householder or servant—is usually on the premises.

The homicidal rampage of Charles Manson's maniacs could as easily have occurred in Beverly Hills as it did a mile away in Bel Air. That the Manson-ordered carnage didn't happen in Beverly was accidental. Manson family members passed through Beverly Hills to reach the Cielo Drive home rented by Sharon Tate, which they attacked under the impression that Doris Day's son Terry Melcher was still the occupant. Melcher was the intended victim because he had repeatedly refused to record Manson's musical doggerel. Had they known that Melcher was living in his mother's Beverly Hills home, that is where the butchery would have taken place.

The gods have also chosen to smile on Beverly in regard to kidnapping. Since 1967 there has been only one attempted and one actual kidnapping.

In January 1966, a member of a gang planning to grab tire magnate Leonard Firestone from his North Alpine Drive home tipped off the Beverly Hills police. The informant was guaranteed safety and immunity from prosecution if he'd bait the two other members of the gang into the Firestone home, where five Beverly Hills cops would be waiting. The tipster agreed. Accounts differ as to what occurred when the kidnappers walked into the house. The official Beverly Hills Police Department version is that the kidnappers sensed a trap and began shooting. The police returned the fire. When the smoke cleared, one man lay dead—the informant. The unofficial version is that the nervous Beverly Hills police fired first and unnecessarily. No one mourned the death of the informant, without whom the case would have had a much different outcome.

A year later, a lone kidnapper appeared late at night at the northside home of Herbert J. Young, president of a savings and loan association. Young's eleven-year-old son Kenneth was taken from his bedroom and held for three days, then released unharmed after Young paid $250,000 in ransom. The kidnapper, a former intelligence agent for the Internal Revenue Service, was apprehended by the FBI and sentenced to twenty years to life.

Asked his explanation for the low incidence of kidnapping when there are so many potential golden-ghetto victims, Chief Cork replies: "We're keeping our fingers crossed. It's dangerous when you kidnap someone because there has to be contact with the victim's relatives. Kidnappers risk exposure in negotiating for and in picking up ransom money. There are just too many ways to get caught. Kidnappers are taking a hell of a chance, and that's a crime most criminals try to avoid."

A more plausible explanation is that of sheer good luck. Considering the world-wide contagion of kidnappings between 1972 and 1976, it would appear that kidnappers do not have the crisp deductive powers of Chief Cork. (Following the much-heralded "abduction" of Patricia Hearst from her Berkeley apartment, a guard was thrown up around the Beverly Hills home of Miss Hearst's uncle, David Whitmore Hearst, a director of one of the family's corporations.)

Chief Cork's logic notwithstanding, fear of kidnapping is one of the reasons many of the rich have left Beverly Hills for less ostentatious areas.

In every felony category except kidnapping, Beverly Hills is experiencing a surge in crime. Arrests for homicide, aggravated assault, robbery, burglary, larceny over fifty dollars, and automobile thefts totaled 2,141 in 1974, up from 1,973 in 1973, an 8.51 per cent increase. More than half those arrested had Beverly Hills addresses.

Next to the school system, the second most-often stated reason for assuming the burdens of owning a home in Beverly Hills is the quality of the protection offered by the police department. The high quality of that protection is questionable—especially for those who live below the tracks.

The headline in the Beverly Hills *Courier* was small but significant—SOUTHSIDERS OPEN ANTI-CRIME WAR. The story's lead paragraph said: "The entire 300 block of South Oakhurst Drive formally declared war on crime Tuesday night, under the approving eye of the Beverly Hills Police Department. Many Beverly Hills residents (in the south) still feel there are not enough police officers cruising the neighborhood streets."

Chief Cork replied that the protection was there, but wasn't visible because officers cruised the area in unmarked cars. (Traditional prowl cars have been abandoned in Beverly, not as a crime-fighting device, but solely because the City Council discovered it could get a better price for the unmarked vehicles at trade-in time.)

The siege of crime was so out of control below the tracks that residents on South Oakhurst and South Canon Drive called block meetings to find solutions. At one of the gatherings, an elderly woman residing on South Oakhurst said that two burly men broke in at three in the afternoon. She saved herself "from being murdered" by blowing a whistle she had bought for such a contingency. Fortunately, the whistle frightened the men off.

Residents in the south decided to organize a citizens' watch program. Groups of householders now keep an eye on homes of neighbors who are away. They've also established a communal burglar-alarm system that alerts families on each block when a prowler is in the area.

Cries of "vigilantism" were promptly voiced by some members of the City Council. But Chief Cork and Councilman Stuchen approved the action, agreeing there was a difference between "citizen vigilantes" and "citizen involvement."

The Beverly Hills power structure has continued to turn a deaf ear to complaints by southsiders that police protection is unequal. Emergency calls from the south sometimes remain unanswered for as long as half an hour, say residents there. In the north, the response is not longer than six minutes.

Another comfortable notion yet to fall completely by the wayside is that it's safe to walk the streets in Beverly Hills. The following are some representative street incidents that occurred in 1974 and 1975, in which both victims and victimizers were all Beverly residents.

"Don't move or I'll blow your brains out" was the inhospitable greeting of a twenty-three-year-old citizen to a seventy-two-year-old citizen one evening at 7:30, on the garbage-strewn sidewalk of North Rexford Drive, a few doors from Nate 'N Al's pastrami palace. The street is regarded as one of the most elegant shopping promenades in Beverly Hills. Among other businesses, it has several jewelry stores that bar their windows and doors with iron gate fences after closing. The accosted senior citizen was relieved of his credit cards, wrist watch, and $50 in cash. The gunman was caught and sentenced to a year in jail. His psychiatrist father sent a stack of letters to the parole board from some of the most substantial people in town, attesting to the noble character of his son, a graduate of Beverly High who was reared and lived his entire life in the golden ghetto. The young man was paroled after serving two months.

"This is a holdup, give me your cash!" The gunman was a Beverly Hills teen-ager and the victims were a sixty-two-year-old man and his wife who were window shopping along Wilshire Boulevard on a Friday evening shortly before eleven o'clock. The young hood lived in a $350,000 mansion above Santa Monica. For his escapade, he received $30 from his victims and probation from the court.

Three fifteen-year-old students of Beverly High were caught by a patrolman while they were beating a seventeen-year-old girl who had been strolling on North Canon Drive. Two of the three young men lived on exclusive North Rexford Drive and North Foothill Drive. The other's home was on South Spalding Drive. They were set free after being admonished by the Juvenile Division of the Beverly Hills Police Department.

One fed-up Beverly citizen, John Cole, wrote a letter to the Los Angeles *Times* in which he made an interesting comparison between street crime and pornography: "I once would have supported police action against pornography, but crime in our streets has become so serious I now say first things first.

"The police should spend every available man-hour 'showing the Flag,' as we used to say in the Navy. By that I mean they will deter serious crime, not by raiding pornographic movies, but by walking a beat in uniform . . . with a weapon on display.

"The policing of morals, except where children are involved, is a luxury we can no longer afford."

Shoplifting costs Beverly's shops and stores some 3.5 million dollars a year, and the crime cuts across class lines. Those who are caught are as likely to be from the north as from the south. A number of famous names—Hedy Lamarr, Judy Garland, Veronica Lake—have been charged with the offense. Most of the shoplifters heist big-ticket items like furs and jewelry, but sadly they have now been joined by Beverly's senior poor who usually steal pathetically small.

"Some of our elderly people who can no longer make ends meet or are too proud to go on welfare are turning to shoplifting," says a dismayed local detective, citing three of the pettiest cases ever reported to the Beverly Hills Police Department.

One oldster was caught in Saks trying to make off with a pair of shorts and a pair of $8.00 sunglasses. Another senior was collared at Bonwit Teller for lifting a $.59 bottle of nail polish. A seventy-three-year-old woman was taken into custody at Robinson's for stealing two jars of spaghetti-sauce seasoning valued at $1.38. Each of the three hapless seniors was given a thirty-day suspended sentence after being arrested, handcuffed, and fingerprinted.

Most juvenile offenders, especially if they are from the north, get off scot-free for anything short of murder. And the Beverly Hills Police Department has never laid a glove on any of the numerous northside families who harbor the cheap Mexican servants who have been brought into the country illegally. Some of Beverly's patricians pay a fee of $500 to smugglers, known as "coyotes," to deliver an illegal alien to their door. Some Beverly Hills matrons have gone to Mexico themselves and brought servants across the border personally, bribing U.S. Immigration officials to let them pass. (In 1974 the FBI investigated two hundred customs officials who had been accepting and soliciting bribes to allow illegal aliens and drugs across the border.)

Beverlyites frequently return from trips to New York, Chicago, Detroit, Philadelphia, and other cities with outraged tales of having had their hotel rooms burglarized. The rest of the country, they aver, is going to hell. They may not know it, but so is Beverly Hills.

A couple at the Beverly Hilton found their rooms ransacked of fourteen thousand dollars' worth of jewelry, cash, furs, luggage, and traveler's checks.

While attending a ball at the Beverly Wilshire honoring Princess Alexandra of England, one guest had her suite plundered of 110 thousand dollars' worth of gems, twenty-eight pieces in all, including a 25-carat sapphire, emerald, and ruby bracelet set with 115 diamonds.

There are as many hotel burglaries, per capita, in Beverly as there are in New York City.

More than 150 forcible rapes are committed in Los Angeles every twenty-four hours. The FBI estimates that only 10 per cent of the actual cases are reported. Chief Cork confirms that, for the most part, the crime also goes unreported in Beverly Hills. From year to year, the number of disclosed rapes in Beverly ranges from two to a dozen, which exceeds the average for a city of its size. And most of the rapists who are convicted are citizens of Beverly Hills.

So great is the fear of rape in Beverly and adjoining suburbs that two hundred women held a meeting in Westwood to ponder how they could best cope with sexual assault. One-third of those in attendance were from Beverly Hills. A petite thirty-two-year-old woman from northside Beverly, who had been a rape victim, called the felony "the most frequently committed crime of violence in America." The women decided to establish a Rape Crisis Line, an around-the-clock telephone service offering aid to victims, including counseling, transportation to a hospital, and advice on legal procedure.

"We especially want to overcome the embarrassment of women confronting salivating police officers who always seem inordinately more interested in the sexual details of the rape than in apprehending the rapists," declared an attractive female attorney.

The glittering area that makes up the west side of Los Angeles County—including Beverly Hills, Bel Air, Westwood, Brentwood, Santa Monica, and Malibu—"has the highest rate of drug-related deaths in Los Angeles County." The surprising information comes from a 1974 survey conducted by the Los Angeles County Santa Monica West Mental Health Service. The survey also said there are probably more drug addicts and drug abusers per capita in west Los Angeles than in any other area of the United States, including New York, Detroit, and Chicago!

In the affluent suburban stretch that is allegedly filled with happy residents, more than one hundred die each year from drug overdose. The number of habituated users totals 57,000, possibly more. Over 3,500 were hospitalized for emergency O.D. treatment. In addition, there were 3,450 heroin addicts, and 3,833 were arrested for possession or use.

In Beverly Hills, about 125 persons are arrested each year on drug charges. In view of the 3,833 drug busts in the rest of west side Los Angeles and Superintendent Peters' admission that seven out of ten Beverly school kids have been users, it would seem that the Beverly Hills Police Department has been somewhat indulgent of its citizens.

The cops awoke temporarily when a fourteen-year-old Beverly Hills boy was arrested for burglary. He proved to be a member of an all-Beverly ring of youthful burglars who stole, the youngster said, "for the thrill of it." Pills were found in the boy's pockets. He admitted buying them from a pusher on the campus of Beverly High.

Information obtained from that arrest turned up another ring, this one, said a police department spokesman, consisting of "a bunch of kids who wanted to get reputations as big dope dealers." In one of the largest arrests ever in the city, thirteen Beverly High boys and one girl between the ages of fourteen and sixteen were picked up. Found on the kids were LSD tabs, cocaine, uppers, downers, and grass. All had been pushers as well as users.

One of the arresting detectives said: "They all come from so-called good homes. They're all nice, clean-cut, good kids, not long hairs." But all displayed "telltale symptoms of problems leading to drug abuse"—attitude changes at home that left them hostile and impossible to talk to, a tendency to cut classes, a decline in the quality of their schoolwork.

"Drug use in this town is very high," the officer said. "I'm not optimistic that the roundup will put a dent in drug use by teen-agers. The kids read the papers and get upset and things slow down for a while. But then they go back to it again."

He added that the police department was "actively seeking" three other local pushers. Nothing came of that investigation. The detective concluded: "We could raid Beverly High every day and arrest almost any kid on sight for use or possession, but what good would it do? It's an epidemic and it's out of hand, and I don't see any improvement in the situation. It's going to get worse, a lot worse, before it gets better, if it ever gets better."

The late Jack Benny did much to create the impression that the Beverly Hills jail was a palace. "You should see the Beverly Hills station house," Benny joked. "If it wasn't for the cars in the driveway, you'd think it was the Taj Mahal. Cecil B. DeMille used to live upstairs. . . . The locker room has Louis XIV chairs and the policewomen all have princess telephones. . . . They're the only cops I know who take their coffee breaks at Chasen's. . . . The jail has Tiffany lamps, floor-to-ceiling drapes, and they change the flowers every day."

The jail, however, is something less than a palace. City Manager

Morgan calls it "a disgrace, intolerable for a city with the prestige of Beverly Hills." *Los Angeles* magazine writer Ivor Davis says the headquarters of the Beverly Hills Police Department is "a cross between a Byzantine cathedral and a Moroccan movie palace, but the sumptuous façade hides a station house that is right out of some run-down precinct in Brooklyn and probably wouldn't be tolerated in Watts." Cockroaches and water bugs abound in the Beverly jail, the food is dreadful, the cells are filthy, the atmosphere unsparingly dingy and depressing.

The jail and other facilities of the police department are unlikely to improve unless a Beverly Hills city councilman is sentenced to serve a jolt there, which may or may not be a possibility for the future.

There have been complaints for two decades about Beverly's outmoded police headquarters and its location. City councilmen, instead of saving Beverly's taxpayers a pile of loot by simply inspecting the building themselves, a five-minute walk from their chamber, hired the prestigious consultant firm of Booz-Allen to write a report on the facility.

After concluding his investigation, Booz-Allen's Richard A. Hughes appeared before the Council and summarized his report. He had found the headquarters overused, poorly arranged, unsafe, inconvenient, and badly lighted.

Councilman Stuchen interrupted Hughes to grumble, "It's a police department, not the executive offices of Sun Life Insurance."

"But it's not San Quentin, either," Hughes responded.

Hughes went on to relate many of the specific things that were wrong: No acceptable accommodations for handling the one hundred to two hundred people who visit police headquarters each day. Rooms for private counseling of juveniles were not available. Security was inadequate. Offices, files, and communications equipment were illogically arranged. All this caused productivity levels to be negatively affected, Hughes said. He recommended that the present headquarters should be scrapped and that a new facility should be constructed in a new location.

That is not about to happen. Cost of a new headquarters would run between two and three million dollars, which would be a heavy financial burden to a City Council already fed-up with the price it is paying for police protection.

The Council and citizenry of Beverly Hills have traditionally taken their police department for granted. Particularly in the north, the force has been treated with condescension. But the concept of a private militia catering to the rich and famous began to change in the late 1960s. The new, young officers quickly turned militant. They were unimpressed by Beverly's reputation and its celebrities. If Beverly Hills wanted the best police force money could buy, Beverly Hills could damn well pay for it.

The City Council disagreed. The solons expected top-drawer police efficiency at bargain-basement prices.

The blowup surfaced in 1973 when a police demand for a 14 per cent wage increase plus other benefits was refused. The Council offered only a 5 per cent hike and insisted on abolishing city payment for educational privileges, which allowed many of the men to attend the FBI Academy and universities offering courses in modern law-enforcement techniques. The police, faced with an immovable Council, threatened a strike. They were dissuaded only when their attorney informed them that state and county statutes outlawed a police strike.

The situation turned so rancorous that seventy-five angry wives of officers picketed City Hall, some with infants in baby carriages. One of the wives carried a placard which read: *Why Should My Husband Die for the Rich of Beverly Hills?* Another, one hand pushing a carriage with three small children, held a sign in the other hand asking: *What Happens to My Children and Me If My Husband Is Killed?*

"I am not demeaning our police by saying this, but they have great, cushy jobs," Councilman Stone told an interviewer. "They very rarely get shot at, and they have no black ghettos to deal with. They have no enormous pockets of poverty, which breed crime, to deal with. Nor must they deal with racial violence.

"Those policemen whose vision isn't distorted by the fact that they aren't getting the benefits they would like to get will corroborate this. They know, as police work goes, this is a pretty good town to work in. It is true our benefits are slightly lower than those offered in the county and city of Los Angeles. But look what the policeman in Beverly Hills receives in return—he doesn't get shot at every time he goes out. His wife can sleep at night. To me, those are offsetting features.

"Sure, we have a murder every so often, but I can't remember the last time we had a shoot-out. There was a policeman shot about a year and a half ago. He stopped a car and was shot, and that's the last time I can recall that a policeman was shot, and that was the first time in years."

Stone's estimate of the "cushy" life of Beverly Hills policemen collides sharply with the view of the men who do the policing. They cruise the streets in fear, contending with malcontents and psychotics from inside and outside Beverly, who each year become hairier, wilder, more obstreperous and dangerous.

While it is true that few Beverly Hills policemen have been killed in the line of duty, it is also true that comparatively few officers are killed anywhere in populous California. In 1974, six policemen lost their lives in the state. It is six too many, but their deaths cannot be related to whether they worked in rich or in poor cities. Watts or Beverly Hills, the risk of being slain is inherent in the job. The possibility of death on the beat in Beverly Hills is ever-present. The cops know it, and so do their wives.

Unrelenting pressure by the police for greater benefits finally forced the City Council to place the issue before voters in 1974. The city overwhelmingly approved the sparse benefits that were offered—the right to retire at age fifty instead of fifty-five, at a rate of 2 per cent of salary for every year worked. Police widows would be awarded one-half their husbands' pensions.

But the policemen were still dissatisfied. The ballot had included no provision for an increase in pay. The cops in the golden ghetto were still earning $2,000 less than their counterparts in Los Angeles.

The job of Chief of Police of Beverly Hills has been one of the most exclusive in the world. Only four men, each with a vastly different style, have held the post.

The first was an easygoing Scotsman, a puckish, soft-faced, ex-jockey named Charles Blair. He was also fire chief and the city's tax collector. Appointed in 1917, Blair began his tenure in the pre-Douglas Fairbanks/Mary Pickford era when Beverly had less than six hundred people.

Crime surfaced quickly in Beverly. In that period, it was residents in the north who complained of inadequate protection. "Impossible," retorted Blair. "One of my men passes every house each hour of the night on his motorcycle." Homeowners were skeptical since they didn't hear the motorcycle. Blair ordered his patrolmen to gun their motors. Four days later the gentry capitulated, declaring the protection was noisily adequate.

When the city was augmented by an inundation of movie people, wealthy businessmen, and socialites, Blair bowed to their pressure for privacy and instituted the policy of "fortress" Beverly Hills. He began the practice of fingerprinting every salesman who entered town. Blair alone decided who was "suspicious." He was a mild-mannered, one-man judge, jury, and executioner, and his punishment seldom involved more than exile for anyone he thought was undesirable. He put the unwelcome guest on the Pacific Electric for a one-way ride, telling the conductor to keep the passenger aboard until the train reached Los Angeles.

Blair gave way in 1929 to one of his subordinates, Clinton H. Anderson, whose approach to the job was similar to the way J. Edgar Hoover ran the FBI. Anderson was fond of personal publicity. He was ruthlessly tough with his men. At the same time, he was unduly impressed by the rich, famous and influential. Many in Beverly Hills believe to this day that Anderson, like Hoover, kept secret dossiers concerning the sex, drug, and drinking habits of every prominent resident in the city, especially movie stars. The allegedly incriminating files supposedly were stashed in a double-locked cabinet in Anderson's office. When Anderson retired, it is presumed he took the files with him. If true, the Anderson notes would make torrid reading. However, Anderson, who remains a familiar figure in Beverly Hills, has denied the existence of such files.

During his forty-year reign, Anderson was without question the most powerful man in Beverly Hills. No mayor or councilman ever questioned his judgment, as no President ever seriously quarreled with Hoover's actions.

Many hard-line conservatives miss Anderson. A legend has grown up that Anderson kept Beverly Hills free of crime. But the legend is bogus. Anderson's own men feared him far more than the criminal element did. His reputation was built on tenacious execution of the law against minor offenders and on the attention he received as a result of crimes involving many of the town's luminaries. However, he seldom cracked a big case.

Anderson was effective in handling such cases as the attempt by an ardent Romeo to gain entrance to Clara Bow's mansion. Anderson boldly arrested the man and received more publicity than the incident merited. He did thwart attempts to kidnap Mary Pickford and heiress Gloria Vanderbilt—but only because he received advance warning in both cases. Anderson was so zealous in his protection of the celebrated that bootleggers during Prohibition never seemed to have trouble supplying their movie-star customers and drove their roadsters up to the celebrities' homes in open daylight.

But, though Bugsy Siegel was mowed down very near Anderson's office, the chief never solved the case. In fact, Anderson and his detectives solved only the most perfunctory cases. When a domestic took a meat cleaver and killed her wealthy employer in a dispute over the carving of a roast, the servant was caught because she sat and waited for the police. But when the dismembered body of a Filipino houseboy was discovered in a Beverly Hills field, the murder was not only unsolved, but was forgotten a week later.

"Eastern racketeers have been attracted to the community for years," a former Beverly Hills prosecuting attorney, C. Richard Maddox, said in 1959. Yet there is no record of Anderson's having rousted, admonished or arrested any organized crime figures, though most of them at one time or another have visited Beverly for business as well as for pleasure. Lucky Luciano and Meyer Lansky, two of the underworld's most notorious gurus, were frequent houseguests of Bugsy Siegel. While hoods could come and go without molestation in Beverly, Anderson brought the policy of intercepting harmless pedestrians to its highest level of efficiency and enforcement.

"Anderson was a hard-nosed guy, and anybody following him would have had a problem," says Councilman Stone. "How could anyone follow God? His legacy was a police department that had no internal leadership other than Anderson. He ran that department totally. He didn't have a single man who, when the exams were given for a new police chief, came within spitting range of being considered chief, because Anderson had blocked the men from educating themselves. Anderson had dominated the department to the extent that nobody knew how to think for himself."

When Anderson retired, Beverly Hills had to look beyond its own borders for a replacement. Hired was forty-three-year-old Joseph P. Kimble, a handsome, well-educated veteran of twenty years in law enforcement. Kimble's brief stay was bizarre and controversial.

Six feet two, weighing 220 pounds, Kimble was as liberal as Anderson was conservative. He was frank, open, and approachable. His office bookshelf was lined with well-thumbed volumes on psychology, criminology, sociology, and history. Another wall held autographed pictures of Supreme Court Chief Justice Earl Warren and former U.S. Attorney General Ramsey Clark, both advocates of balanced justice for rich and poor. One of the first orders Kimble issued was that his grimy, linoleum-floored office be carpeted and the walls paneled. He hung modern paintings and had classical music piped in.

Nobody on the Beverly Hills Police Department knew what to make of their new chief. Accustomed to the taut, dictatorial, non-intellectual atmosphere of the Anderson regime, it was difficult for the force to get a fix on Kimble. If anything, he seemed a man who would be more at home as a professor than as a police chief.

The dismay and bewilderment at headquarters turned to decided disapproval when Kimble began holding rap sessions with hippies, expressing sympathy for blacks, and visiting such places as The Classic Cat, a bottomless and topless dive on the Sunset Strip. Kimble also attended fashionable parties in the north, where he comported himself as an equal, discussing ideas with great gusto and perception. (On the rare occasions when Anderson attended social functions, he had felt out of place. He had been more at home at a Kiwanis meeting than in a living room filled with intelligent, witty people.)

Kimble committed the unforgivable sin of pointing up Beverly's hypocrisy toward minorities and of attempting to end Beverly's insularity. "My premise," Kimble said, "is that my officers in a nearly all-white community, through negative contacts with minority people, can shoot down the hard work of adjoining communities that have significant problems with those members of society who are less fortunate."

He eased the strictures against the promiscuous persecution of pedestrians. He did not automatically consider long-hairs, blacks, and Mexican-Americans as suspicious. He was fair, compassionate, and regarded the Constitutional rights of every citizen as sacred, no matter what his social standing, color, or income. For the first time in Beverly Hills, there was a chief of police who considered a suspect innocent until proven guilty.

Though Kimble had his supporters, his attitudes were too soft for the local Establishment. After less than two years on the job, he was fired.

The grounds for his dismissal were as vague as they were unfair. The major charge against him was that under his rule crime had gone up. But crime had also increased under Blair and Anderson.

"Kimble was glib, charming, and we wanted someone in step with the times," recalls Councilman Stuchen. "Anderson was a great chief, but his era was passing, and when the kids and the dope problem came up, he knew something was happening but he never understood what.

"Kimble fixed up his place like a matinee idol's office. He gave the kids what they wanted—no dope arrests—and played up to them and their parents.

"He was the ultra-liberal symbol, and anyone against him was a Fascist. If Kimble arrested a guy he'd call in the TV cameras. He'd show up at premières with his own photographer. He wanted to run the town."

Councilman Stone's recollection is less harsh. "The Kimble situation was essentially a breakdown of administrative control. What happened was that you had a department head who was not disciplined personally and had nobody over him to see that he got back into line. So all the ideas that he had, and he had lots of good ones, were lost."

From the long shadow of Anderson's hegemony emerged B. L. Cork, fifty-one years old, 194 pounds of terse, rule-book cop. Cork succeeded Kimble as chief—although, in Councilman Stone's view, Anderson had left no worthwhile heir. Cork, a Texan raised on a ranch near Lubbock, had worked under Anderson for twenty-one years.

Heavy-set and not overly friendly, Cork is far closer to Anderson than he is to Kimble. He occupies Kimble's "matinee idol's office," which in fact is less lavish than the quarters assigned to most corporate secretaries in Beverly Hills. Music is no longer piped in, and the walls of cheap, brown paneling are now bare of paintings. Cork appears to be a man who would prefer Anderson's linoleum to Kimble's carpeting. He is quick to show his distaste for his predecessor. "Our crime rate is way down since that other fellow left, I forget his name."

Cork presides over a department that provides less protection than the citizens of Beverly Hills believe they have. Of his 119-member force, 93 are officers assigned to the streets. That gives Beverly 31 policemen per shift, less than one for every 1,000 residents. Cork says as few as five unmarked cars may be cruising the town at any given time—which does much to explain the high rate of burglary. At maximum, Cork can put seventeen cars into action. But such maximum visibility is hauled out only to police street demonstrations or to guard important visitors.

Nevertheless, Cork insists that a squad car can answer an emergency call in as little as five seconds. "Sometimes, if our units are tied up, it may take a little longer." In practice, it takes a lot longer, as anyone in the south will attest.

Cork readily voices his attitudes concerning local law enforcement. "No one gets special favors, and I mean no one. . . . I don't buy pressure. . . . I don't fix parking tickets, and I don't have the power to fix a ticket. . . . Everyone gets the same protection, north or south. . . . Beverly Hills is a prime target for criminals. . . . Most of our thieves are from outside. . . . Our reputation prevents a lot of people we don't want to see from coming into town. . . . I'm just a chief of police trying to get along. . . . Our policy is to use brains rather than brawn."

But Cork's treatment of young people isn't much different from Kimble's. "In juvenile cases, we work with the parents. I don't want to take kids and put them through the meat grinder. *Some of our juveniles are only arrested after they commit three or four crimes.*" Such permissiveness, in fact, exceeds Kimble's leniency.

It is a misconception, says Cork, to think that young people in Beverly have everything. "They have cars and money, but Mom and Pop are in Europe. The problem is that they don't have family. So they relate to their peers, and their peers can get them into trouble—'Let's go steal a car.' Or: 'Let's go to a pot party.' "

Cork earns $26,000 a year and says he has no desire to be a millionaire. "I'd worry if I had a million dollars. I don't envy millionaires. I feel sorry for them. They have more problems than I have. They can't relax. They have a $3,000 payment on a mortgage to meet every month. I'm happier than they are."

Under Cork's stewardship, Beverly's attitude toward gambling and prostitution is extremely liberal. "We have no roving vice squad," Cork says. "In gambling and prostitution situations, we act only on complaints."

There's been very little complaining. In 1972, Cork's first year as chief, not a single gambler was arrested in a town noted for heavy action. Only seven prostitutes were nabbed, though scores of successful call girls live in Beverly and practice their trade daily in the city. They are augmented by others who weekend in town.

"There was sex before I was born, and it'll be here after I leave," the chief notes. "We can't prevent prostitution, only control it."

Cork beams his first smile as he reveals the existence of what he terms Beverly's "full moon club."

One woman, he says, calls the department frequently to complain that Communists are coming through the woodwork. "She even has pans covering the holes in her walls. She literally believes this." There is the woman who phones and says someone is trying to steal a fortune she doesn't have. Another woman has a habit of dancing on the sidewalk every Sunday after church, and complaints are received about her. A man calls Cork's secretary at least once a week and curses her for no discernible reason.

"Seems like they come out whenever the moon is full," Cork sighs. "We talk to them. We pacify them. It's a funny town."

Cork takes a final swing at Kimble. "The last chief didn't understand the community."

And surprisingly, he also takes a swing at Anderson. "Anderson's book [*Beverly Hills Is My Beat,* 1960] was a lot of bullshit. He wrote mostly about dead people. He was scared to write the real story of Beverly Hills."

What is the real story of Beverly Hills?

"I'm retiring soon, so I don't want to make waves. But if I ever write a book, they'll have to bind it in asbestos covers."

11.
"This Piece of Geography"

MIKE SILVERMAN, real-estate broker to the stars, has dated Jayne Mansfield, Judy Garland, Joan Crawford, Marie McDonald, and a cast of thousands.

At the moment, a knockout redhead, legs crossed, sits on the cream-colored sofa in Silverman's mahogany-paneled office, lapping up his every word. The standard coffee-table books pepper his sanctuary, art volume reproductions of the works of Leonardo, Michelangelo, Picasso, and Winslow Homer. "We are terribly cultured, terribly," says Silverman.

Befitting his Beautiful Person status, the millionaire realtor has spent Christmas at Merle Oberon's white marble villa overlooking Acapulco Bay, and he has photographed Bengal tigers in India, where he was a houseguest of a maharajah. Silverman denies asking his royal host to use his influence to obtain an exclusive listing on the Taj Mahal. "Still and all," says Mike, maybe kidding, maybe not, "the Taj *would* make an attractive focal point for one hell of a subdivision."

Silverman, who has a bachelor pad in Beverly to which he commutes by Cadillac, is possibly the only hawker of homes in America with a press agent to keep his name in the gossip columns.

On Silverman's way up, Louella Parsons was a loyal chronicler of his social life, and he has all of Louella's nuggets in his scrapbook. Among the exclusive items she revealed to her millions of readers:

"The handsome man who escorted Joan Crawford to the Academy nominations is Mike Silverman, young realtor."

"Jayne Mansfield was at Ciro's Saturday night with real-estate man Mike Silverman. A photographer snapped their picture from the rear! Surprise! Jayne is flat-chested in back!"

"Realtor Mike Silverman picked up Judy Garland after her TV rehearsal the other night and held her hand all during their late supper date."

Coincidentally, Silverman subsequently sold the homes of Miss Crawford, Miss Mansfield, and Miss Garland.

"Being a bachelor is very helpful," explains Big Mike, "because the whole thing is moving around and making contacts." Professional contacts, presumably.

Mike Silverman is not a man who forgets important friends. "I was at Louella's memorial service," he says respectfully. He pauses for three seconds. "Louella was a lovely, lovely person."

Silverman's social calendar is now recorded in the Hollywood trade papers, the *Hollywood Reporter* and *Variety*, and wherever else his press agent can plant an item. Everybody in Beverly knows when Big Mike has been to a party and who his date was. "The whole thing is moving around and making contacts," he repeats.

At forty-nine, the self-made Silverman is still handsome. A six-footer, he is one of those men for whom gray hair and heavy, black eyeglass frames add a distinguished touch. He is as slim as the king-size cigarette the redhead on the couch is smoking.

Big Mike has built a business that grosses more than $30,000,000 a year, which isn't chopped liver for a kid from the Bronx who worked his way through jobs at two Madison Avenue advertising agencies. "I was the original huckster." He left advertising to study art in Mexico, and then, on a whim, dropped into the southern California scene —with $29 in his pocket—to "sniff the air."

"It was a complete career change, an *opportunity*," Silverman says of his decision to enter real estate and open his own office in the magic kingdom.

His long, rectangular shop where Beverly's dream houses are for sale is located on North Canon Drive, next door to the Bistro. From his window on a clear day, Silverman might see anyone from Henry Kissinger to Princess Margaret.

Of the real-estate brokers in Beverly, Silverman is not the richest or the most successful. That distinction probably belongs to low-profile, seventy-four-year-old George Elkins, a former oil-field hand from New Mexico, who harks back to the days of Rudolph Valentino and E. L. Cord. The Elkins firm today is an operation with a yearly handle of 100 million dollars in retail sales, 25 million dollars in mortgage banking, and another million dollars in fees garnered for managing several thousand apartment-building and office units.

Silverman, however, is *the* fashionable broker in Beverly. He has the most pizazz. And he is never out of touch with his clientele, a lesson that was expensively learned.

"Some chap was at the airport in Washington, D.C., and he was interested in a big piece of commercial land. His plane was about to take off, and he put in a call to me to see if I could take an offer on the property. He was on his way to Europe and just couldn't wait. I lost that particular deal because I was in the john. So I installed a very elaborate telephone contraption in there. I don't lose any more deals because of not getting out in time."

Silverman has the listing on Merle Oberon's home. Called *Ghalal* ("to love," in Acapulco Indian), the price is 2.2 million dollars, less Silverman's commission. The normal broker's commission in Beverly Hills is 6 per cent. "Sometimes it's negotiable," says Silverman.

How will Mike Silverman sell the splendid *Ghalal?*

"We have world-wide connections. We're in contact with royalty, with powerhouse executives all over the globe, who might purchase such a house. Plus we do extensive advertising in all the world capitals for the proper properties."

For Miss Oberon's house and others in the same price-range, Silverman uses an office slide-projector and screen.

"The slides are helpful to show a client shots of thirty or forty houses. They narrow down the choices. In Merle's case, it's not a simple matter to get on a plane to Acapulco and show her lovely, lovely home. So we have about nine shots of it that we show here."

Some of Silverman's listings are not advertised. In the trade they're called "pocket listings." He has one in Beverly Hills priced at $2,-250,000, another at a bargain $1,000,000. "These are houses that are quietly on the market. They are shown only to qualified buyers, which are like two, or very few. They may not sell tomorrow or the next day. It may take a year or five years. Anyway, we have them in the back of our minds for that one lone buyer who will come along."

How does Silverman handle unqualified buyers, the riffraff house-voyeurs?

"We are very wary of that, and we've developed a qualifying technique that eliminates most of these people. We very often know a little bit about the people coming to us because they are recommended. If they aren't, we find out their affiliations, enough of their general background so we can ascertain whether they are real buyers or people who merely want to look. Those who are polished in this business, give them fifteen minutes and they can tell who is or isn't a buyer. We are polished pros here. All we need is one name and we can make a phone call and check them out. Besides, we know just about everybody in this town, coming in or going out."

Silverman readily admits why he's been successful in dealing with movie stars. "We cultivate them," he says. "They cultivate us. Over a period of years, we have come to know these people quite well. It takes a lot of careful handling, and sensitivity is needed in handling the type of client we have. We consider ourselves masters of the soft sell."

When Greer Garson decided to put her home on the market, she called Silverman, who inserted a "soft-sell" ad in *Variety*:

> GREER GARSON'S
> ENGLISH COUNTRY MANOR
> ½ BLOCK. Privacy behind
> electric gates. 50' pool.
> 2 acres of enchanting
> gardens. 4 bedrooms, maid's.
> Gracious, livable home!

Says one of Silverman's associates: "The house was a white elephant. A big barn that takes three servants to run. We finally dumped it."

Mrs. Minniver's manor took more than a year to dump. The buyer was a doctor, who paid, per Miss Garson's insistence, entirely in cash—$325,000.

Silverman claims the fifteen salespeople in his office can earn from $30,000 to $150,000 a year. He selects employees by "psyching in on them."

"If they look good to me," he says, "I take them out for a drive in their car. I can tell so much about their real-estate business personality by the way they drive, whether they are aggressive or Caspar Milquetoasts. A half-hour's drive can tell me an enormous amount about a person because driving is a projection of the personality."

Ed Kelly, Silverman's chief aide, wanders into the office. Kelly is a salesman and vice president of the outfit. A rotund, good-natured fifty-nine-year-old man with show-business contacts of his own, he joined Silverman after fifteen years as a music publisher and ten years managing Peggy Lee's career. In thirteen years with Silverman, Kelly has sold in excess of 25 million dollars' worth of property.

"We create an image," says Mike Silverman. "For example, Ed Kelly has been cultivating Frank Sinatra and his friends for years. Every time Mr. Sinatra gets married, he calls Mr. Kelly to buy a house from him. Every time Mr. Sinatra gets divorced, he calls Mr. Kelly to sell his house. As a result, Mr. Kelly has made approximately six real-estate deals with Mr. Sinatra."

Asked if a "for sale" sign on a star's home is an asset, Silverman replies:

"There *is* a mystique to such a house that can actually be interpreted in dollars and cents. We find that people associate with and enjoy the glamour of a star's name being attached to a piece of property. We put a price that is maybe somewhat a little higher on a star's house, a higher price than we think the house will eventually bring, because that's the standard game in Beverly Hills. No matter what the asking price, people always offer less. But a star's being the seller excites a larger number of potential buyers, and we have a better roll of the dice then, more prospects for that celebrity's house."

On some occasions, a star's home will sell sight unseen. According to Ed Kelly, Sinatra's Coldwater Canyon place was sold in this manner.

One evening Kelly was having dinner with broadcasting executive John Kluge.

"I understand you have Frank's house for sale," Kluge said. Kelly confirmed the fact and Kluge wondered, "What do you think it's worth?"

"Four hundred and fifteen thousand dollars."

Kluge made an offer close to the asking price.

"When would you like to see the house?"

"No need to see it. If it's good enough for Frank, it's good enough for me."

Kluge left town that evening, and the next day Kelly approached Sinatra with the offer.

"Frank was in a good mood, and he accepted the deal. I phoned Mr. Kluge, who was somewhere up north, and said, 'Congratulations, you've just bought yourself a house.' "

Silverman says that celebrities and their houses can sometimes pose unusual problems.

"Elvis Presley's problem was that his house was too close to the street when he lived on Hillcrest Road in Trousdale Estates. Every time he returned home at night, there would always be a gang of youngsters waiting outside. So Elvis wanted something more secluded. We found a private estate for him with lots of ground, lots of acreage and more privacy. It once belonged to Julie Andrews. So we made that switch."

Perhaps the knottiest problem ever faced by a realtor confronted Silverman when he was trying to sell Jayne Mansfield's home after her death.

"It was quite opulent and pink. She loved pink. The whole house was painted pink and the carpeting that ran from floor to ceiling was pink. The bathtub in the master bedroom suite was heart-shaped and Jayne's husband Mickey Hargitay had arranged for lettering at the bottom of the pool which said, 'I Love You Jaynie.' Our problem was to find a buyer with a wife named Janie, so they could use the pool writing.

"Our search for a buyer with a wife named Janie was perfectly serious. But we weren't able to accomplish exactly that." The house eventually sold for $200,000. The buyer again was a doctor. His wife's name was Priscilla.

Mike Silverman also sold Judy Garland's home after she died. "Judy had thirteen mortgages on her home. I put it on the market at a price somewhat above the total of the mortgages. I then received an offer somewhat less than the total of the mortgages. So what I did was gather up all the people who were owed money on the house. I got them into the office, closed the door, shut the windows to make them a little uncomfortable, blew a little cigar smoke around the room, and turned the heat up a bit. I said to them crisply and cruelly, 'The chances of you people collecting one hundred cents on the dollar for what is owed you is rather slim. I have an offer for the house. It will mean taking less on the dollar than is owed you, but this is the only offer we have, and it's a clean cash deal. If you'll go along, maybe I can put the deal together.' It was brought to that point and this large group of people agreed to go along. They did take less, and I made the deal."

Miss Garland's home was in Holmby Hills, a tiny bastion that shelters the richest of the richest, located just west of Beverly Hills and south of Bel Air. Silverman calls Holmby the "quintessence of opulence." Comedian Ken Murray says Beverly Hills is a holding pattern for people hoping to be rich enough to land in Holmby.

Developed prior to World War I, the tab per acre even then was $25,000. Nothing can be touched in Holmby today for under $500,000.

Former residents have been Louis B. Mayer, Humphrey Bogart and Lauren Bacall, and Art Linkletter. Among those residing there now are Jerry Lewis (in Mayer's former home), composer Henry Mancini (in Linkletter's former home), Sue Carol (the widow of Alan Ladd), and Hugh Hefner, who paid 1¼ million dollars for his Bunny hutch and spent almost as much on refurbishing. Though it is considered part of the city of Los Angeles and is far less known than Beverly Hills, Holmby, by local standards, is 1,000 per cent more prestigious than the golden ghetto.

Silverman has four times unloaded one 27-room Holmby manse, first owned by opera star John Charles Thomas during his brief, unsuccessful fling in silents in the 1920s—to Dick Powell and June Allyson as their honeymoon cottage; to stripper Margie Hart; to Frank Sinatra and Mia Farrow as their honeymoon cottage; and to the present owner, a thirty-one-year-old tycoon named Gregory McKay, who paid $500,000 for the place.

Silverman says that he's often turned over the same home as many as five times. "There's a great deal of mobility among our clients."

As fortunes have waxed and waned, Silverman has bought and sold homes for an unending array of stars, among them Anna Maria Alberghetti, Tony Curtis, Eddie Fisher, Zsa Zsa and Eva Gabor, Jill St. John, Elke Sommer, Sonny and Cher, Bob Wagner and Natalie Wood, and Dana Wynter. "All of these people are lovely, very, very lovely people."

Silverman pushes his real estate with the aid of what he terms "a gimmick that no one else has, that we use exclusively."

Said gimmick is hiring a helicopter at $150 an hour, so that clients can view their potential homes.

"It's quite an exciting tool. We show the client a vista, an angle of the property that he could see no other way. We used it in selling the Tony Curtis house. At that height, the client can see in one fast glimpse where the schools are, what the streets look like. We point out the supermarkets, and he can also see if his swimming pool is larger than that of his next-door neighbor. Incidentally, from the helicopter you can see Jayne Mansfield's heart-shaped pool, even the writing 'I Love You Jaynie' is still there."

According to Silverman, most of the stars can afford their homes at the time they buy them. "What happens is that after a period of time they may get into financial difficulties. Then their whole position changes."

Silverman is ready to help stars avoid such catastrophe. He's enlarged his business to include tax-shelter purchases for high-income showfolk while they are earning their high incomes. He sold a medical building to Henry Mancini, and he sold 1,000 acres of raw land to Rock Hudson on the outskirts of Riverside, California.

"They make such acquisitions with soft dollars, which can go up in value through the years. They also benefit from depreciation write-offs. It is not so much what they make, but how much they can keep after taxes."

Silverman also arranges for celebrities to rent and lease homes in Beverly Hills.

"Rex Harrison called me while he was doing *Doctor Dolittle* on location outside London. He said he was coming in and he wanted me to find a house for him. We had a very bad connection and things were going badly for Mr. Harrison. It had been raining for ten days, and he was in a foul mood. He said, 'I can't hear you. I want you to come over here and we'll discuss the arrangements.' "

Silverman was on a plane that night, met Harrison on the set, spent the weekend watching him shoot the picture, and closed a deal for Harrison to lease Greta Garbo's former house for $4,500 a month.

Silverman says it's more difficult to sell a $30,000 house than a $300,000 house.

"Emotions fly a little easier among people who buy the expensive homes. The affluent will not make an issue of certain upkeep problems that would be germane in a less costly home. In the lower-priced house, every dollar counts, the property tax counts, the mortgage payment is of great importance. All that is not as true in the $300,000 range."

Silverman's gross has increased each year, and he explains why so many are anxious to purchase homes in Beverly Hills.

"Number one, we have an excellent school system and police force. Number two, we have peculiarly in Beverly Hills, this piece of geography, a lower tax rate as against Los Angeles. Number three, the aura of Beverly Hills is very attractive as indicated by the supply and demand. There is always more demand than there are available houses in Beverly Hills. Also, the background of Beverly Hills as the focal point of whatever movie industry there is now lingers and is another important plus."

What is the lowest-priced home he lists?

"We like to keep them above $100,000." He shifts gears quickly, preferring to dwell on one of his more expensive listings. "We have a one-bedroom house for which we are asking $625,000. As a matter of fact, it's not a bad deal. What we have here is five acres, a superb location on the top of a shaved-off mountain. A talent agent built this sort of super-custom house in Beverly Hills for resale value."

Is there a snob factor involved in living north of Santa Monica?

"Yes, there is a prestige factor involved there, especially above Sunset, where the houses have a bit more land, and land is what gives those homes the extra quality that people like. Land allows room for tennis courts. Land allows room for moving around. The homes are more elegant in the north, no question."

Silverman says that the least-expensive homes in Beverly Hills are in the $50,000 to $60,000 range. They are located in what he describes "as the fringe area, south of Wilshire, the Olympic Boulevard area." He predicts that eventually such houses will be torn down and replaced by luxury apartment buildings and dwellings that will cost $100,000 or more.

Won't that keep poorer people from living in Beverly?

Mike Silverman, tall, rangy, confident, but suffused with sensitivity, rises from his ebony leather chair. The silent redhead uncoils herself and also gets to her feet. They make an attractive couple as they head out for an evening on the town that will be duly recorded somewhere in the press in the next day or two.

At the door leading to the parking lot where his Cadillac is waiting, Mike Silverman says, "We don't like to use the words 'poorer people.' In Beverly Hills, there are rich people and less rich people. Good areas and better areas. The word 'poor' isn't in our vocabulary."

12.
Couch Canyon

JUST AS THE Gabrielinos assumed their shamans could hold conversations with Quaoar and deliver supernatural healing, the status-conscious patients who stream into Beverly Hills today from all over the world harbor the conviction that the city's doctors are miraculously superior to doctors elsewhere. That reputation is so entrenched that conned patients have created the planet's wealthiest collection of doctors and psychiatrists. The payoff is extraordinary for care that is seldom excellent, usually average, often below the level available elsewhere, and in too many instances criminally negligent.

Even the town's 165 dentists charge *ten* times the going rate, although their competence is no better or worse than dentists in any other city.

"There are good dentists in Beverly Hills, but not all of them are first-rate by any means," says Dr. William T. Deardorff, who practices in a Burbank medical building across the street from the Disney studio and NBC.

The same if not superior jacket job for which Dr. Deardorff charges $3,000 will cost an incredible $30,000 in Beverly. Among Dr. Deardorff's show-biz clients are Gene Autry, Yvonne King, of the singing King family, actress Diana Rigg, and a number of producers, directors, and writers. Diana Ross, who lives in Beverly, travels to Dr.

Deardorff's office for her dental work. These showfolk are very fussy about their jackets, fillings, and smiles. But they are also canny enough to ignore the status of Beverly's dentists in favor of financial common sense.

Beverly Hills boasts 550 medical doctors—one for every 60 residents. The national average is one for every 612!

However, there isn't a single doctor in Beverly of the stripe concocted by their Hollywood writer-patients—such imaginary, dedicated, deeply caring medics as Dr. Kildare, Ben Casey, and Marcus Welby. Nor is there a single doctor in Beverly whose name carries national or world-wide esteem as either practitioner or as inspired researcher. There has never been—and it is doubtful that there ever will be—a Pasteur, a Madame Curie, or a Semmelweis in Beverly Hills.

The overhead in the ghetto is too high to devote long years to research that may prove financially unrewarding. The type of doctor attracted to Beverly Hills isn't interested in research—or even in healing. Their sights are set on money, climbing the city's social ladder, golf, country clubs, the new limo every year or so, private planes, and three-day weekends at the second home in Palm Springs. The favorite reading matter of Beverly's doctors is not the American Medical Association *Journal* but their own bank accounts.

What is more deplorable than Beverly's failure as a breeding ground for medical genius is that the socially oriented doctors are among the worst in the nation. Chasing busily after the fast buck and the sweet life leaves them little time to keep abreast of new medical knowledge. As a group, they are at least five years behind most of their peers throughout the country.

When a Beverly doctor sees a patient with a serious illness, one he knows he cannot help, he'll still "treat" him for as long a period as possible. Eventually the patient will be referred to a medical facility or a specialist outside the ghetto, where more-conscientious treatment may or may not be successful. It is a costly system of medicine by referral, gouging, fee-splitting, and loss of critical time. Beverly's cancerologists, neurologists, and cardiologists are especially notorious for following this procedure.

The patients of Beverly's doctors pay as much as $50 for a routine office visit. Sometimes it runs as high as $100 if the doctor is seeing a movie star or a known millionaire. The same office visit in surrounding communities is $10 to $15.

Beverly's medical patients pay at least twice or three times the national average for even such uncomplicated medical procedures as an appendectomy or the birth of a baby—and the fleecing fees aren't a recent phenomenon.

Back in 1934, Bing Crosby's wife Dixie gave birth to their twin sons, Philip and Dennis. Crosby was just beginning to make it big, so his Beverly sawbones socked him with a bill for $2,500. The tab for the delivery of a pair of babies in that Depression year was a top of $20 anyplace else in the country. Crosby chafed and scowled, but instead of protesting the outrageous fee he challenged his doctor to eighteen holes of golf—double or nothing. Crosby won. And that's probably the last occasion anyone received something for nothing from a Beverly Hills doctor.

Beverly's doctors make—but hardly earn—more money than most film luminaries. High incomes in Beverly Hills have shifted dramatically from the movie industry to the medical industry. Unlike faded stars, Beverly shelters no has-been doctors. And theirs isn't a profession subject to the pendulum of public taste. For the doctors, the money rolls in as regularly and consistently as sunrise and sunset. Annual incomes average $150,000 to $300,000. Many earn over $500,000 a year. About fifty are in the $1,000,000-per-annum club—and there are no house calls, just the same long wait in reception rooms.

Though inundated by every imaginable type of specialist, Beverly's medical renown stems primarily from its concentration of psychiatrists and plastic surgeons.

Plastic surgery began to flourish in Beverly Hills because of the film business. There's hardly an important male or female star who hasn't been touched up, though none, except Phyllis Diller, has admitted it publicly. In Miss Diller's case there was no choice but to acknowledge her transformation in public, since her face-lift was so striking.

Plastic surgery is a far more limited specialty than is commonly realized, and therefore thousands of out-of-town patients arrive in Beverly every year for the fountain-of-youth treatment. There are only thirteen plastic surgeons in Beverly, but that is more than the total in *all* Los Angeles, which has eleven.

Cosmetic rejuvenation—performing nose jobs; the lifting of breasts, necks, and chins; as well as the reconstruction of birth defects and traumatic injuries—can cost up to $50,000 in Beverly, again double or triple the fees charged in Los Angeles, Chicago, or New York for identical work by equally competent men. Any plastic surgeon who hangs out a shingle in Beverly Hills can become a millionaire in five years. It generally takes about eight to ten years for a Beverly G.P. to reach that plateau. Part of the responsibility of a $150-a-week assistant to a Rexford Drive plastic surgeon is to deposit her boss's take in the bank each afternoon. "It's so much," she says, "it's vulgar."

Vulgar, too, is the high incidence of shoddy work. The plastic surgeons always demand payment in advance because there have been so many complaints, and because many dissatisfied patients have refused to pay their bills.

Then there are the disasters that have caused malpractice lawsuits to be filed against one-third of Beverly's M.D.s and plastic surgeons. Negligence is so pervasive that the Hartford Insurance Group, which underwrites most of the physicians in Beverly Hills, hiked premiums by 75 per cent in 1974—that on top of increases totaling more than 400 per cent between 1968 and 1970.

The doctors cried foul but blithely passed their increased premiums on to patients. While the doctors claim that threat of malpractice action inhibits them, there is usually good reason for the suits that are brought before a jury. Here are some examples, supplied by one local attorney who specializes in malpractice cases, of horrors committed by Beverly doctors.

Movie star Jeff Chandler died in 1961, in a hospital bordering Beverly Hills, as a result of medical incompetence. While he was undergoing minor surgery for a ruptured disk, Chandler's aorta was punctured. He bled to death. The damages awarded were in excess of $500,000.

A young Mexican swimming champion who had been training at the Los Angeles Health Club complained of spinal pain. During surgery, his aorta was also punctured fatally. Damages collected: $300,000.

A Beverly Hills doctor, while performing a routine circumcision with an electric knife known as a cautery, "burned the hell out of the kid's penis," says the attorney. "They had to chop part of it off." The parents and the infant were awarded more than $1,000,000.

A $300,000 settlement went to the wife of a man in his early fifties who had a "somewhat nasty" gash in his forehead when he walked into the office of the Beverly Hills doctor who'd been treating him for years. The patient had been in a minor car accident, and his doctor checked him into a hospital for suturing and observation. Forgetting that his patient had a history of heart trouble and needed daily doses of oxygen, the doctor neglected to order the inhalation therapy. As a result, the patient died.

An eye-specialist performed a retinal detachment operation on a woman in her seventies. The operation was successful. For the post-operative period, the ophthalmologist wrote a prescription for a drug that was supposed to keep her eye dilated. However, her lawyer proved in court that the prescription was the opposite of what his client required, that it contracted rather than dilated the eye, and that it was responsible for the loss of the eye. Damages: $175,000.

A twenty-five-year-old woman, the wife of an airline pilot, had suffered a lump on her breast for about a year. "The damn thing kept growing," the attorney recalls, "even after she visited her doctor. The worried husband suggested a biopsy to the doctor. The doctor wouldn't see the husband and sent word through his secretary, 'Let him fly the planes and I'll take care of the medicine.' " Mastitis developed during the next year, the inflammation spreading to her lungs. "They lost her when she could so easily have been saved. There was no excuse for not doing a biopsy on her breast. We settled for $170,000."

"The most fantastic case I've ever had involved a plastic surgeon," says the attorney. A forty-six-year-old woman, accompanied by her niece, went to a Beverly Hills beauty doctor for a face-lift—price, $5,000. The doctor began the operation in his office at 9:00 A.M. By 3:00 P.M. the procedure was finished, but the patient hadn't snapped out of the anesthetic.

The doctor told the niece, "I'll get the janitor to help you get her into your car." And he left.

With the aid of the doctor's nurse and the building's janitor, the unconscious woman was strapped into a wheelchair, taken down the elevator, out the back door, and lifted bodily into the front seat of the car.

"What am I going to do if my aunt hasn't revived by the time I get her home?" the niece asked the nurse. "I'm not strong enough to carry her upstairs by myself."

"Leave the window down as you drive, and maybe she'll wake up before you reach home. If she doesn't, stop at a fire station. Firemen are nice people and they'll probably help you carry her into the house."

Since her aunt hadn't awakened as they neared home, the niece did stop at a fire station. The accommodating firemen followed them home and carried the still unconscious woman to her bed.

The niece went downstairs to prepare dinner. When she returned a short time later to check her aunt, she found her dead.

"The violent thing about it," declares the attorney, "was just dumping the woman out into the street without waiting for her to revive, without further examination, without taking her to a hospital, without calling in a consultant, without considering the possibility of giving her emergency or follow-through care."

During the trial, the plastic surgeon testified, "This was perfectly normal and natural, nothing unusual here."

"You mean to tell me," the attorney countered, "that you have the janitor in your building help carry out all your patients through the back door?"

"Well," the doctor admitted, "*that* hasn't happened before."

Says the attorney, "I hate to tell you what we settled for. There was no insurance, no children. The niece was the only heir. Wrongful death damages are based primarily on how much support would be given the heirs. We couldn't prove very much. We got $25,000.

"Doctors object to malpractice suits as an affront to their integrity," the attorney asserts. "They just don't want anybody looking over their shoulders.

"A lot of doctors consider themselves little gods because they frequently make life-and-death decisions. But they do not always make the correct life-and-death decisions. Unlike God, doctors are human to a fault; they damn well need someone looking over their shoulders.

"Doctors in Beverly Hills are no better than doctors anywhere else. But what you find in Beverly Hills is astonishing medical arrogance. And there are more doctors in Beverly than anywhere else who really believe they are gods."

This affliction—doctors believing themselves gods—is much greater among the city's head shrinkers than among M.D.s. Despite the fact that psychiatry has proven itself a false idol, it still has considerable force in Beverly Hills. The city is home for the highest per capita concentration of psychiatrists anywhere, including mental hospitals. The number is so massive that Beverly Hills boasts in excess of 250 psychiatrists and 110 psychologists in its scant 3,346 acres, larger than the total of twenty-two of our states. To judge by the number, the golden ghetto must be the sickest city in the world, its residents the most overly psychoanalyzed on earth. The demand is so great in Beverly Hills that the number of therapists moving into town increases monthly.

The city's champions claim most of the head shrinkers' patients are from out of town. But estimates vary from doctor to doctor as to how many of their patients live in Beverly Hills. Some say virtually all their clients are hometown folk. Other practitioners draw from 20 to 50 per cent of their patients from Beverly.

Whatever the exact statistics, it is clear that a vastly disproportionate amount of Beverly Hills' population has been, are, or will be in therapy.

Because Beverlyites believe so deeply in psychiatry, they are more scrupulous about paying their shrinks than their servants, and the widespread disenchantment with shrinkery has not yet penetrated the golden ghetto.

Dr. Karl Menninger, American psychiatry's biggest gun, says, "I used to believe that psychiatry was the great hope for America. But now I feel it's failed, and I don't really know why. People in analysis don't really seem to get better, as I once hoped and thought they would."

In Europe and Asia, faith in psychiatry never caught on among the educated and those in upper-income brackets. English-reared Pamela Mason says she never heard of psychiatry until she moved to Beverly Hills. Though Miss Mason has a wide circle of friends who've been through analysis, she has seen none that were measurably helped by the treatment. She puts it all down as "nonsense." Harsher critics assert that the only sane thing Hitler ever did was to outlaw psychiatrists as "unnecessary."

Following World War II, the shrinks began moving into Beverly Hills in force. There was an immediate rapport with the Beverly citizens. The therapists were amazingly successful in convincing Beverly residents that emotional well-being could be had for a price, so much so that even today, whenever a Beverly Hills psyche finds itself with a real or imagined anxiety, the only course of action is to visit a therapist. The response is instant and automatic, a syndrome that has served to make the shrinks of Beverly extremely rich.

Most of them reside in a part of Beverly Hills nicknamed "Couch Canyon," which stretches from Wilshire Boulevard to Bedford, Camden, and Roxbury Drives. Couch Canyon is one of Beverly's most renowned phenomenon.

The greater the number of Picasso and Braque lithographs on the walls of the shrink's office, and the more luxurious the furniture and appointments, the larger his bill will be. Princely surroundings and high-rent locations are not matters that have been left to chance. They have their own psychological justification.

"One way to raise patients' expectations is the building used for the healing," maintains psychiatrist Dr. E. Fuller Torrey. "The more impressive it is, the greater will be the patients' expectations. That has been called the 'edifice complex.' "

A far better way to raise the expectations of the emotionally ill would be for shrinks to work harder at curing patients. Abandonment of the edifice approach would lower the psychiatrist's overhead and possibly drive down the outlandish fees he has to charge. There is no evidence that a psychiatrist in Beverly occupying a $1,500-a-month office is more effective in aiding a patient than a therapist elsewhere in the country paying $200 a month in rent. If the edifice routine had any relationship to excellence, patients in Beverly Hills would be cured in wholesale lots. Yet Beverly's shrinks almost always fail.

As is the case with medical doctors, there isn't a single analyst in Beverly Hills devoted to research. There is not even one psychiatrist in Beverly Hills who has a reputation that comes anywhere near that of Karl Menninger, generally regarded as the leading psychiatrist in the United States.

The cure rate at Menninger's clinic in Topeka, Kansas, by far the most famous psychiatric hospital in the United States, is no better than the cure rate in Beverly Hills. But at least Menninger has a body of important, solid, and selfless achievements to his credit. He has devoted years to research—seeking, if not finding, answers to the elusive reasons "people in analysis don't really seem to get better." Menninger pioneered preventive psychiatry, led the fight to clean up the snake-pit atmosphere of mental hospitals, worked for penal reform, provided shelter for homeless, emotionally disturbed children, and was one of the few males who attempted to deal with the special problems of women long before the women's lib movement.

Menninger has two other attributes unshared by any Beverly Hills therapist: he is honest enough to denounce his profession as a failure; and he charges less not to be cured in Topeka than it costs not to be cured in Beverly Hills.

The chief distinction of Beverly Hills psychiatrists is that they charge the highest prices in the nation, up to $200 an hour, for their well-nigh 100 per cent failure to heal any emotional wounds. Moreover, their effectiveness is no greater than that of their primitive ancestors, the Gabrielino medicine men. In fact, their curative powers do not surpass those of present-day witch doctors.

A Canadian psychiatrist, Dr. Raymond Prince, after spending seventeen months in Nigeria studying forty-six "primitive" healers, concluded that the cure rate of witch doctors was virtually identical to that of therapists in the West!

According to Dr. E. Fuller Torrey, an anthropologist and psychiatrist who has done research in Ethiopia, Sarawak, Bali, Hong Kong, Colombia, and among Indians in Alaska, "Witch doctors and psychiatrists perform essentially the same function in their respective cultures. They are both therapists; both treat patients using similar techniques, and both get similar results. Recognition of this should not downgrade psychiatrists—rather, it should upgrade witch doctors. What I learned from these doctor-healers was that I, as a psychiatrist, was using the same mechanisms for curing my patients as they were—and, not surprisingly, I was getting about the same results."

Unfortunately, the "results" almost invariably spell catastrophe for the clients of Beverly's analysts. It is bad enough that they waste huge amounts of money, that they generally aren't cured, that their emotional pain continues to be an unassuaged burden that handicaps them in daily life. The worst of the tragedy is that—at the end of the long, getting-nowhere road that is formal psychiatry—the patient's hope for recovery has been dashed.

Many patients, therefore, cling to their shrinks in the forlorn expectation that their anointed wonder-workers sooner or later, somehow, in some manner, will deliver the resurrection of personality.

There are hapless patients in Beverly Hills who have paid their way through 300, 500, 700 (and more) hours of therapy and remain as fouled-up as ever, at least in the opinion of their shrinks. Among the Freudians particularly, the term "cure" is an anathema.

With characteristic pomposity, a Camden Drive disciple of the Viennese *Wunderkind* says, "The only cure for a patient in Freudian analysis is the grave."

But benefits to the shrinks sometimes extend beyond the grave. One Beverly matron was so "grateful" to the Camden Drive charlatan who kept her in therapy for the last twenty-two years of her life that she willed him $250,000.

The extremely convenient "no-cure" Freudian hypothesis, borrowed by the practitioners of most other psychiatric schools, serves to keep the appointment books of Couch Canyon therapists full. The fuller the appointment books, the richer the shrinks.

The typical shrink in Beverly is so deeply committed to money that it is in his best interest *not* to cure. Why pronounce a patient cured when that would mean losing him? The therapist builds a steady, reliable clientele, and he feels comfortable and secure dealing with the same patients year after year. By keeping the patient on the couch for a lifetime, the therapist also keeps himself closely attached to the patient's bank account for a lifetime—and that's the point, the only point, of Beverly Hills psychiatry. It is a cash-and-carry business. The patient forks out the cash and carries home the same troubles he arrived with.

At most Beverly Hills parties, there is usually one token shrink on the guest list, and he is thus accorded an acceptance he does not deserve and hasn't earned. The shrinks rank incredibly high in the class structure of Beverly Hills, which is odd, since achievement means so much in Beverly Hills and they are prime underachievers.

In comparison with all other professionals, including medical doctors, lawyers, clergymen, and entertainers, psychiatrists have a higher rate of drug addiction, alcoholism, suicide, divorce, and promiscuity. Scores of Beverly therapists are secretly being treated for every imaginable hang-up (and some unimaginable ones) by other psychiatrists. There is much truth in the notion that only highly neurotic individuals are attracted to the psychiatric profession.

Another curious behavior pattern among the Beverly Hills shrinks is that they display the same awe-struck adoration for a star as would a fourteen-year-old groupie.

Show-business patients are well-represented along Couch Canyon. Among them: Tony Curtis, who has spent $30,000 in analysis. Dyan Cannon, ex-wife of Cary Grant, pays $1,000 a month for primal scream therapy. Bob Newhart went to a therapist to end his fear of flying, but the treatment proved unsuccessful.

Comments Dr. Charles William Wahl, clinical professor of psychiatry at the UCLA School of Medicine, "The celebrity's analyst can be as image-conscious as the layman. Frequently a man of middle-class background, he finds it hard to develop an effective therapeutic relationship with a rich and famous patient he secretly envies or idolizes.

"It is perhaps understandable, if unacceptable," Dr. Wahl continues, "that an occasional departure from grace may take the form of 'name-dropping,' which is perhaps a subtle indication on the analyst's part that he is prized and valued by the great."

Such "humanness," concludes Dr. Wahl, often involves more than a breach of ethics. Too often it results in unsuccessful therapy. He cites the case of one celebrity who went through two analysts with his problems intact. The star complained, "Both of the doctors were more like friends than doctors. They fawned on me, and one of them even asked me for an autograph for his daughter."

Couch Canyon failure with celebrities is most starkly illustrated by the tragedies of Marilyn Monroe and Judy Garland. Charged Beverly Hills prices through years of treatment, both stars nevertheless ended as suicides. Ostensibly they were receiving the best therapy money could buy.

The problems of the two stars were serious but not terminal. Miss Monroe wrested with nymphomania, career insecurity, fear of aging, and inability to succeed in marriage. Miss Garland had similar travails, compounded by drug addiction. Yet countless others with the same difficulties—and even those in worse emotional shape—do not commit suicide.

A striking trait of all Beverly shrinks is that they prefer patients with mild neuroses, as mild as possible. There are also those along Couch Canyon who specialize in cases where there are *no* problems. As one puts it, "I work only with patients without presenting symptoms, who are interested in exploring the exciting, fascinating life of the subconscious. These are people who aren't sick at all, but aware that through analysis they can improve their lives, grind off a few of the rough edges, and square a couple of the corners of their emotional life. They have all the money they'll ever need, so the only thing left for them to do is improve the quality of their lives. They are functioning at perhaps 90 per cent capacity. I try to bring them up to 100 per cent functionality."

It is rare to find a shrink in the Canyon treating anyone with a serious emotional ailment, an advanced case of schizophrenia or paranoia, a catatonic or manic-depressive. Such patients are not only considered incurable, but they are upsetting, and Beverly Hills shrinks prefer not to get upset. The best way not to get upset is to refuse patients with upsetting problems. Contending with a heavy drug-user, for example, can intrude on the sweet life—can hamper one's golf swing, can make bitter the taste of one's Château Lafite-Rothschild at Chasen's, can drive one to an emergency appointment with one's own analyst.

One psychiatrist, a Bedford Drive Jungian, faced a young drug addict in daily meetings for two weeks. The shrink became so unglued that he swore to a friend, "Never again! No more hopheads! It's too much work, too much strain on *me*. It isn't worth it."

The psychiatrist referred the addict to "the best man in the field," who happened to be an old school chum and happened to practice in Long Beach, about a forty-five-minute drive from Beverly Hills.

That was one trip the addict never bothered to take.

His sister says, "My brother felt rejected by the psychiatrist. We put so much faith in that doctor. His office was only five minutes from our home. No one in the family had time to drive my brother to Long Beach, and since he was always so strung out, he couldn't be trusted to drive himself."

The eighteen-year-old youngster took a fatal overdose of Nembutal two days after his Beverly Hills shrink dismissed him.

"He wasn't treated; he was murdered," thunders his sister.

Beverly Hills is also America's leading center of group therapy. As it is practiced by Beverly's therapists, the group concept is the total head-shrinker snow job. It is designed not to cure but to be a moneymaking machine for the shrinks.

When a patient has been sucked dry in private therapy and can no longer afford to pay a bill that may add up to several thousand dollars a month (depending on the number of sessions a week and on the status of his shrink), he is tossed, ready or not, into the cattle pen of group therapy.

Standard group therapy is an immensely profitable racket in Couch Canyon. The charge ranges from $300 to $500 a month for one two-hour session a week. Several psychiatrists in town conduct as many as six group sessions a week, which brings in an extra monthly income of $18,000 to $30,000.

"What I found in group therapy," recalls a staff writer for a television comedy show, whose salary was $50,000 a year when he ran into emotional flak in 1969, "were six other unfortunates who had problems with no relationship to mine. We were seven rats in a cage, all running in different directions.

"One was an actress whose fast-fading career had prompted her to try suicide twice. She'd had three nervous breakdowns. Her illness was diagnosed by the psychiatrist as 'the Marilyn Monroe syndrome.' One was a stunning blonde, once a well-known Beverly Hills socialite. Her husband had lost most of their money through bad business investments. She spent virtually all her time visiting her father's grave at Forest Lawn. Her father had been dead for six years. The only other guy in the group was a homosexual. Of the three other women there, one was suffering mild depression due to the after-effects of a divorce;

one was terrified of driving a car; the other hated everybody, including her husband and children. My problem was alcoholism. We were quite a heterogeneous collection of neurotics. None of us were cured."

The type of group therapy to which the writer was subjected was the worst possible, and he hinted at the reasons. The members of his psychiatric cell had problems that were too diverse. They had too little in common. They were a heterogeneous rather than a homogeneous group.

At this point in man's knowledge of the mind, group therapy is considered the best cure for many emotionally rooted problems. But not the kind of hapless group groping that is practiced in Couch Canyon.

One group therapy that works is based on the formation by laymen of their own self-help organizations. The vacuum created by no-cure Establishment psychiatry has been filled effectively by people's psychiatry. And the laymen are often better at it than the certified, high-priced doctors are. Without diplomas and deluxe edifices, the self-help groups have been amazingly effective in resolving the emotional problems of millions. Their solution has been to band together in groups in which all are under the duress of the *same* affliction.

Founded in 1935, the Big Daddy of self-help groups is Alcoholics Anonymous, which has had a phenomenal success among its members, who currently number a half-million. Similar results have been achieved by hundreds of anti-drug groups, by Gamblers Anonymous, Weight Watchers, Overeaters Anonymous, and Parents Anonymous (which contends with fathers and mothers who batter their children). All these self-help groups have chapters in or near Beverly Hills. And not only is their cure rate higher than anything being accomplished in Couch Canyon, but there is little or no charge at the self-help groups.

The self-help group is not a universal panacea. Not everyone who joins magically manifests improvement or cure, but the overall record is more successful than what exists in the psychiatry of Couch Canyon. Still, despite the availability of self-help groups, the witch-doctor whangdoodle remains the fashionable solution to problems in Beverly Hills.

What each seeker of emotional joy will be sold in Beverly depends on which office he strays into. The Canyon's psychiatric bazaar offers a bewildering maze of treatments. In addition to having their choice of the established Freudians, Jungians, Adlerites, and eclectics, patients in Beverly may dabble with such other fads as transactional analysis, transcendental meditation, biofeedback, aggression therapy, nutritional therapy, behaviorism, reality therapy, primal screaming, nude encounter groups, assertion training, Gestalt awareness, Satsang, humanistic psychology, psychodrama, sensitivity training, transpersonal psychology, and psychosynthesis. There's also rolfing, feldenrkrais, and bioenergetics. Another "school" of Beverly Hills shrinkery advocates reading pornography, attending X-rated movies, and participating in extramarital affairs for couples whose marriages display stress. "Marriage enters into a new vitality when husband and wife agree to separate adulteries," one of this movement's psychologists asserts.

Faced with this variety of treatment, one wonders how the shrinks can cure anyone of anything when the profession is so splintered, when the shrinks themselves can't agree on which method to follow. Admittedly, mental disturbances do not lend themselves to snug, repeatable diagnoses and cures. A doctor may learn to set a broken leg or remove an appendix, and it's pretty much the same procedure for him every time out. By now, the therapists should have reached the point where they can offer patients more than tranquilizers, conflicting theories, and a lifetime on the couch. Many psychiatrists agree on that—there are apostates aplenty in the psychiatric profession—but none of them reside or work in Beverly Hills.

"Psychiatry as it's now being practiced in this country is a scandal," says Dr. Martin Shepard of New York, who gave up his practice because therapy is a "racket" and a "rip-off."

Dr. Abram Hoffer, of Saskatoon, Saskatchewan, claims there are ten times as many psychiatrists around as are needed. He says he sees 600 patients a year who have been diagnosed by other psychiatrists as psychotics, but only 10 per cent of them actually need psychiatric counseling.

"I wouldn't dream of wasting their time delving into their childhood," he adds. "Yet the standard procedure with the majority of psychiatrists is to put their patients on the couch and try to encourage memories of traumas. Many people have been kept in psychotherapy for years without improvement."

Among Beverly Hills shrinks, there's never been so much as one small cry of criticism about their profession, except to put down a colleague.

"I've spent most of my life treating people and teaching young doctors to do so," says eighty-one-year-old Dr. Karl Menninger. "But more and more I see the still greater importance of doing something preventive. Psychiatrists should eventually work themselves out of business by preventing illness or disorganization. But there's no money in prevention!"

In searching for the reasons why psychiatry has failed in America, Dr. Menninger says, "Perhaps psychiatrists have become too arrogant, without love or compassion in their work."

Dr. Menninger's criticism is precisely on target so far as the shrinks of Beverly Hills are concerned. To arrogance, lack of love and compassion, Dr. Menninger should have added greed.

13.
The Beverly Clippers

THERE ARE 104 beauty salons in Beverly Hills. None has a monopoly on celebrity customers. Few of the famous matrons in the golden ghetto display lasting loyalty to any stylist. Patronage depends on whose "look" is momentarily fashionable. Consequently, the salons come and go.

A similar state of impermanence exists with most of Beverly's thirty-one barber shops, although Rothschild's, the most singular tonsorial parlor in the world, hangs in there. Through the years it has retained most of its celebrated customers because of the personalities of the two likable, somewhat iconoclastic sixty-seven-year-old artisans who own and run the shop.

The House of Rothschild, Beverly's *in* barbering oasis, never advertises itself. Everyone who presumably matters knows where to find it. To reach Rothschild's, it is necessary to enter the uncrowded Monte Factor haberdashery on North Bedford Drive; thread past the $415 suits, $225 sports jackets, and $35 shirts; veer left to an inconspicuous corner; and climb a flight of sun-colored wooden steps to the huge, sumptuous, usually very crowded waiting room—larger than the shop itself—which has twelve $1,500 red-leather chairs, two manicurists, and a bootblack who shines shoes.

Women are welcome to wait for husbands and lovers. They are served coffee and cigarettes, and reading matter from *Vogue* to *Reader's*

191

Digest. Reading, however, is not the favorite pastime in the waiting room. All eyes are glued to the entrance. Is that Burt Lancaster? Tony Curtis? What's-his-name? Chances are, it is.

A haircut at Rothschild's is a happening. Despite inflation, the price remains $4.00, a bargain considering that the entrepreneurs of the shop, Harry Gelbart and Morry Mandel, freely dispense gossip, philosophy, jokes, and career advice.

The partners have been inseparable friends for more than three decades.

"It's amazing," notes Morry, "but ninety per cent of our customers think we're brothers. If you stay partners long enough, maybe you do begin to look like each other."

Nonetheless, there are obvious differences between them. Harry is five-feet nine-inches tall; Morry five-seven-and-a-half. Says Morry, "Harry is a much bigger man in Beverly Hills than I am."

London-born Morry has blue eyes, a brown mustache, a razor-sharp wit, and is an outspoken kibitzer. "Business is fantastic! But we're hoping it will get better."

Harry is brown-eyed, has a salt-and-pepper mustache, and his kibitzing is gentler. "I was born in Latvia and worked in Chicago for twenty years," he says. "How did I get to Beverly Hills? I didn't walk."

The moths of the underworld have always been drawn to the flame of Harry Gelbart's scissors. A case in point is Johnny Stompanato. By the time he hit Beverly Hills, Stompanato had a long police record. A former bodyguard and muscleman for a string of mobsters, Stompanato and his talents found fertile ground in Beverly Hills. He shook down wealthy businessmen, whose choice was to pay or die. With rich women, the handsome hood would love them and then beat them to a bloody pulp if they refused his blackmail demands. In Harry Gelbart's chair, however, Stompanato was a pussycat.

"He was a barber himself years back," says Harry. "We used to talk about it. I cut his hair for a long time. He had nice wavy hair to cut. He was an average tipper."

Harry saw him for the last time a few days before Stompanato was stabbed to death in Lana Turner's bedroom. "I read about it in the newspapers, like everybody else," Harry says, with a shrug. "He didn't come to tell me he was dead."

Harry also goes way back with Mickey Cohen, and illuminates a side of the fierce, short-tempered Cohen personality that few know.

"Mickey was in a fight in prison and when he was paroled he was a cripple. He has to walk with two canes.

"We had a manicurist who was in an automobile accident just before Christmas in 1972. She was paralyzed from the waist down. Mickey heard about it; and though he hardly knew the girl, only enough to say hello, he went to the hospital three and four times a week to visit her. It's probably a fifty-mile trip from where he lives. Since she got out of the hospital, he takes her to dinner a couple of times a week. One night he took the girl and her whole family to dinner. I don't think much of his way of life. What he did with his life is his business. But what he's done for that girl is a very fine and unselfish thing. She's still paralyzed, but she doesn't feel sorry for herself . . . because of Mickey."

Another good customer was Bugsy Siegel. Harry cut Siegel's hair for the three years the gangster was a resident of Beverly Hills.

"Benjy was a neat dresser and when he got off the chair he'd wet his fingers and check the press and crease in his pants." Harry Gelbart was possibly the only person in the world besides Siegel's mother who was allowed to call him Benjy, an intimacy granted by one not-very-nice Jewish boy to a very nice Jewish boy.

"I used to give him a shampoo, which you had to do very gently. Benjy was very vain and hated the fact that he was losing his hair. Before I lifted his head from the sink, I'd remove all the hair that had fallen out. If he saw a guy in the shop with a nice full head of hair, he'd say, 'Look at that S.O.B. Why does *he* have all that hair?'

"Benjy would sit in the chair and the biggest people in Beverly Hills would bow to him. A man who was a vice president and a big producer at Twentieth Century-Fox would wait to chauffeur him around town. Everybody was scared to death of him, except me," says Harry. "To them, Benjy was a celebrity."

Siegel would answer to a variety of names—anything except Bugsy. Calling him *that* was courting mayhem, as a strapping six-foot-two multimillionaire, a Beverly Hills auctioneer, discovered.

"One day I have Benjy in the chair," recalls Harry Gelbart, "and this fellow comes up and says, 'Hello, Bugsy.' On his best days he was not very friendly with people, Benjy wasn't. His face got red like fire and he said to this man, 'What did you call me?'

" 'Bugsy,' the fellow said again."

Siegel told him: "When I'm finished with my haircut, I'm going to blow your goddamn brains out and throw your fucking, stinking body out the window."

It dawned on the auctioneer that he had made a blunder that might cost him his life. He stood transfixed, speechless.

"Look, Benjy," Harry Gelbart interceded, "I never asked you for a favor, have I?"

"No," Siegel said, still visibly upset.

"Now I'm going to ask you a favor."

"Anything you want."

"This guy here you just bawled out, he didn't mean it the way you took it. He thought he was being friendly. He felt friendly toward you, and he's a wonderful man. Benjy, I want you to shake hands with him and forget it."

Siegel considered a moment. "For you, Harry, I'll do it."

Harry Gelbart's intervention probably saved the auctioneer's life. The auctioneer thinks so. He's still one of Harry's most loyal patrons, and leaves a twenty-dollar bill after each haircut.

Morry Mandel also had a near-lethal experience with Siegel.

Prior to the opening of Siegel's pride and joy—the Flamingo Hotel, in Las Vegas—Morry was invited to organize the gambling spa's deluxe barbering facility. He also served as Siegel's private barber.

Morry spent four months in Vegas, living rent-free and earning $200 a week.

"The Monday before we were due to open," Morry recalls, "I flew back to Los Angeles with Siegel, his girl friend Virginia Hill, and her brother Chuck. It was a Saturday night. As we landed, Siegel said, 'Morry, let's go to Jack's at the Beach for dinner, then to my place in Beverly so we can talk some more about the opening. I want everything to come off perfect.' "

"My mother's in the hospital with a brain hemorrhage, and I want to visit her," Morry explained. "Let's talk tomorrow."

"Sure thing," Siegel said.

When Morry arrived at Siegel's home the next morning, the place was surrounded by police. Siegel had been murdered. "If I'd gone to his house that night," Morry adds in an almost needless postscript, "I would have been in the living room when he got shot. I might be dead, too."

While Morry ponders the past event, Harry Gelbart says of the current barbering business, "It's a living. We're not getting rich."

But for Harry's son, Rothschild's provided a launching pad for riches. Harry describes how it happened, how his son, Larry Gelbart, became one of Hollywood's top-flight, best-paid writers.

"I cut Danny Thomas's hair back in Chicago yet, when he was making fifty dollars a week," says Harry. "After we both came to

Beverly Hills, I had Danny in the chair one day. As I was giving him a nice close shave, I said to him, 'Look, my son Larry is going to Fairfax High School and he's very bright. He writes for the school newspaper. Are you going to give him a job?' "

Thomas told Harry to see his head writer. "Think your kid could write for Danny?" the writer asked doubtfully. He gave Harry an old script, which Harry took home and gave to his son. Larry spent a Sunday afternoon locked in his bedroom studying the script, and emerged at last with a sheaf of jokes, which Harry delivered to the head writer.

The head writer was surprised. "Danny can use some of these!" he said, and Larry Gelbart's career was in gear.

Larry's first check as a gagman brought twenty-five dollars. He was earning forty dollars per batch of jokes when the powerful William Morris agency signed him at the age of seventeen.

A year later, Larry Gelbart was writing for Bob Hope. Then for Ed Gardner on *Duffy's Tavern*. After service in the army during World War II, he rejoined Hope, and soon was earning $1,000 a week. He went on to write for Sid Caesar on the *Show of Shows*, considered by many to be the most inventive comedy program in television history. Larry Gelbart's credits now include the hit film, *A Funny Thing Happened on the Way to the Forum*, and the hit television series, *M*A*S*H*, for which he wrote the pilot.

"That's what comes from holding a razor to Danny Thomas's throat," Harry Gelbart says, smiling satisfaction.

In Harry's estimation, his profession takes second place to no other calling, not even that of classical music. Several years ago, Jascha Heifetz was combing through a copy of *Reader's Digest* in the waiting room while Harry labored on another customer. An impulse came over Harry. Interrupting his work, he approached the distinguished violinist, and said, "Mr. Heifetz, can I disturb you a minute?"

Heifetz looked up. "You already have. What is it?"

"It's really a shame. With those fingers, so artistic, you could have become a fine barber."

"Better than fine," Heifetz shot back, "I would have been a *great* barber!"

In late 1963, a fire destroyed Rothschild's. There had been no insurance on the shop. A great many influential citizens were crestfallen. "The Beverly Hills Committee to Save Our Barbers" was formed; and, on January 21, 1964, a fund-raising dinner was arranged at the Friars

Club. In the crowd that night were such Gelbart-Mandel customers as Lee J. Cobb, Jackie Cooper, Kirk Douglas, Leo Durocher, Peter Falk, Spike Jones, Harry Karl, Peter Lawford, Tony Martin, Ricardo Montalban, Gary Morton, Ken Murray, Danny Thomas, and Robert Young. The affair raised $20,000, and Rothschild's was back in business. As warm a gesture as the money-raising dinner was, the most satisfactory moment in Harry Gelbart's life had nothing to do with the barber shop.

When Prime Minister Golda Meir was in town to ask support for Israel, her reception in the ballroom of the Beverly Hills Hotel was emotional. The tables were packed with many of the wealthiest celebrities and tycoons in Beverly Hills. As the appeal for pledges began, there were promises of $1,000; $5,000; $10,000; $25,000. When the spotlight fell on Harry, he found himself with only a $100 bill, which he promptly sent up to the dais.

After the pledge-taking ended, Harry left quietly. The next morning, producer Dore Schary called and asked, "Why did you leave so quickly? Golda Meir wanted to meet the barber who gave one hundred dollars."

Harry isn't at a loss for an explanation of Mrs. Meir's interest in him. "It proves cash is one thing, promises another," he says.

Morry Mandel remembers his first customer at Rothschild's. He had just been hired, and his initial appointment was to cut the hair of Jack Benny.

"I was so excited I couldn't sleep that night. I'd been a barber in London and New York and was used to working on poor and obscure people. To give Jack Benny a haircut was, oh, my God, the height for me. It was unbelievable."

The trimming was uneventful, except that Benny, in contrast to his skinflint image, tipped the price of the haircut, a liberal one dollar.

"That was quite a tip in 1937, when most other shops were charging fifty cents just for a haircut. In the late thirties and into the forties, guys like Bing Crosby and Fred MacMurray would tip fifteen cents. Groucho Marx, twenty cents. Later on they did better. Fifty cents from Bing and MacMurray, thirty-five cents from Groucho."

Morry began cutting Frank Sinatra's hair gratis when the singer lived in a $27.50-a-month room at the Casa Argyle Hotel in Hollywood. Sinatra was then eking out an existence, earning $75 a week.

"Besides Sinatra, I used to take care of all his friends for nothing on Sunday. There were about ten of them, guys like the composers, Sammy Cahn and Jule Styne; Phil Silvers; George Evans, Frank's publicity man; and Irving Weiss, his musical arranger.

"I was Sinatra's personal buddy. We had a good relationship. I was considered one of the family. Then Frank hit it big. Later, his career slipped. When he won an Academy Award for *From Here to Eternity*, he was a star again, and I was still cutting his hair.

"The day we opened the shop, the place was a madhouse, packed out with at least five hundred people milling around. All our friends were here. Everybody wanted to give us a start. Some put money in the register without getting their haircuts. In the midst of all this confusion, the phone rings, and it is Frank."

Sinatra said, "Morry, I want you to come to the studio and give me a haircut."

"This is our opening day and we're mobbed. I can't make it."

"Okay," said Sinatra, hanging up.

"The next day the same thing happened," says Morry. "Frank called again and I told him I couldn't get away. We were still crowded, but I'd come to his house that night."

"Never mind," Sinatra said.

"I never saw him again. I found out that he had bet somebody at the studio ten bucks that I would leave everything and come over and cut his hair.

"When he was down and out, Frank was a great guy. But he was never as liberal with his money as most people think he is or say he is. When he became an absolute king, he was a different type of person altogether from when I first knew him. You could never cross him. You had to agree with him on everything. You had to bow to him, and that was it. He became that kind of fellow. I used to go to his house off Coldwater Canyon. The price for a haircut outside the shop was ten dollars. He'd give me fifteen dollars, which wasn't a great amount of money for a man in his position. There were many others who gave more when you went to their homes. Kirk Douglas would give twenty-five dollars."

Morry recalls an episode in 1960 at Douglas's mansion on North Canon Drive. The star had just completed *Spartacus*, investing his own money in the film. Financing it himself was the only way he could get it made.

"He'd busted himself out and was down to less than his last quarter," says Morry. "If the picture bombed, he'd have to start again from the ground up."

As Douglas settled down for his haircut, Morry chided him, "It's a fine, goddamn thing. You send tickets to the *Spartacus* premiere to Harry, and me you don't."

"You didn't get your tickets?" Douglas appeared surprised. "Hand me the phone and I'll call my secretary. I want everybody to see the picture; I want *you* to see the picture."

"Never mind," Morry replied. "I'll wait a week and watch it on television."

Douglas turned pale. "My God," he said, the humor of Morry's remark having escaped him. "You're kidding. You've *got* to be kidding."

Happily for Douglas, *Spartacus* was a smash at the box office.

Some of Morry's "house calls" have taken him considerable distances from Beverly Hills.

The phone rang late in the shop one Saturday night. Buddy Fogelson, Greer Garson's immensely wealthy oilman-rancher husband, was calling from Dallas. "Morry, what are you doing tonight?"

"I'm tired, and I'm going home to bed."

"No, you're not," Fogelson said. "You're flying to Dallas. I'm playing poker with four friends and I've told them what a great barber you are. I want you to fly in right away and give us haircuts."

"I don't even know if there's a plane to Dallas tonight."

"I'll take care of it."

Morry went home and packed. Within an hour, a chauffeured limousine arrived to take him to the airport. Besides himself, only the pilot and co-pilot were aboard the chartered commercial airliner.

"I gave Fogelson and his friends their haircuts," says Morry. "Buddy gave me five hundred dollars and flew me back the next day. I was the only passenger that time, too."

Another phone call led Morry to an adventure with shoe magnate Harry Karl.

"I'm going to an important party, and I have to look good," said Karl's voice from Hawaii. At the time Karl was courting Debbie Reynolds. He'd rented a house for her in Honolulu, and he was staying at the Royal Hawaiian Hotel. "My hair looks terrible," Karl complained. "I'm reserving a suite for you here at the hotel. Fly in right away and give me a haircut. I'll pay all your expenses and throw in a free ten-day vacation."

Returning to his chair to finish with another customer, Morry confided that Harry Karl was flying him to Honolulu for a haircut.

"It would be funny if you got on the plane, then slipped and broke your arm," the customer remarked idly.

"That gave me the germ of an idea," says Morry, never averse to a practical joke. "The more I thought about it, the more it fractured me. So I had a friend of mine make up a sling and a beautiful cast that fit perfectly. I had everybody in the shop sign it. When I arrived in Honolulu, there was a chauffeur and car waiting for me at the airport."

Answering Morry's ring at his hotel door, Karl looked like he hadn't had a haircut in two months. He was half asleep as he said to Morry, "Am I glad to see you." Abruptly he came fully awake as his glance caught Morry's sling and cast.

"What's that?" Karl demanded.

"Would you believe it, Harry, an hour after I talked to you, I fell and broke my arm."

"So what are you doing here? Why do I need a barber with a broken arm?"

"As long as you were nice enough to send the ticket, I thought I'd enjoy myself and take a vacation."

Karl screamed: "Do you realize what you've done to me? I'm taking Debbie to this big affair, and now without a haircut."

"Why don't we go to the shop in the hotel and I'll tell the barber what to do," Morry suggested.

"I spent two thousand dollars for you, and I can't call the hotel barber myself? Why didn't you send your partner?"

"He's never cut your hair."

"You're an idiot, a bastard, a dumb, no good son-of-a-bitch," Karl raged.

"Look," Morry countered, "I've been on the plane all night. The least you can do is invite me in and get me some breakfast."

"Get your own fucking breakfast."

"Okay, if that's the way you feel, I'll go back."

Karl reluctantly relented, brought Morry into his suite and called room service.

"For twenty minutes he was hysterical," says Morry. "He cursed me and held his head in his hands, mumbling, 'What am I going to do? Look what you've done to me.' "

The waiter arrived and set the table.

Said Morry: "Harry, would you mind cutting my ham?"

Karl hacked away angrily. Then he slammed Morry's plate down in front of him, and the pieces of ham spilled onto Morry's pants.

"Harry, would you mind scooping my eggs?"

Karl picked up the dish of soft-boiled eggs and threw the eggs at Morry, staining his jacket.

Still unruffled, Morry said, "Harry, would you mind passing the toast?"

"You broke your arm; you didn't break your ass. Get your own toast."

Morry slipped out of his sling and cast and reached for the toast.

"Harry is looking at me. He doesn't get it yet. I said, 'It's a miracle, Harry. You've just seen a man with a broken arm healed before your eyes.' Harry started to laugh uncontrollably. He laughed so hard and so long that I finally had to call the house doctor, who gave him a shot. Even then, he was still hysterical. To this day Harry has that cast in his house. He's saving it. He says it's the greatest gag that was ever pulled on him in his life."

When Tony Curtis was scheduled to shoot a film in London, he invited Morry along as his personal barber. Morry begged off, explaining that he was just back from a trip and couldn't leave the shop again.

"Do you know anybody in London who can cut my hair?" Curtis asked.

"I'll call Ben. He's an old friend of mine. I'll give him exact instructions."

Two months later, Morry's annual vacation rolled around. He decided to spend it in London, visiting relatives. Curtis had kept in touch with Morry by mail, and Morry was compelled to pay a delicate professional call on Ben, who assured him that Curtis couldn't be in better hands. "As a matter of fact," Ben said, "I'm going to the Dorchester tonight to do his hair."

"I'll go with you," Morry said. "I'll carry your bag."

"I hate to tell you this," Ben replied, "but I think he likes my haircut better than yours. Maybe you shouldn't go."

Morry insisted. When they reached Curtis's suite, the star's male secretary pulled Morry aside. "This guy is ignoring your instructions. He's killing Tony's hair. He doesn't know what to do with it. Tony is very unhappy. Wait till I tell him you're here."

"No, let's surprise him," Morry said, and he hid behind a screen as Curtis entered.

"Ben," said Curtis, "I don't know what you're doing to my hair. I like full sideburns and you keep cutting them thin and short. I hate the way my hair sticks out every which way. I like it flat to my head. Everything is wrong."

As Ben started to cut Curtis's hair, Morry came up from behind, took the scissors and gave the haircut. Then Morry passed Curtis a hand-mirror.

"Great! Great!" said Curtis. "That's just the way Morry does it."

Morry turned him around and said, "You're damned right that's the way Morry does it." And Curtis kissed him right on the mouth.

The next day, Curtis had a photo session for publicity pictures, and the pictures were widely printed in the world press.

"Everybody in London went wild and everybody wanted a Tony Curtis haircut," says Morry.

A reporter came to interview Morry.

"You're the barber who cut Tony Curtis's hair?"

"Sure."

"Do you know, Mr. Mandel, that everyone's calling you a genius."

Morry looked startled.

"How did you originate the Tony Curtis cut?" the reporter inquired expectantly.

"First," Morry answered, "you get a guy that looks like Tony Curtis."

"Then what?"

"Then you give him a haircut!"

That concluded the interview.

Morry, however, was more informative with another interviewer, describing the Curtis cut as "the sides real thick, and short on top with a curl in the center."

The Mandel creation, said a British newspaper, "caused an international sensation." Morry was buried in mail for months from would-be customers and from other barbers who wanted the precise formula. Says Morry now: "Any barber could duplicate the haircut, but first you still have to find a guy that looks like Tony Curtis."

One day in 1960, Peter Lawford called and said his brother-in-law, John F. Kennedy, was in town and wanted a haircut. Could one of them come to his Malibu beach house as soon as possible?

It was a Sunday, warm, sunny, pleasant. The partners, who both lived in apartment buildings south of Santa Monica, were enjoying a relaxing afternoon at the pool.

Morry said to Harry: "Why don't *you* give Kennedy a haircut?"

Harry said to Morry: "Why don't *you* give Kennedy a haircut?"

"I'll never forget it," says Morry, "because any barber in the world would give his right arm to cut Kennedy's hair, but neither one of us wanted to leave the pool. Here we were arguing over who *wouldn't* give Kennedy a haircut. We tossed a coin. Harry lost, but I went along anyway."

Kennedy was in the midst of his Presidential campaign. When they arrived, he said, "My hair's been unmanageable for years. It grows too fast and it's always falling over my eyes. Now my people tell me I look too boyish and it's going to cost me votes. It's very important that I get rid of the boyish look. I have to look more mature. Maybe another style would do it."

Morry did the restyling. As he picked up his razor, the seven Secret Service agents in the room moved closer and breathed harder.

Kennedy told them to relax.

"I got rid of that forelock and made his hair lie down by giving him an all-razor cut," says Morry. "I cut his hair straight across his forehead. It did make him look older. It changed his whole appearance and image."

For what Morry Mandel had done, Lawford handed him a twenty-dollar bill, a very reasonable price for assisting a man into the White House.

"Some say the last Presidential election was won not by a whisker, but by a haircut," wrote reporter John Krueger in the armed-forces newspaper *Stars and Stripes*. "The man who brought the unruly Kennedy locks into line was screenland's number one male-hair specialist, Morry Mandel."

Other newsmen also commented favorably on the haircut, and Kennedy's press secretary, Pierre Salinger, another Rothschild's patron, estimated it was worth more than a million votes. (Kennedy defeated Nixon by 119,450 ballots.)

Both Morry and Harry were invited to the Inauguration, and when they shook hands with Kennedy, he said, "Thanks for the help."

Subsequently, Morry and Harry alternately cut Kennedy's hair when he came to California.

Once, after Harry did the honors, the pleased Kennedy remarked, "I think I'll fly out here for all my haircuts."

"Mr. President," said Harry, "you don't have to do that. You can always draft me."

Morry remembers, "The times I cut Kennedy's hair he usually read a newspaper. Sometimes I'd tell him jokes. When we talked, it was mostly about broads. Kennedy loved the broads. That's what helped make him President. He liked them and they liked him, no question about it." Tactfully refusing to mention names, Morry adds, "We all know who the broads were that he saw in Beverly. He was a swinging President. Can you imagine a guy like Nixon banging some young broad?" Morry smiles thoughtfully. "It would probably have done him a lot of good."

Harry remembers, "The President promised he would send me an autographed picture. I waited a long time. Then it finally came. It came on a Wednesday. The following Friday he was assassinated."

Harry had made a practice of saving Kennedy's discarded hair and giving the locks to young, worshipful admirers of the President. "After he died, somebody approached us about gold-plating the scissors and comb we'd used to cut his hair. He wanted to put them on display somewhere. I didn't think much of the idea. No, we didn't do it."

With the advent of long hair, business at Rothschild's has fallen off 40 per cent. Loyal customers haven't abandoned the shop. But instead of coming in for a trim every ten days or so, they wait a month to six weeks.

In its palmiest period, Rothschild's had a dozen barbers working at full clip. Now, on its busiest days, there are ten—five traditional barbers and five hair stylists.

"The hair stylists are a new breed," says Harry. "They are the coming thing. We had to bring them in and charge ten dollars for their services in order to survive."

"The old-timers still want us," says Morry, "but when they're gone, there will be no one to replace them. The younger ones all go for the styling."

Though rooted to contemporary realities, the partners still have an inclination to dwell on the past. A few years after the incident in Hawaii, Harry Karl took Morry with him on a boat trip to Europe. The voyage aboard the *Michelangelo* was without incident, except for Karl's spending.

"I shaved him and cut his hair," Morry recounts. "He brought along another fellow just to comb his hair. Each of us had a private room at Claridge's in London, a driver, a car, salary, and expenses. The three-week trip cost Harry close to fifteen thousand dollars."

That kind of spending is rare nowadays, Morry and Harry agree. So are big tips. Their average tip is $1.00 to $2.50.

Although Morry, Harry, and some of their customers try their best, the high jinks at Rothschild's are mostly a thing of the past. Years ago, for instance, Harry had finished giving Harry Ritz a haircut and, as the comedian was paying his bill, he spied an unshorn man with a briefcase enter the waiting room. "My God," Ritz yelled in mock pain, "seventy-five dollars for a haircut!" The would-be customer left in a hurry.

The new-breed hair stylists at Rothschild's are polite, proper, efficient, businesslike. They are also dull, and none possess the imagination or chutzpah to pull off the Caper of the Twin Shaves. That stunt was cooked up in 1964, with Leonard and Bob Goldstein, movie executives who were identical twins.

"Unless you knew them well, you couldn't tell them apart," Morry says.

As prearranged with Morry and Harry, Leonard Goldstein walked in and went to a barber who had just been hired. "Shave me very close because my beard grows quickly. You wouldn't believe how fast my beard grows."

Completing the shave, the barber inquired, "Is that close enough?"

"I hope so," said Leonard Goldstein.

Less than an hour later, Bob Goldstein appeared—sporting a heavy beard. He made a beeline for the barber who'd shaved his brother. "It's all grown out again. You gave me a lousy shave. This time I want a close shave, a very close shave."

Morry, feigning anger, told his new employee, "The policy at Rothschild's is that the customer is always right. Please give this man a proper shave."

"It's impossible," sputtered the hapless barber. "I just shaved him smooth as glass."

"Well, look for yourself," Bob Goldstein said.

Sweating bullets, the barber shaved the "same" customer again. Clarity came to him a week later, when Leonard and Bob Goldstein arrived together. Studiously ignoring their victim, Leonard calmly went to Harry's chair and Bob wordlessly sat down at Morry's station.

Occasionally, the old spirit still flares at Rothschild's. Burt Lancaster told an unimpressed Morry Mandel in 1974 that he was going to Israel to star as Moses for a six-part television special.

"That's the worst case of miscasting I ever heard," Morry said.

"Why?" Lancaster demanded.

"You can't even part your hair right. How are you going to part the Red Sea?"

The shop, say the partners, will inevitably be sold.

"It's hard to put a monetary figure on it," Morry sums up. "Whoever buys it has to lose unless we are working here. Because *we* are the shop. The people come in because of us. The bottom would fall out if we weren't here."

So it would; so it will.

14.
Wall Street West

IN A CITY where the greenback is the all-consuming preoccupation, logic would seem to dictate that making money is Beverly's thing. It would also seem logical that Beverly's moneymen would be so skilled that there would be no need for them to cut corners or engage in larceny.

Certainly the Beverly Hills Chamber of Commerce assures readers of its brochures that the financial wizards of Beverly earn fortunes for themselves and for their investors. "The City is the Wall Street of the West, and there is no limit to the monetary marvels on our Island Mountain of Finance," the Chamber declares. "Beverly Hills can look forward to the prospect of still greater financial wonders in the City of Wonders."

The awful truth is that the town is still reeling from an outrageous series of past "financial wonders." In fact, an investor should approach Wall Street West with the advice of Thomas Jefferson in mind: "I do not believe with Montaigne that fourteen out of fifteen men are rogues. But I have always found that rogues would be uppermost."

Applied to the money-handlers of Beverly, Montaigne's percentage is more accurate than Jefferson's. The city hosts the most rapacious financial underworld this side of the Mafia.

"Economic crime is a pervasive cancer eating away at our society, and it is many times more destructive than theft, robbery, muggings,

205

or even homicide," says U.S. Justice Department Prosecuting Attorney Nathaniel E. Kossack. "It is almost impossible to assess accurately the monetary loss we Americans suffer from so-called white-collar criminals. But one expert has set the figure at more than forty billion dollars every year, and I'll buy that."

Beverly Hills contributes more than its share to this looting. The thieving by its professional moneymen is unequaled anywhere else in the United States. And the thieving by its average citizen is also unequaled. Beverly Hills is so notorious as a tax-cheating mecca that the Internal Revenue Service has kept a particularly sharp eye focused on its residents.

On August 23, 1953, special IRS tax investigators ran a door-to-door survey of Beverly. *Every* return in town was audited on the spot! More than six million dollars in undeclared income or disallowed deductions was unearthed. The raid and what it unearthed speaks eloquently of Beverly's financial morality.

A special set of circumstances exists in Beverly that provides little or no incentive for honesty. Local crooks in custom-tailored business suits are aware that only the most conspicuous offenders are caught. And even if they are caught, they are secure in the knowledge that restitution is rarely demanded. And thanks to a combine of shrewd local lawyers, misguided judges, and the city's status, punishment for Beverly's white-collar lawbreakers is lenient.

Most of the 587 attorneys of Beverly, masters at driving a truck through a loophole, earn their huge fees by overseeing the legal paperwork involved with home-hatched financial crime. On the rare occasions when their clients are nabbed, the lawyers prove to be masters at getting them off with probation or with extremely light sentences. (Largely because of such specialization, Beverly Hills hasn't produced a single home-grown legal star. Not one lawyer has burst forth to carve a national reputation for excellence. There are no Clarence Darrows, Percy Foremans, F. Lee Baileys, Louis Nizers, or Melvin Bellis in Beverly Hills.)

The local judiciary and the Beverly Hills Police Department are not equipped with either the power or intelligence to cope with the Beverly Hills money pirates. The Beverly Hills Police Department seldom if ever uncovers or makes an arrest for sophisticated financial crime, despite city statutes against the commission of fraud in all its guises. Federal or state government investigators are responsible for those who are apprehended in Beverly Hills. They are then tried in Los Angeles superior courts or in the federal system. Remarkably, the judges in these courts are still swayed by the atavistic prestige of a Beverly Hills address and follow along with the notion that Beverly's criminals are not as guilty as criminals who live in lesser neighborhoods.

Here are some recent samples of justice.

A Wilshire Boulevard operator who palmed himself off as a stock-market consultant functioned for eight years in a large, wide-windowed office, sitting behind a $2,000 hunk of mahogany whose sole adornment was a copy of *The Wall Street Journal,* which coyly covered a corner of his desk. Investors with portfolio trouble put themselves into his hands when he promised to double their wealth in six months. His fee: 10 per cent a month (120 per cent a year) deducted from the face value of each portfolio.

He amassed additional revenue by bucking shareholders from one stock to another, or out of one stock and back into the same issue, sometimes within twenty-four hours. A Beverly Hills widow of a cowboy star was bought in and out of the identical stock thirty-seven times in three months! The consultant was eventually convicted of illegal stock manipulations and accepting illegal kickbacks from Beverly Hills stockbrokers on the commissions engendered from so much trading. All the witnesses at his trial testified that they were attracted to him in large measure because his office was in Beverly Hills. Able to hire a clever member of the Beverly Hills Bar Association, the consultant was sentenced to a year in Chino (a comparative country club as penal institutions go in California), and he was out in less than five months, still a wealthy man. The judge had not demanded he make restitution of the $450,000 he stole.

A Beverly Hills businessman, according to his indictment, used a false invoice and inventory scheme to bilk a supermarket chain "of approximately $400,000 and a provable theft well in excess of $200,-000." Found guilty, he received a two-year suspended sentence. He, too, still has the money he stole, a gift from another generous judge who apparently never heard of restitution.

A pillar of Beverly Hills, a well-known real-estate developer residing on North Alta Drive, listed no income for 1972 through 1974, and claimed he had lost a total of $47,462 during that period. But IRS investigators discovered he had earned a tidy $508,915 in unreported capital gains and a comfortable $131,875 in unreported income through interest. He made good $79,325 in back taxes and penalties, was fined $6,250 and placed on three years' probation.

In 1974, a Beverly Hills lawyer was convicted, if that's what it can be called, of failing to turn over $185,000 to a client from a judgment in a damage suit. The attorney was given a suspended sentence and exempted from restitution. Nor was he disbarred.

"Society does not severely punish those who sin severely, but those who sin and conceal not cleverly," said Judge Learned Hand. With that thought in mind, anyone planning a big-buck rip-off would be well-advised to set up shop in Beverly Hills and memorize the phone number of a local attorney. He then will become the beneficiary of favorable legal discrimination based on the odd notion that anyone convicted of operating illegally out of Beverly Hills is somehow more susceptible to rehabilitation.

Beverly Hills excels as a taker and not a giver of money. The loot that tumbles into town—at least 80 per cent of it from outside investors—is seldom returned at a profit, or returned at all. The money has a way of disappearing into a funnel that runs into the silent obscurity of Swiss bank accounts, dummy corporations, safe deposit boxes, and tax shelters.

Not even the banks of Beverly Hills can be trusted.

The Beverly Hills Chamber of Commerce boasts that there are twenty-six banks in town. The Chamber, however, cannot boast about the integrity and the management skills of its bankers. Beverly has established an unenviable record of near and actual bank failure, and a regiment of the local banking fraternity has been quietly fired (with only a few landing in jail) to hush up such peccadilloes as embezzlement, phony loans, shady bookkeeping, tax avoidance, and failure to report secret assets. And such thievery isn't a recent thing.

On June 4, 1932, the First National Bank of Beverly Hills neglected to open the doors of its insolvent premises. It was a casualty not of the Depression but of its thieving president, Richard L. Hargreaves. The expansive, socially active president dated Lupe Velez and Jean Harlow, was a darling of local society, and a member of the Chamber of Commerce in impeccable standing until his hand was caught in a giant cooky jar.

"Take some and leave some" was his axiom. He took the bank for $7,000,000, and left only $32,321 in cash, the sum found in the vault by receiver H. R. Shilling.

Convicted in 1934 on eight counts of filing false reports and misapplication of funds, Hargreaves' punishment—three years in jail—didn't quite fit his crime. As the $7,000,000 was never recovered, he wound up with better than $2,000,000 for each year he spent in prison.

A survey conducted by two local consumer groups in April 1974 reached two conclusions about the banks of Beverly Hills. One was that all of them practiced discrimination against women and minorities in loaning money. The other was that two-thirds of Beverly's banks were violating regulations of the Federal Truth in Lending Act by failing to provide borrowers with honest, specific, and accurate information regarding the real cost of their loans. The banks were accused of blatant gouging, so much so that the consumer groups decided to press the California State Legislature for a bill that would remove the exemption of banks from state usury laws. The citizen activists pointed out that, while other businessmen could charge a legal top of 10 per cent for credit, banks were writing loans that paid off at 25 to 75 per cent in hidden interest and fees. (The rate is comparable with that charged by loan sharks.)

The survey had been undertaken because of unsettling discoveries made in 1973 about two Beverly Hills banks.

Beverly Hills National had been around for a half-century and had presumed assets of 135 million dollars in loans and cash. The bank had been acquired in 1968 by a publicly held holding company, the Beverly Bancorp, whose principal businesses were real-estate syndication and loaning money to building contractors. The bank was to be operated independently of the holding company. However, in 1973, five years after it acquired the bank, Beverly Bancorp was threatened by its creditors with involuntary bankruptcy; they charged that the now-insolvent holding company had used the solvent bank as a front.

One example of the mismanagement of Beverly Bancorp was its extremely generous loan to Urbanetics, a Beverly Hills condominium builder. The 10.8-million-dollar loan was considerably larger than the holding company's total 7.8-million-dollar worth. Beverly Bancorp managed this excessive amount by borrowing funds from an Eastern mortgage trust, using as collateral a condominium project under construction by Urbanetics. But when Urbanetics itself went into bankruptcy, Beverly Bancorp was forced to the wall.

The bank itself was saved by selling it to Wells Fargo, the nation's eleventh largest banking institution (304 branches), for 12.2 million dollars. But the money derived from the sale of Beverly Hills National did not solve the holding company's cash problem. It was still saddled with an additional debt of at least 13 million dollars because of other bad loans and investments.

The SEC carefully investigated the relationship of Beverly Hills

National and its former parent company, Beverly Bancorp, in an attempt to determine if the bank's funds had been misused.

When anguished creditors held a meeting at the Beverly Hills Hotel, one woman said an officer of Beverly Hills National had induced her to invest in Beverly Bancorp by assuring her that her money was backed by the bank. That did not prove to be the case, and she was smarting under a $100,000 loss.

Another woman complained that the interest on her $75,000 investment in Beverly Bancorp was the sole support of her school-age children and herself. "I might as well go on welfare now," she said.

The creditors filed a 10-million-dollar class-action suit against Beverly Bancorp. The charge was fraud. Another 6.7-million-dollar suit was initiated by a former officer of the holding company. He claimed that the company had engaged "in schemes to falsify, fraudulently and illegally inflate the firm's earning and income figures," and that the company had failed to act properly even after he had uncovered the schemes and voiced his alarm to his superiors in late 1972.

The failure of Beverly Bancorp, however, was small compared to the biggest bank failure in U.S. history—398.4 million dollars' worth of failure. This was brought about by financier C. Arnholt Smith, a seventy-six-year-old one-time grocery-store clerk from San Diego. Smith was a personal friend of Richard Nixon and had been a member of Beverly Hills society for more than forty years. He alternated his residence among homes in Palm Springs, rich La Jolla outside San Diego, and a sumptuous apartment on Doheny Drive in Beverly Hills. He has often claimed Beverly Hills to be his favorite city, and he has spent as much time as possible there. Beverly can—and does—claim him as one of its own.

When the Fidelity Bank of Beverly Hills, chartered in 1952, was a step away from collapse after twenty years of financial brinkmanship, Smith stepped into the breach, acquiring control for an undisclosed sum. He proudly forged Fidelity into his huge banking chain, U.S. National, in turn a subsidiary of his Westgate-California conglomerate, which owned or had a piece of: an airline, tuna fleets, a cannery, wholesale produce companies, an insurance company, a luxury hotel, and the San Diego Padres baseball team. In addition, Westgate had important holdings in farming and real estate. Together these enterprises were supposedly generating annual revenues of 130 million dollars.

The most valuable part of the Westgate conglomerate appeared to be

U.S. National, the ninth richest bank in California, ranked eighty-sixth in the nation. Its Beverly Hills branch was, for Smith, the most prestigious of U.S. National's sixty-five branches.

Abruptly, on October 18, 1973, U.S. National was declared insolvent. James E. Smith, U.S. Comptroller of the Currency, said the bank had been felled by "a significant volume of unsound loans."

Television and newspapers had spread word of the insolvency, and the next morning there was panic outside U.S. National's Beverly branch. Long, anxious lines of depositors had formed. The scene was reminiscent of Depression bank failures. Said one Beverly senior citizen, a part-time cab driver, "I'm scared as hell. I don't have that much money to lose, but it's all I've got."

A woman from North Beverly Drive in a straw hat and sunglasses had a French poodle in one hand and a brick in the other. "I'm going to throw this through the window if they don't open. My life's savings are in that place."

The bank did open on schedule, and all checking and savings accounts and time deposits of whatever size were honored. The feat was accomplished by some very quick footwork by the Federal Deposit Insurance Corporation, the government agency that insures the funds of savers. The FDIC had been named receiver of the bank, and within hours it had sold U.S. National to the 360-office Crocker National Bank of San Francisco for 89.5 million dollars in cash, a distant cry from its presumed value of 1.3 billion dollars.

Although the money of depositors was safe, the hundreds of Beverlyites among the 4,600 minority shareholders in U.S. National (Smith himself owned 36 per cent of the bank's common stock) had no guarantee whatever of safety. There was only a slim chance that any portion of their investments would be recouped.

A major proviso in Crocker's purchase of U.S. National was that it would not assume responsibility for the questionable loans okayed by Smith and his associates. Those questionable loans totaled a towering 398.4 million dollars. A spokesman for the FDIC said he had "no idea" how much of the bundle would ultimately turn out to be losses that the FDIC would have to cover. "It could take years to straighten it out," he added.

The failure of U.S. National triggered a torrent of legal action. In a scorching indictment against Smith and twenty-two of his directors, the Securities and Exchange Commission declared: "Those in control of a vast corporate empire have demonstrated an almost total disregard for their obligations under the securities laws and for their obligations as fiduciaries to the public stockholders by engaging in a scheme to divert corporate assets for their own use . . . and to falsely inflate Westgate's earnings over a number of years."

The massive fraud, alleged to have been directed by the top management of Westgate, also involved nearly $20 million in "manufactured" profits reported by Westgate "in the name of subsidiaries."

After filing the action, the SEC offered Smith a deal. All charges would be dropped against him and his associates if he resigned as board chairman of Westgate. He reluctantly agreed. But that hardly ended Smith's troubles. Westgate filed for bankruptcy, and Beverly's Congressman Tom Rees asked the House Banking Committee to investigate the U.S. National debacle. The U.S. Justice Department, with the aid of eighteen FBI agents, was looking into possible criminal action in Smith's operation of Westgate. Furthermore, the IRS was hot on Smith's tail, demanding payment of a 22.8-million-dollar claim on his personal income tax for 1969—according to the IRS, the largest ever filed against a single individual for a single tax year!

On top of all that, U.S. National stockholders instituted three suits against Smith for a total of 199.5 million dollars. And the trustees of Westgate filed a 1.5-billion-dollar damage suit against Smith and several of his associates, alleging "systematic" looting of the publicly held conglomerate.

Smith seemed unruffled by the massive litigation and the incredible tax bill he might have to pay. Cheerfully unconcerned about his role in the biggest bank failure ever, he continued his social activities unabated. He tossed a party at a Beverly Hills restaurant for Marje Everett, a major stockholder in the Hollywood Park racetrack. Celebrities among the 150 guests included actor David Janssen, director Mervyn LeRoy, and jockey Willie Shoemaker. Cary Grant telegraphed his regrets.

While Smith continued to live high, his former employees at his former Wilshire Boulevard bank were faring less well. After the takeover of U.S. National, a Crocker official informed the hired help at a labor-management meeting: "You are as new employees—starting out fresh."

Later, one teller responded: "What that means is that many of my fellow employees have lost twenty to forty years of seniority, pension and hospitalization benefits and will now have only Social Security on which to get by. I saw grown men and women entirely innocent of any wrongdoing break down and cry."

Said another employee wistfully: "Anyone anticipating retirement with pleasure has nothing to look forward to any more. And we have no union protection."

Unperturbed C. Arnholt Smith blamed his difficulties on a "shocking display of bureaucratic power and arrogance." He said, "At some bureaucratic levels, I am being attacked as a friend of President Nixon. It's strange that the people around the President who have been actively supporting him and raising money for him have been targets. I can't help but feel that I am on some bureaucrat's list of enemies, and I must be Number One plus, or something."

Smith's paranoia wouldn't wash. In April 1975, he was convicted on two counts of making illegal political contributions to the 1970 campaign of Senator George Murphy. He was given the maximum fine—$10,000. The jury deadlocked on two other charges against Smith involving illegal contributions to Nixon's 1972 campaign.

Added up, the morality of Westgate was remarkably similar to the morality of Watergate.

"I'm sorry, you have reached a disconnected number. Please be sure you are dialing correctly. This is a recording." The phone company's mechanical, flat-voiced finality was the greeting received after May 10, 1973, by callers still trying to reach a Beverly Hills baron. It was extremely difficult to reach Harold Goldstein because he was in jail. He was also in bankruptcy, his liabilities estimated at 76 million dollars.

While Goldstein was operating out of Suite 522 at 8920 Wilshire Boulevard, his phone jangled incessantly and was answered eagerly on the first ring. Investors couldn't wait to place their money with Goldstein, and Goldstein couldn't wait to take it. Some days as much as $800,000 in cash and checks floated into the premises of Goldstein, Samuelson, Inc., a commodity options firm in which Goldstein was the sole shareholder.

In 1972, the bespectacled six-footer, who favors wide-lapel suits and paisley ties, sold a smashing 42 million dollars in largely bogus options and that much again in January and February 1973. Already the biggest commodities trader in the nation, he'd only begun. Until his firm was dissolved, he was on his way to raking in 200 million dollars a year in Beverly Hills and the seventy-five other offices he had set up throughout the U.S. and abroad.

In perfecting his hoax, Goldstein knew he had to offer a gimmick to entice investors into the volatile, dangerous commodities market, where daily price fluctuations are wild. Traders must contend with any number of pitfalls locked into the harvesting of crops and minerals. An act of man—such as a strike—or an act of God (hurricanes, windstorms, droughts, floods, unseasonable snows) can shoot an investor's money down the tube overnight.

In normal commodities trading, buyers receive a fixed price on a futures contract in a specific product, anything from barley and butter to lead and tin. If and when the market price subsequently exceeds the amount paid for the option, clients cash in and take a profit. If the price of the commodity drops during the life of the option, usually confined to about six months, clients suffer a loss.

For Goldstein, the traditional system was unpromising. Conducting an honest business would mean he'd be just another commodities salesman. So he iced the cake with his extra gimmick—assuring clients that their investments were guaranteed against loss, by insurance policies or bonds he carried on every option that was purchased. There was no way the client could lose. Which is why Goldstein was so successful.

The joker was that Goldstein had no such insurance or bonds. "He practiced deliberate fraud," said an SEC attorney. "The operation of the [Goldstein] company only tangentially involved commodities —they were just window-dressing that lured people in."

The herculean success of Goldstein's company, the fact that it had grown so swiftly, proved his undoing. SEC and postal inspectors began a routine investigation, which left no doubt Goldstein was running a con game. His firm was quickly closed. A grand jury issued a sixteen-count indictment and a warrant for Goldstein's arrest.

Goldstein, however, didn't want to be arrested. He much preferred skipping the country to join his money in Switzerland. But before he could make it to the airport, he was spotted in his car by a pair of postal inspectors, who proceeded to chase him all over Beverly Hills. Goldstein tried to shake his pursuers by weaving in and out of alleys in the residential north. When the chase led to downtown Beverly Hills, Goldstein tore through red lights and stop signs, and cut across parking lots, wheels squealing, brakes screeching. The postal inspectors were pushing hard to keep up with him, with the unmarked cars of the Beverly Hills Police Department nowhere in sight. Finally, the federal men cornered him. He was handcuffed an option's throw from his office.

The judge set Goldstein's bail at $500,000, which he was unable to raise. He languished in a county jail cell for fifty-four days, during which time the government recovered about $300,000 from his Swiss bank account and $100,000 secreted in a Miami bank. His bail was then reduced to $175,000. Goldstein's wife provided $100,000, his parents $65,000 and his brother $10,000.

Goldstein was now free to contemplate how he would answer the charges against him. The first fifteen counts alleged that he had written fraudulent letters soliciting customers. The last accused him of perjury, making a false statement to investigators when he said he had a million-dollar insurance policy with Lloyds of London that would protect those who invested with him. Language in the indictment also said Goldstein had masterminded "an intricate scheme to defraud the public of millions of dollars."

Goldstein figured there was no way to squirm loose. Conviction on all charges could result in a prison sentence of eighty years and a fine of $85,000. He decided to plead guilty on three counts of mail fraud, for which the maximum punishment was fifteen years with a fine of $3,000.

Prior to his sentencing, Goldstein claimed: "Initially, we were taking money and putting some of it into the market, but when you're doing more silver trading than the exchanges and more coffee than the coffee exchange . . . you rely on new premiums to pay off the old ones."

Goldstein had robbed Peter to pay Paul. In order to keep his racket going, he constantly had to have a fresh influx of investors to cover the expired options of previous clients.

"In the long haul it couldn't have lasted," Goldstein admitted, observing as well that there is no way to make money legitimately in the commodity options market if the investor gambles long enough.

On November 9, 1973, to the amazement of observers, Goldstein was given the maximum fifteen-year sentence. Never before had a white-collar crook from Beverly Hills been treated so harshly. However, the sentencing proved a charade. The fifteen-year maximum penalty actually opened the door for a much lighter sentence. California law stipulates that a convicted felon may undergo a ninety-day psychiatric examination if the maximum term for his offense is imposed. After psychiatrists contemplate his psyche once or twice a week for three months, he can return to court and ask the judge for a reduced sentence.

And that's precisely how it went. The shrinks examined Goldstein and concluded he wasn't a hardened criminal. Their recommendation was for mercy. On the basis of the psychiatric report, the Los Angeles Probation Department recommended immediate parole!

When Goldstein appeared in court for reconsideration of sentence, the only discordant note was sounded by U.S. Attorney Richard Kirschner. "The ease with which [Goldstein] justifies his criminal activity makes him quite a hazardous individual for the property and valuables of the ordinary citizen," the prosecutor said.

The judge ignored Kirschner's warning. Before him stood a defendant, bereft of remorse, who had gulled investors of 76 million dollars, who had 50 million dollars in lawsuits filed against him by those he'd duped, and whose swindle had prompted the U.S. Congress to consider tighter laws to police the 500 billion dollars per year commodities market. Yet the judge reduced his sentence from fifteen years to eighteen months. He made no demand that Goldstein return any of the money he'd stolen, and Goldstein was not barred from re-entering the commodities business.

By 1975, after serving his sentence, Goldstein was in trouble again. The Securities and Exchange Commission filed a fraud complaint alleging that he'd mulcted about one million dollars from investors in a phony gold scheme.

Apparently, the judge, the probation department and the shrinks had all been wrong. It appeared that Goldstein was not a promising candidate for rehabilitation, and no matter how the second case turned out, Goldstein could look forward to a long investment career in Beverly Hills. He was only thirty years old.

Huge as Goldstein's swindle was, it is dwarfed by the con of another Beverly Hills operator, one who once supped at the White House with President Nixon and Golda Meir.

The Beverly Hills con-artist was forty-eight-year-old Stanley Goldblum, who—as chairman of Equity Funding Corporation of America—pulled off the largest theft in American corporate history, a two-billion-dollar heist of assets, a sum that far exceeds the $1,351,128 of assessed valuation for the entire city of Pittsburgh, Goldblum's birthplace.

The Goldblum family moved to southern California in the 1930s. Young Stanley grew up in nondescript circumstances. He graduated from Los Angeles High and served a hitch in the Army Signal Corps. After his discharge, he entered UCLA, planning to major in pharmacy. However, he dropped out before earning his diploma. Stanley Goldblum went into the junk and scrap-metal business in 1949. He probably would have stayed a junkman all his life if the venture hadn't failed. He was so strapped for funds that he was unable to invest in another business, and was reduced to taking a job in a packing house, where his primary duty was hauling carcasses.

Equity Funding was born in 1958, brought to life by Gordon C. McCormick, a pioneer in a risky money-making plan, selling all comers what seemed an irresistibly attractive mutual fund–insurance package. Goldblum joined Equity as a clerk after a decade of meandering through a series of unsatisfactory jobs. At Equity, he quickly found his milieu.

Stanley Goldblum's climb in Equity was swift, but he was soon chafing at the company's slow progress. It was a small, unknown straggler, way behind in the long parade of American business behemoths. Goldblum saw tremendous, untapped potential in the idea undergirding the company. However, it could come to full fruition only through mass-merchandising.

Goldblum had proven his ability as a salesman and executive, and a mere two years after he'd walked through the door for the first time he and three associates bought the company for $60,000. Goldblum's investment was $3,500.

Under Goldblum's deft guidance, Equity was transformed into a juggernaut, becoming the financial supermarket the former junk-dealer had envisioned. The company reached behemoth status in a few lightning years, its sales force mushrooming to 4,000. Its device was to get clients to invest in an Equity-controlled mutual fund, then use their shares in the fund as collateral to borrow on a life-insurance policy issued by an Equity-controlled insurance company. In effect, the investor was receiving free insurance along with the promise of earning money from the mutual fund. Equity's salesmen never failed to point out that the mutual fund–insurance marriage was an unmatchable two-for-one bargain, and foolproof.

The foolproof wrinkle was workable only as long as Equity's three mutual funds made money. Mutual funds are supposed to make money by investing profitably in a diversified portfolio of common stocks, the theory being that the fund can't get hurt badly if the risk is spread. The theory holds together while stocks are booming, but it disintegrates when stock prices drop.

The arrangement offered by Equity was thriving because Stanley Goldblum's outfit was riding piggyback on a bull market. Since stock prices were constantly increasing, mutuals were also enjoying a handsome price rise. Until the 1969–70 stock-market downslide, Equity was operating honestly, and everyone connected with it was prospering.

Prospering most of all was Stanley Goldblum, now a multimillionaire living on tree-shaded North Whittier Drive in Beverly Hills. Early in the game, as Equity was surging forward, Goldblum had bought out the associates who had helped make it possible for him to parlay $3,500 into millions. (Of his original colleagues, he said, "They just didn't have it and they had to get off a moving train.") By now, Equity had become a public corporation, and in May 1969, its shares reached a lofty peak of 81⅝.

When the 1969–70 market disaster struck, the worst since the crash of 1929, 15 billion dollars' worth of common stock was swept away. One of the victims was mutual funds. Of 470 mutuals charted by the Arthur Lipper Corporation from January 1, 1969 to May 7, 1970, only four showed an increase in price. At the same time, the profits of insurance companies dipped severely.

Despite the nightmare engulfing Wall Street—East and West, Equity seemed to be swimming against the tide. It seemed recession-proof, outperforming the market, its income never higher. Stanley Goldblum was hailed as a wizard. One Wall Street analyst was beside himself with praise for Goldblum's gold mine: "Almost alone, Equity remains a shining star of the financial community."

In 1972, the market picked up slightly, and Equity was still outperforming everything in sight, its profits continuing to zoom. Late that year, Stanley Goldblum, who had contributed a great deal of money to Israel, was invited by Nixon to dine with Golda Meir at the White House. It is doubtful if Mrs. Meir had the undivided attention of either man as she discussed Israel's perilous situation in the Middle East. Nixon was already worried about Watergate. And Goldblum was worried about Equity.

Equity cracked wide open early in 1973 when two disgruntled employees began talking to the SEC, the FBI, and the Justice Department. Astonished government investigators learned that Equity had persisted as "a shining star of the financial community" by counterfeiting—the indictments said—100 million dollars in corporate bonds which it could put before auditors as "proof" of its stability. With the aid of a computer, Equity had also manufactured more than 60,000 phony insurance policies, many in the names of dead people. A startling two-thirds of all its policies were spurious. In 1970–71, Equity had sold 5.7 million dollars' worth of the false paper to other insurance companies. The victimized firms were "reinsurers." (The practice is common in the industry; it involves buying policies from the prime insurer at a discount.) The effect of all this, the indictments further stated, was to allow Equity to raise quick money by selling the worthless policies, thus inflating the value of its business.

Equity had actually been hit harder by the recession than perhaps any other company. The drastic fall in its mutual-fund income had made the larceny necessary.

With Equity bankrupt, Goldblum and a troop of his executives resigned on April 1, 1973. Thousands of ordinary investors had been bilked, their Equity mutual-fund shares and insurance policies worthless. The reinsurers were stuck with millions in good-for-nothing policies. Seven thousand stockholders and several Beverly Hills banks and brokerages found themselves in possession of millions of dollars in valueless Equity shares.

A storm of suits, adding up to almost three billion dollars, were slung against Equity, Goldblum, and his executives. The largest was a class-action suit for 1.5 billion dollars, which consolidated 117 separate individual suits filed by stockholders. When trial of this legal action began in April 1975, more than one hundred attorneys packed the courtroom. It was dubbed "the court battle of the century." Judge Malcolm M. Lucas jokingly suggested that all the participants pose for a group photograph to mark the "historic moment."

Pending his felony trial, Stanley Goldblum had no difficulty posting bail of $200,000. He was quietly spending almost all his time inside the Beverly Hills home that Equity had bought—a $495,000 fully air-conditioned townhouse with a $100,000 private gym he had added. Shortly after his trial began, Goldblum, facing a thirty-year sentence but a maximum fine of only $31,000, pleaded guilty.

U.S. Attorney William D. Keller implored the judge to give Goldblum at least a twenty-year sentence as a deterrent to the "other would-be Stanley Goldblums of this country." Keller laid part of the blame for the epidemic of white-collar crime on courts that have been "all too willing to put them [white-collar criminals] back on the streets after their protestations of 'I'm sorry.' "

Picking up the cue, Goldblum told the judge he was sorry. "My motives were not venal," he said, "and I regret my actions."

The judge's sentence was eight years, and not a nickel in restitution. Goldblum would be eligible for parole after serving one-third of his term.

In the wake of the Equity case, many observers wondered what the Stanley Goldblum saga might mean in the context of American business.

In the judgment of historian and author Page Smith: "The Equity Funding scandal strikes at the heart of the American business ethic. For many members of the American business community, I suspect, the episode . . . has been far more demoralizing than the Watergate revelations, which have also shown up business in a less-than-flattering light.

"It dwarfs Wall Street's celebrated Richard Whitney affair, in which the president of the New York Stock Exchange managed to misappropriate client's funds for years.

"The Equity Funding scandal represents cheating of a magnitude never before revealed in the United States."

Plainly, Stanley Goldblum had never left the junk business.

15.
Fade-Out

"THE NAME of Hollywood has never had any real meaning within the film industry. People in show business all know that Beverly Hills is in fact the heart of the industry," stated March Schwartz in the *Courier*. "This is where most of the biggest and best directors, writers, and actors live today and where they have lived for years."

The comment from the editor-publisher of the Beverly Hills paper is a combination of wishful thinking and a remembrance of things past.

To a large extent, the generation of movie princes who followed the hallowed founders bought the Beverly ballyhoo, settling there in large numbers to embrace the good life.

But the current crop of filmdom's famous and influential are conspicuous by their absence. New Hollywood's rejection of Beverly is virtually 100 per cent, a dramatic shift in home-style as well as life-style. Contemporary film-makers have been content to forego the ostentatious northside Beverly mansion. They've put their mortgage money somewhere more quiet, happy to leave the tinsel of Beverly Hills to the affluent doctors, shrinks, dentists, lawyers, promoters, and businessmen. For the top movie people, Beverly is now unchic, unnecessary, and undesirable. William Friedkin (*The French Connection* and *The Exorcist*) is the only in-demand director who lives in Beverly, and he doesn't much care for the town.

221

The seven top screenwriters, men who earn $100,000 to $250,000 per script, are Dalton Trumbo, Stirling Silliphant, William Peter Blatty, Jules Epstein, Lorenzo Semple, Jr., Wendell Mayes, and Francis Ford Coppola. Only Silliphant lives in Beverly Hills.

None of filmdom's top ten box-office stars has a Beverly Hills address. Able to afford to live anywhere, they have all chosen to abide anywhere but Beverly Hills. The top ten and their choice of residences are as follows: Clint Eastwood, in Sherman Oaks in the Valley; Ryan O'Neal, in Malibu; Steve McQueen, in Malibu; Burt Reynolds, in Hollywood, off the Sunset Strip; Robert Redford, in Utah; Barbra Streisand, in Holmby Hills; Paul Newman, in Westport, Connecticut; Charles Bronson, in Bel Air; John Wayne, in Newport Beach; and Marlon Brando, in Tahiti.

Little realized is that a great many of the biggest Hollywood names either never resided in Beverly Hills or moved away, disgusted and disenchanted, early in their careers. Clark Gable leased a house briefly in Benedict Canyon while he was married to Carole Lombard. Neither was enchanted with Beverly Hills. They bought a San Fernando Valley ranch in Encino. After Miss Lombard's death in a 1942 plane crash, Gable spent the remainder of his life on the ranch.

When Bob Hope signed his first contract with Paramount, he rented a Beverly pad for about a year and then made tracks for the greener pastures of Toluca Lake, a posh San Fernando Valley enclave. Dorothy Lamour, the Disney family, Ann Blyth, Richard Boone, Frankie Avalon, and television's Redd Foxx, Andy Griffith, and Jonathan Winters also live in the hidden, low-key and relaxed village, a thirty-minute drive and a world away from the hurdy-gurdy atmosphere of Beverly Hills. Toluca Lake was home base during the years of Hollywood stardom for William Holden, Bing Crosby, Bette Davis, Audie Murphy, Gene Autry, Ann Sheridan, W. C. Fields, Richard Arlen, Janet Gaynor, Mary Astor, and Al Jolson.

Beverly Hills, the city that once boasted, like MGM, that it had more stars than heaven, has, for the moment, only four names who can work with any degree of regularity: Marlon Brando, Kirk Douglas, Jack Lemmon, and Charlton Heston. But Brando is never in Beverly, except when he's filming interior scenes at a studio. He prefers Tahiti, which he lists as his official residence, and New York. Douglas's home, at a price tag of $695,000, is up for sale. Lemmon spends most of his time at his Malibu beach house. Heston's house is also for sale, at the right price. When that foursome formally sell their homes, Beverly Hills will not have a single important present-day star living within its borders.

The reputation of Beverly Hills as a chichi shopping quarter is also fading fast. Wilshire Boulevard, the town's toniest thoroughfare, has 983 boutiques, 87 jewelry stores, 32 furriers, and 6 department stores. It was named for H. Gaylord Wilshire, the conjurer of the I-on-a-co "magic horse collar," a piece of electrical hocus-pocus touted in the early 1920s as a cure for everything.

Worn like a horse collar around the neck, waist, or legs, I-on-a-co consisted of two coils of insulated wire. A small flashlight bulb attached to the rim of one coil lit up when the device was plugged into a light socket. The same current that lit the bulb allegedly passed through the body and cured illness by "magnetizing the iron in the blood." The control-switch, held in the palm of one hand, could be adjusted to low, medium, or high, purportedly permitting the afflicted person to regulate the speed of recovery.

Consumers swore to its effectiveness in advertising testimonials:

"John A. Mooney, 514 El Molino St., Pasadena, claims to have had nothing but gray hair on his head until he used I-on-a-co, when about one-third of it 'miraculously returned to the original color'; and he further reports that his hair 'grows twice as fast as formerly'!"

"Ramon Martinez, a fruit packer in Dallas, Texas, claimed to be paralyzed from the waist down, legs being always cold. Used I-on-a-co. Circulation restored; legs no longer cold!"

"Otis Williams, 322 South Spring Street, Los Angeles, cured of cancer of the neck by I-on-a-co."

Mass-produced at a cost of $4.10 each, hundreds of thousands of the I-on-a-co devices were sold nationwide via newspaper and magazine mail-order ads for $58.50 cash or $65.00 on time.

I-on-a-co reaped a fortune for its inventor and promoter, and Wilshire, an eccentric Socialist millionaire, used the profits to indulge his passion for acquiring southern California real estate, much of it in Beverly Hills.

Sired by a con man with a taste for extravagance, Wilshire Boulevard is facing a day of reckoning, and retailers along the boulevard are finding that the penchant for extravagance in Beverly Hills is diminishing.

The town's tradesmen are hampered by a restrictive business code, lack of room for expansion, scarce and expensive parking facilities, murderous rents, the high cost of licenses and fees, and unkempt sidewalks. Inflation and the high incidence of shoplifting (three times more frequent in Beverly than in Los Angeles) are other factors that add to their woes. Most significant, though, is the proliferation of new, jazzy, shopping centers nearby, where there are no charges for parking, where prices are one-third to 50 per cent lower, and where there isn't, as in some Beverly restaurants, a forty-cent charge for a glass of water (with a tip expected).

Says writer Jim Murray, "The day of the Beverly Hills character in the ascot scarf, putties, and 'Mittel' Europe accent walking into Martindale's demanding 'a wall full of books' and when asked, 'What kind?' answering, 'Red ones,' is gone."

More books supposedly are sold in Beverly Hills today than in any other city its size in the world. But local taste in reading matter is still showy—and plebeian. Solzhenitsyn, Galbraith, Michael Harrington, Ralph Nader, and reprints of classics sell poorly. Most popular are tomes on sex, dieting, gambling, and show business. Expensive art books, rarely consulted, are bought mainly to decorate coffee tables.

Gone from Beverly are most of the big spenders. While elegant Tiffany's is forced to pinch pennies by charging a dollar for its catalogue, Wellington Jewels, which sells fake diamonds in its North Rodeo Drive boutique, advertises "free brochure upon request." Prices there start at a comparatively modest forty dollars a carat, about one-thirtieth the cost of a genuine diamond. Throughout Beverly Hills, more phony diamonds, cheap pearls, and zircons are purchased than emeralds and rubies, because few women dare to wear genuine stones and because there isn't that much money around. There are now three pawnshops in Beverly Hills, all of them doing very well. The most common item hocked: diamonds!

There's a thrift bakery in town that sells one- and two-day-old bread at a 50 per cent discount. Customers stream in from both sides of the tracks, and the store does a roaring business. So does Newberry's, where a comb and a host of other items can still be bought for under one dollar. Dresses at Lerner's cost as little as $12.99, and the shop is more profitable than the haute couture beachheads at Robinson's and I. Magnin, where an Oscar de la Renta goes for $300 and a Norell is priced at $6,000 (alterations not included). Furriers rent or provide storage for more sable and chinchilla than they sell. Boutiques come and go like Arab tents, many of them fly-by-night operations run by businessmen who move in for a quick buck but are usually disappointed.

At any given time, between 10 and 25 per cent of Beverly's retail locations are vacant. Congressman Tom Rees reports numerous letters of complaint streaming into his Washington office concerning unrentable stores. The problem, he says, generates more mail from Beverly Hills than any other issue. But he isn't sure what action he's expected to take. He's not about to introduce a bill asking federal aid for his district's landlords.

According to the last available figures compiled by California's State Board of Equalization, gross retail sales in Beverly Hills during 1973 totaled almost 190 million dollars. In 1974, the take was 180 million dollars, a drop of 10 million dollars. Every retail category was down, except for purveyors of booze and drugs, which added about five million dollars and four million dollars in sales respectively. The principal rise in drug sales was for tranquilizers.

As their careers have petered out, a number of celebrities who still have recognizable names have gone into business for themselves or are fronting for various Beverly Hills enterprises. Zsa Zsa Gabor and Polly Bergen both sell cosmetics to Beverly Hills department stores. Eva Gabor, whose career is almost entirely devoted to appearances on television talk shows, markets wigs. Gloria Swanson, a former $25,-000-a-week star, has a line of dresses. No longer sought after, Cesar Romero has a men's clothing chain. Jill St. John, once considered the most strikingly beautiful girl who ever shook a derrière through Beverly Hills, displays Indian jewelry. Mary Carlisle, a popular leading lady of the 1930s and frequent co-star of Bing Crosby, called it a career in 1942; she's now in charge of Beverly's Elizabeth Arden salon. Even so recent a popular personality as Donna Douglas, who played Elly May on *The Beverly Hillbillies*, is a victim of diminished income; while waiting for "my chance to get back into the business," she's selling real estate out of a Canon Drive office. Elvis Presley's ex-wife Priscilla runs a Beverly Hills women's wear boutique.

Beverly's shop owners, at a moment's notice, will supply a long list of stars who've patronized their establishments, and they aren't shy about revealing the names of scores of past and present celebrity deadbeats. Diana Barrymore, Judy Garland, Jayne Mansfield, and Marilyn Monroe died owing fortunes to Beverly Hills merchants.

A Beverly haberdasher remembers an episode involving John Barrymore, who sauntered into his shop one morning shortly before his death in 1942. Barrymore selected three hats, ordering the purchase charged to his account.

The Great Profile was nonplused when a clerk failed to recognize him. Through clenched lips, Barrymore gave his name.

"Is that one *r* or two?" the clerk asked.

"I believe the last time I looked, it was two."

"First name again, sir?"

Exploded Barrymore, "Ethel, you ass!"

Barrymore was further chagrined when the manager refused him credit. The star, who once had picked up a check every Friday at MGM for $10,000 already owed the store $2,000.

Few show-business veterans are richer than multimillionaire Art Linkletter. A certified tycoon, he owns sheep and land in Australia and an importing business based in Hong Kong. He is a member of the board of directors of eight corporations and has income from heavy investments in electronics, oil, publishing, toys, real estate, home construction, airlines, and cattle. "I'm one of the biggest bull-shippers in the country," he laughs. Nevertheless, his bulging bank account was not taken for granted when he bought a gorgeous new home in 1972.

"One of my biggest surprises," he recalls, "was when the van delivering a load of furniture arrived. My wife wanted to charge the bill. But the delivery men refused. Next, Lois offered them a check, which they also refused. It was a startling experience to realize that a great many celebrities who live in Beverly Hills, in tremendous homes with huge grounds, have absolutely no credit rating. Stores have been stung so often that it's meaningless to them that you live in a $300,000 house, because you may not own any of it, and you may be behind in all your bills. So credit checks for everyone, including the biggest stars, are ruthless."

Sitting in the corner office of his fifth-floor suite in the Buckeye Building on Wilshire Boulevard, Linkletter at sixty-two is tanned, loquacious, easygoing. A faint veil of weariness clouds his square face, betraying the tragic elements of his life—the loss of his daughter Diane, who fell to her death from a Hollywood apartment in 1969, and the suicide of his son-in-law, John Zweyer.

Linkletter says, "I was talking to the president of one of the biggest banks in Beverly Hills the other day. We were discussing the fact that people around here who put out financial statements of their worth put into those statements every dream and every eventual payoff for whatever their hopes are.

"I know stars who've slowly built their way up from $10,000 to $200,000 a picture and aren't working but are living in big homes in Beverly, Bel Air, and Holmby Hills. They have big cars and their wives have jewels and furs, but they don't have any money at all. They would love to have a job, but if they're offered a picture at $100,000 and they desperately need it, they can't and won't take it, because they've worked their way up to $200,000.

"They won't cut their price because they know that there is no way for it to be confidential. It doesn't matter if the producer says, 'No one will know about it except you and me.' Everybody in town knows the minute he leaves the office that the star has placed a new, lower price on his services."

The Linkletter style is unpretentious, although he's been very rich for a very long time. He is not the average Beverlyite.

"You can be a show-business star and still be happy with the things most people have," he says. "You don't need gold-plated faucets or a Mercedes-Benz. From the point of view of the average person, I suppose I do many glamorous things. I might fly to Switzerland to go skiing, which most people wouldn't just do offhand. And I live in a very comfortable home. Other than a few things like that, I have never enjoyed putting it on. I've never owned a foreign car and fifty suits or had a retinue of sycophants. I don't need yes-men or gofers.

"I'm very happy flying commercial airlines. If I'm in tourist, for one reason or another, I don't care. If I carry my own bag, and hang it up in the airplane, it's all right with me. I don't expect anyone to carry my bag for me."

Of his reputation for reading the right-hand side of a menu first, Linkletter says, "I still tend to do it. I'll never get away from it. Because of the poverty of my childhood, it's just my nature to be thrifty. I look at prices in restaurants, and if I see something on a menu that I think is too expensive, I won't order it. I will eat something less costly. It is just like turning out lights. I don't like to see lights burning. And I don't like to see food left over on anybody's plate after a meal. Those are things that kids who were poor never forget. There's no way of erasing it. Some people, of course, try to erase it by spending wildly, gambling wildly, overdoing everything. But ostentation means nothing to me. Appearance means nothing to me."

Appearance of another sort does not seem to matter to many in

Beverly Hills. Councilman Stone recently declared that his luncheon walk up North Beverly Drive had been spoiled by the sight of the "filthy, atrocious" sidewalk, and an old battle between City Hall and the merchants quickly flared anew. The sidewalk issue had last been fought in 1969, and it had been fought on numerous occasions before that.

Stone was so annoyed that he told the City Council: "It's all right for the city to clean the sidewalks on an annual basis, but that's not enough. The merchants should clean up at least once a week in front of their establishments. Let's tighten the [clean sidewalk] ordinance so we can enforce it."

Nothing, of course, was done. The merchants, complaining that they already supplied the bulk of Beverly's taxes, were not anxious to incur new costs and wanted the city to pay for cleaning the sidewalks. The sidewalks, as a result, remain untended and filthy.

Dirty golden-ghetto sidewalks are one thing, but an army of rats in Beverly Hills is quite another matter—perhaps the most astonishing surprise in a city of astonishing surprises. The rat problem is so serious that there are more rodents in the city than people.

Before her term as mayor ended, Phyllis Seaton emphasized the rat invasion in speeches before the Chamber of Commerce, civic groups, and in City Council debate. In one oration on the subject, she said, "There are more rats in Beverly Hills than Watts! They live, nest, and love among us. Some day they may spread bubonic plague!"

She described the tree-rats native to Beverly Hills as mating and growing bolder each day in dead palm fronds and overgrown ivy patches. She cited complaints of residents and merchants who found rats in their swimming pools and shops. Many Beverlyites, she said, are bitten by rats every year. "I hate rats, and yet our city is overrun with them."

Mayor Seaton proved to be no Pied Piper. Her recommendation to eliminate rats from Beverly Hills was ignored by the Chamber of Commerce, the civic groups, and the City Council. The only action taken was publication of a booklet by the Beverly Hills Sanitation Department entitled, "Prevention and Control of Rodents in Beverly Hills." A copy was sent to all residents and merchants in the city, who were otherwise on their own in contending with the rats.

Since the City Council has refused to appropriate funds to rid the city of rats, the creatures continue to thrive, especially in the north. Recently a resident of North Hillcrest Road reported sighting "a pair of huge rats thirty-six inches long and covered with red spots."

As a symbol of Beverly Hills, the rat is eminently appropriate: the primary characteristics of the rat and the city are identical. Both are sly, fierce, and aggressive. Those characteristics have made Beverly Hills a city afflicted with unending social and financial warfare—a mean, grasping, selfish place filled with institutions that have failed, and with people who have failed in spite of the ability of some to earn great sums of money.

Jerusalem, Athens, and Florence gave the world the Bible, democracy, and the Renaissance. Beverly Hills, on the other hand, hosts a breed of citizen who knows the price of everything and the value of nothing. It has failed to provide a climate for any native son or daughter to excel. Except for a few movie stars, it has not attracted as a permanent resident one first-rank citizen whose name looms large in any profession. To cite but one contrast, Princeton, New Jersey, with a population of 12,311, about one-third that of Beverly Hills, has been the home of two Presidents—Grover Cleveland and Woodrow Wilson —and a pair of pre-eminent scientists—Albert Einstein and J. Robert Oppenheimer.

By any test or standard, Beverly Hills has failed as an idea and as a city. But Beverly Hills is no more than a microcosm of America in its inability to wash itself clean of crime, poverty, noise, and pollution, and to treat its elderly with dignity. It is not unique or "something special."

The future for Beverly Hills is bleak. "We're going nowhere," admits March Schwartz. And Councilman Stone says that if federal, state, and county governments continue to impose tax burdens on the city, "they have the power to destroy us as a unified community. They can bankrupt us overnight and wipe us out completely."

It doesn't much matter. Beverly Hills is a city past its prime. With the stars who gave it glory all but gone, a resurgence in its vitality is doubtful.

Those with keen eyes have never seen Beverly Hills in a flattering light.

Novelist Herman Wouk called the town a "compound of the temporarily well-paid."

Says a Beverly chauffeur who works for a service that rents Rolls-Royces to stars and tycoons, "We have people here with money, but no class."

For Candice Bergen, who grew up in Beverly Hills, the city is a "non-place, a suburb with vinyl trees, artificial grass, and no garbage cans in the streets."

Director William Friedkin says, "You make a lot of money, you buy a house in Beverly Hills, and the only guys you ever see are your butler and your cook and the guy who drives you to the studio. You leave an air-conditioned house to get into an air-conditioned office, from which you go to an air-conditioned screening room. And you never touch a dog on the street or talk to a guy in a bar or on a subway or know what the hell he wants, and that's why a lot of guys don't know who their audience is.

"Success is a bitch. You get the big buck and you say, 'Boom, I got to be alone here, because now I've got to really think about what I'm doing.' And you lose touch with the people. You lose touch with what people are thinking. When you're in the street, you damn well know what people are thinking, because you're the people. You are them. In Beverly Hills, you can block all that out."

The pit of Beverly's failure and folly is that it is a place that has everything it needs—except everything it needs.

Index

231

240   *Index*